Assistive Technology for Young Children

Assistive Technology for Young Children

Creating Inclusive Learning Environments

by

Kathleen Curry Sadao, Ed.D.
Supporting Early Education Delivery Systems (SEEDS) Project
Sacramento County Office of Education
Sacramento, California

and

Nancy B. Robinson, Ph.D., CCC-SLP
San Francisco State University
San Francisco

·P A U L·H·
BROOKES
PUBLISHING Co ®

Baltimore • London • Sydney

Paul H. Brookes Publishing Co.
Post Office Box 10624
Baltimore, Maryland 21285-0624
USA

www.brookespublishing.com

Typeset by Broad Books, Baltimore, Maryland.
Manufactured in the United States of America by
Sheridan Books, Inc., Chelsea, Michigan.

The individuals described in this book are composites based on the authors' experiences. In all instances, names and identifying details have been changed to protect confidentiality.

Permission to reprint the following material is gratefully acknowledged:

Page 75: "Speech Disorder," by Carin Westerlund, from Williams, M., & Krezman, C. (Eds.). (2000). *Beneath the surface: Creative expressions of augmented communicators* (p. 55). Toronto: ISAAC Press; reprinted by permission.

Library of Congress Cataloging-in-Publication Data

Sadao, Kathleen C.
Assistive technology for young children: creating inclusive learning environments / by Kathleen Curry Sadao, and Nancy B. Robinson.
   p.   cm.
  Includes bibliographical references and index.
  ISBN-13: 978-1-59857-091-5 (pbk.)
  ISBN-10: 1-59857-091-9 (pbk.)
1. Children with disabilities—Education (Early childhood)   2. Teaching—Aids and devices.   3. Self-help devices for people with disabilities.   4. Inclusive education.   I. Robinson, Nancy B.   II. Title.

LC4019.3.S25 2010
371.9'045—dc22
                                                     2010031509

British Library Cataloguing in Publication data are available from the British Library.

2014   2013   2012   2011   2010

10   9   8   7   6   5   4   3   2   1

Contents

Contents of the Accompanying CD-ROM

About the Authors

Kathleen Curry Sadao, Ed.D., Program Specialist, Supporting Early Education Delivery Systems (SEEDS) Project, Sacramento County Office of Education, P.O. Box 269003, Sacramento, CA 95826

Dr. Sadao has been in the field of early childhood special education (ECSE) for more than 25 years. She received her doctorate in educational administration from University of Hawaii at Manoa in 1995. During the 1980s and 1990s she traveled the Pacific Islands providing training and technical assistance to newly developed ECSE programs as a Head Start Technical Assistance consultant and later a National Early Childhood Technical Assistance Center coordinator. Her research focus has been on interagency collaboration, parent involvement, inclusive practices, and cross-cultural issues in education. In 2007, she coauthored a book with Dr. Nancy Robinson focused on interagency collaboration and evaluation. Since 1997, she has spent her time in California focused on preservice and in-service training programs in ECSE as a faculty member of the University of the Pacific, Gladys Benerd School of Education, and as an administrator of an early intervention program. Most recently, under the auspices of the Supporting Early Education Delivery Systems (SEEDS) Project at the Sacramento County Office of Education, she has worked as a program specialist developing training materials for the field and facilitating a state-level assistive technology (AT) work group creating web-based AT training products. Currently she and her SEEDS Workgroup on Early Education Technology (SWEET) team have been field-testing the AT training modules around the state of California. She has presented her work at the Council for Exceptional Children, Division on Early Childhood, conference and other state, national, and international conferences and has published several articles on the SWEET AT efforts.

Nancy B. Robinson, Ph.D., CCC-SLP, Associate Professor, San Francisco State University, Department of Special Education and Communicative Disorders, 1600 Holloway Avenue, San Francisco, CA 94132

Dr. Robinson is a speech-language pathologist (SLP) and special educator with a focus on early childhood education. She completed her graduate work as an SLP at Portland State University in 1975 and earned a doctorate in special education at the University of Washington in 1987. For many years, she worked at the University of Hawaii at Manoa with the Center on Disability Studies with a team of faculty who developed interdisciplinary education models with students in education, health, and social sciences. Dr. Sadao and Dr. Robinson began their collaborative work at the University of Hawaii at Manoa and established an interagency systems evaluation initiative through technical assistance and training in the Pacific Islands. In 1998, Dr. Robinson joined the faculty in communicative disorders, first at California State University, Chico, and then at San Francisco

State University. Within communicative disorders, Dr. Robinson developed course work and clinical training in augmentative and alternative communication. In 2005, she became a consultant to the SEEDS Training Project at the Sacramento County Office of Education and participated as a member of the SEEDS Workgroup on Early Education Technology to assist in development and delivery of AT training in early childhood settings throughout California.

Foreword

Congress passed the Technology-Related Assistance for Individuals with Disabilities Act of 1988 (PL 100-407), which expanded the availability of assistive technology services and devices for individuals of all ages with disabilities. The intent of the Tech Act was to promote a systems change or service delivery model that will ultimately result in full access to appropriate assistive technology (AT) devices and services for individuals with disabilities. It also defined AT in a broad sense that has now become universal for most federal, state, and local institutions. Most recently the Individuals with Disabilities Education Improvement Act (IDEA) of 2004 (PL 108-446) continues the requirement that educational teams consider AT for all students with disabilities. This "consideration requirement," determining whether an AT device or service is required, must be made on an individual basis as part of the individualized education program (IEP) and individualized family service plan (IFSP) process. Professionals are responsible for helping children and families select and acquire AT devices and equipment as well as instructing them in their use. Because of these mandates, agencies that serve young children have recognized the need for AT and struggle to meet the challenge in a manner that provides appropriate technology, train professionals and families in the use of AT, and demonstrate unique ways for families to access AT in a timely and reasonable manner. It is reasonable to assume that if teachers and other professionals in the field of early intervention have inadequate skills and knowledge about technologies, then they are failing to consider and use AT with young children.

Assistive Technology for Young Children: Creating Inclusive Learning Environments addresses these challenges by taking the field a step further by illustrating recommended practices in developing AT for young children with disabilities to gain access to and participate in natural environments. Sadao and Robinson have produced a fresh perspective on AT assessment for young children with the Functional Evaluation for Early Technology assessment process. This book integrates and translates information about the law, policies, and research into practical, day-to-day AT strategies to promote learning and development within an inclusive environment. This practical focus is reflected in the scenarios, case studies, activities, and AT resources that give the information real-world applications. Separate chapters focus on particular functional areas for young children, including communication, play, computer access, and emergent literacy. This culminates in a rationale for developing and implementing AT toolkits with young children across daily routines. This special feature provides an AT solution that gives young children immediate access to meaningful experiences and allows them to participate in classroom activities more effectively. This book makes a valuable contribution to the field of early intervention (EI) for this reason and also because it is well organized, thoughtfully written, and comprehensive.

The future of AT depends on the extent to which individuals who provide services to young children and their families have the knowledge and skills to access and use technology services. This book appeals to the needs of a wide range of readers who seek to increase their technology competencies in order to improve access to learning for children with disabilities. It is a privilege to write this foreword to a book of this quality. I applaud the authors for creating a resource that provides solutions for using AT for young children.

Sharon Judge, Ph.D.
Professor and Associate Dean
Old Dominion University
Norfolk, Virginia

Acknowledgments

The genesis of this book began on a dinner napkin at a restaurant in Niagara Falls, at the Division of Early Childhood conference in 2007. Our friend and colleague Susan Sandall at the University of Washington encouraged us to consider synthesizing our ideas into a publication. She introduced us to Heather Shrestha and Johanna Cantler at Paul H. Brookes Publishing Co., who listened and saw possibilities in applying assistive technology (AT) resources in early childhood settings. We then began to take steps to create a resource for families and providers to bring consideration of AT supports into the educational process for every child. Our brainstorming at the dinner table served as the initial outline of the proposal that was further developed, peer reviewed, and ultimately accepted for publication.

While we come from different disciplines, representing early childhood special education and speech-language pathology, we share common professional philosophies based on core values that include the acceptance, inclusion, and full participation of young children with disabilities and their families in all aspects of daily living. Although the field of early childhood has embraced and recommended full inclusion for young children with disabilities, it is not fully implemented across the nation. With the goal of inclusion in mind, this book offers a vehicle to demystify AT as a specialized service and make it practical to infuse into the daily routines of all children. Our intention is to align AT with current and future trends in early childhood, such as universal design for all learners. In doing so, we hope to shift attitudes from a deficit model to capitalizing on child assets in order to move children with disabilities from the periphery into the hub of educational experiences.

The conceptual framework for this book grew out of a collaborative effort sponsored by the Supporting Early Education Delivery Systems (SEEDS) Project, based at the Sacramento County Office of Education and funded by a contract with the California Department of Education, Special Education Division. We want to thank Gary Scott Johnson, SEEDS Project Director, for his vision to establish AT as an initiative for training and technical assistance throughout the state of California. Our involvement in this effort provided the context for understanding the potential contribution for AT in ECSE.

The authors wish to further acknowledge the support and opportunity provided by San Francisco State University (SFSU) for sabbatical time for Nancy Robinson to devote to completion of this project. Much of the research for this book began under the auspices of a collaborative effort funded by the U.S. Department of Education, Office of Special Education Programs, and directed by

Dr. Gloria Soto at SFSU. Dr. Soto's generous mentorship in the field of AAC contributed significantly to our focus on language development and literacy. Many other colleagues at SFSU in the Department of Special Education and Communicative Disorders also made this book possible by covering Dr. Robinson's duties during her sabbatical and we extend our deep gratitude to them.

In addition, we want to thank each of our colleagues in the SEEDS Workgroup on Early Education Technology (SWEET), developed through the SEEDS AT initiative. The members of the SWEET team have been designing and implementing AT training products and materials for young children with disabilities and their families for the past several years. We first would like to acknowledge Catharine Mikitka, SEEDS Program Specialist, for her unique ability to recognize training needs and match them to local programs. Furthermore, her insights about families and children continues to enrich our beliefs about AT for children to promote access to inclusive environments. Jennifer Brown, OTR/L, pediatric occupational therapist for the Sacramento County Office of Education Infant Program, deserves recognition for her unfailing enthusiasm and energy to create adaptations for children to grow and learn with their peers. Debbie Grant, Speech-Language Pathologist and Assistive Technology Specialist, Santa Barbara County Education Office, has inspired us to explore and identify the most recent AT tools and trends to keep us at the forefront of the field. In addition, we appreciate her generosity in reviewing and critiquing earlier versions of this book. The SWEET team has been instrumental in navigating the ever-changing landscape of AT.

We have both benefited from many mentors and leaders in the field of AT for young children. Sharon Judge has written extensively in the field and guided our conceptualization of evidence-based approaches to family-centered and activity-focused AT services with young children. We thank her for her willingness to write the foreword to this book. Pip Campbell and M. Jeanne Wilcox and their Tots 'n Tech Research Institute Team grounded us in the current research and resources for children, families, and providers. Susan Mistrett contributed extensively to the field of AT and play with young children. Her work is evident throughout the design of the assessment model described in this book. There are many other mentors, too many to recognize, throughout each of our professional lives that have impacted our thinking and led to this work.

The completion of any book is a labor of love and a long-term commitment. We spent many hours, together and apart, writing and sharing our work until we were satisfied with the result. Our families were part of this journey and the support of each person made it possible for us to continue and to occasionally pause for renewal. We cannot forget the wonderful barbeques prepared by Lothain Sadao that rewarded us at the end of each day of collaborative writing.

To all readers of this book, whatever your background or occupation, we hope that the resources to follow will provide the impetus for you to embrace AT. The chapters are offered to you as a way to create adaptations for children with disabilities to fully participate in the multiple opportunities of learning.

For our families and especially Sean, Nicole, and Angelica

Introduction

Technology has revolutionized the world in which we live. Social networks, instant messaging, and e-mail connect people around the world with each other as long as the user has access to the Internet. In 2003, 76 percent of school-age children in the United States had computer access at home (Lieb, 2005). Families use computers for communication, games, word processing, publishing, and connecting to the web. Young children are exposed to computers in infancy and toddlerhood either formally through the introduction of baby software programs or informally when exploring their parents' computer keyboard. Battery-operated toys and games are advertised on television programs geared toward a juvenile audience. Car keys are no longer just keys but automated gadgets that can be activated with a touch of a button. Photograph frames are able to hold multiple digital pictures flashed intermittently instead of a static single photograph. Advances in technology have simplified how we do our work and live our lives. Because of these advances, infants and preschoolers have access to many new avenues for learning, and early exposure increases their likelihood of academic success.

When a newborn enters the world, she comes equipped with a sensory system that develops over time as she responds to and manipulates the multiple environments in which she lives. When there is a problem in any of the infant's sensory pathways used to develop communication and knowledge, including hearing, vision, motor, and touch, she is immediately limited to how, what, when, and where she can explore the world around her. Participating in daily routines, such as eating, bathing, and playing, allows young children opportunities to learn about their environment, opportunities that are critical to later school performance. What happens when a young child is restricted from seeing, listening, vocalizing, reaching, grasping, and fully participating in the daily activities that take place in the home or community setting? Typically, her early experiences are significantly compromised, which may in turn inhibit her overall growth and development. Modifying young children's environments by using assistive technology (AT), defined as any tool, device, or adaptation that allows them more ways to gain access to the people, places, and settings where they can be exposed to typical developmental activities, increases opportunities for learning. In addition, all children can benefit when universal design, an approach by which a setting is modified or enhanced to provide access for all children to curriculum and materials, is considered when creating materials for use in the home and in the classroom. This empirical observation supports the basic tenet that AT adaptations are fun and appropriate for everyone. For young children with disabilities without AT supports, however, access to learning is significantly affected and not regained through later special education remediation.

RATIONALE FOR ASSISTIVE TECHNOLOGY WITH YOUNG CHILDREN

AT for young children with disabilities and their families is now recognized as a vehicle to access learning environments that are typically out of reach for them due to the multitude of sensorimotor issues and physical barriers encountered (Langone, Malone, & Kinsley, 1999; Mistrett, 2004; Sawyer, Milbourne, Dugan, & Campbell, 2005; Sullivan & Lewis, 1995). Young children explore their environments through play, communication, and movement to increase their learning capacity. AT devices can be used to help support young children with disabilities access natural environments to develop functional skills in all developmental areas. AT includes a range of low-technology adaptations such as adding page turners to a book or creating picture schedules of a child's day. Similarly, middle-technology options are primarily inexpensive adaptations that typically include a mechanical component such as battery adapters for toys or voice-overs to create 10-second messages. Higher technology solutions such as sophisticated voice output communication systems or a computer with a touchscreen are discriminated from the simpler modifications because they require a significant amount of training and expertise to implement and usually come at a much higher price.

AT devices have been identified as a way to connect young children with learning opportunities within their daily routines (Wilcox, Guimond, Campbell, & Moore, 2006), which meets the requirement of the Individuals with Disabilities Education Act (IDEA) of 1990 (PL 101-476) and its amendments that young children with disabilities must be served in natural environments. Inclusion for children with disabilities using augmentative and alternative communication (AAC) systems in general education settings has been acknowledged as recommended practice for full participation in natural environments (Hunt, Soto, Maier, Müller, & Goetz, 2002). AT is defined by several federal mandates, including the Individuals with Disabilities Education Improvement Act (IDEA) of 2004 (PL 108-446). AAC is included along with AT and is focused on the communication needs of the child. The legal mandates require that AT be considered for young children with disabilities.

Although documentation of the benefits of AT use in early intervention settings can be found in the literature since the mid-1980s, information on the need for training on effective practices for AT has appeared only recently (Campbell, Milbourne, Dugan, & Wilcox, 2006; Wilcox et al., 2006). Furthermore, this research has demonstrated that underutilization of AT in early childhood settings is due to lack of or differences in parent and professional knowledge about its use. Providers have limited opportunities to gain access to training to increase their skills in incorporating AT strategies in the individualized education programs (IEPs) of young children (Judge, 1998; Mistrett, 2001; Sawyer et al., 2005; Weintraub, Bacon, & Wilcox, 2004). Judge surveyed 62 early childhood special educators and found concerns for lack of funding, training for AT device use, family involvement in AT decision making, and the limited support for ongoing technical issues in AT use. As mentioned by Wilcox et al., "Policy and the growing empirical database both support the use of AT for very young children, but if infants and toddlers are to benefit from AT's promise, it will also be necessary for early intervention providers to understand the potential use of AT" (2006, p. 34). In a study they conducted on perceptions of early intervention providers, Wilcox et al. found that 922 survey respondents from across the United States reported an increased utilization of AT when they had more training on AT's benefits in early intervention. Most troublesome is the tendency of districts to focus on training provisions focused on more mainstream topics such as behavior problems or only well-known, high-prevalence disorders such as autism, keeping AT from being adequately addressed in personnel development plans.

AT provided to young children with disabilities can act as a bridge to developing language and play through linking them to participation in daily routines (Campbell et al., 2006; Langone et al., 1999; Mistrett, 2004; Sullivan & Lewis, 1995). Pretti-Frontczak and Bricker (2001) reported on findings that support the practice of embedding language and learning activities within daily routines that results in positive learning outcomes. AT tools then need to be readily available and easily implemented in home and school milieus in order to ensure that language and learning opportunities are accessible for young children with disabilities. Mistrett considered the functional nature of participation in multiple environments and activities such as eating, bathing, changing (clothes or diapers), playing, and reading by categorizing AT tools and strategies into three groups: movement, communication, and use of appropriate materials for daily activities. Similarly, Judge (2006) and Judge, Floyd, and Jeffs (2008) emphasized the importance of materials to be in the hands of the providers who serve young children by offering a toolkit approach divided into three developmental domains: communication, movement, and learning. Sadao, Robinson, and Grant (2007) and Sadao (2008) structured AT training into six modules based on Mistrett's functional learning model: overview, assessment, early literacy, communication, play, and computers. Furthermore, Sadao, Brown, and Grant (2009) organized AT tools to support assessment and intervention in early childhood special education programs by identifying toolkit items matched with developmental areas such as social-emotional, communication, literacy, play, motor, academic, and recreation, with possible learning outcomes. Although these authors provided a framework for AT use for young children with disabilities by linking low-technology devices and materials with both functionally based and developmentally appropriate outcomes, evidence-based research supporting the use of AT devices and AAC systems with young children is limited. However, current research has shown very positive results in using AT to enhance learning opportunities (Grant & Singer 2004; Hitchcock & Noonan 2000; Weikle & Hadadian 2003).

Grant and Singer (2004) explored using computer-assisted instruction (CAI) in a 3-year series of case studies with infants and toddlers with disabilities. They found that a touchscreen was as good as or better than using laminated pictures. The study offered a glimpse at the benefits of CAI use with infants and the future possibilities to consider. Hitchcock and Noonan (2000) found CAI use with preschoolers increased their preacademic skill levels and motivation for learning. Weikle and Hadadian (2003) summarized several promising AT efforts focused on infants and toddlers with disabilities. Their review flagged several efforts that have advanced the practice of employing computer technologies to benefit both emergent literacy skills and receptive and expressive communication. Parette, Boeckmann, and Hourcade (2008) recommended several software programs for teachers to consider when attempting to provide techniques to improve the reading skills of young children with disabilities. Furthermore, the literature to date has proposed several toolkit approaches to assure that AT is readily accessible for use in early intervention settings (Judge, 2006; Mistrett, 2004; Sadao, Robinson & Grant 2008, Sadao et al., 2009).

DEFINING ASSISTIVE TECHNOLOGY

AT is defined by several federal mandates, including IDEA 2004. An AT device is described as

> any item, piece of equipment, or product system, whether acquired commercially off the shelf, modified, or customized, that is used to increase, maintain, or improve the

functional capabilities of a child with a disability. The term does not include a medical device that is surgically implanted, or the replacement of such device. (34 C.F.R. §300.5)

AAC overlaps with AT and includes technology processes and tools that focus specifically on the communication needs of the child. Furthermore, the complementary nature of AAC and AT can be conceptualized as overlapping and divergent fields because AAC includes multiple communication modalities that do not involve technology, such as natural gestures, vocal sounds, speech, and sign language (Cress, 2006). More information on AAC can be found in Chapter 5.

A variety of AT considerations can be used in daily routines for minimal cost and documented on the IFSP.

> For children under three, if assistive technology is identified as part of a child's individualized family service plan (IFSP) and if the family has exhausted all other possible sources of funding, such as Medicaid or health insurance, it must be provided at 'no cost' under Part C of IDEA (34 C.F.R. §303.527). No eligible child can be denied an assistive technology device or service because of a family's inability to pay. (Hanline, Nunes, & Worthy, 2007, p. 5)

A section devoted to AT considerations is required in an IFSP, which is used to document services for children with disabilities who are under 3 years old, and an IEP, which is used for children between 3 and 21 years old. Therefore, the legally mandated policies and procedures related to AT use provide a foundational structure for professionals to refer to when charting a course for AT supports with young children with disabilities.

TYPES OF ASSISTIVE TECHNOLOGY OPTIONS FOR YOUNG CHILDREN

Categorizing AT devices and materials provides a framework for selecting AT devices for young children. Table 1.1 lists types of AT available for different technical levels. No technology refers to the individual body of the child such as sign language or a simple gesture for bridging the access to the learning environment (Hanline et al., 2007). Implementing AT and AAC includes both high- and low-technology opportunities for young children as vehicles to enhance access to communication and learning in natural environments that they may not be able to gain access to on their own due to sensory challenges (Sadao et al., 2007). Before considering AT, programs need to determine the working definition they will adopt when deciding which tools are most appropriate. Some staff may only consider high technology as AT and not include other low-technology options on the IFSP or IEP.

Although there are both low-technology and high-technology AT and AAC options available for young children with disabilities, parents and professionals often possess differing attitudes toward the benefits of AT use with young children. In addition, they may be at the novice level in understanding how to include AT as a support in the educational plans of young children with disabilities (Judge, 1998; Sawyer et al., 2005; Weintraub et al., 2004). Studies examining both parent and professional perceptions of the potential of AT revealed varying amounts of information available about AT and inadequate training options for gaining an increased awareness of AT (Judge, 1998; Sawyer et al., 2005). Even though program staff indicated some familiarity with AT devices, in general, early intervention programs offering services to young children with disabilities typically were missing plans for increasing awareness about AT with parents and professionals (Dugan,

Table 1.1. Types of AT

Technical level	Purpose	Functional area	Cost and training needs	Sample tools
Low	Increase access to books, games, and activities	Communication, motor, play, and literacy	Low: under $100; no training required	Page turners, slant boards, communication symbols, communication boards, daily schedules
Mid (light)	Provide a voice for nonverbal; offer access to learning and social opportunities	Communication, motor, play, and literacy	Under $500; minimal training required	Adapted toys, basic switch, single-message device, multiple-message device, software, and touchscreen
High	Provide a vehicle for language development and learning through alternative speaking methods	Communication, literacy, and play	Expensive; training required	Augmentative and alternative communication system either dedicated or on a computer, iPod Touch, or iPad

Milbourne, Campbell, & Wilcox, 2004; Judge, 2002; Lane & Mistrett, 2002; Sadao et al., 2007). Furthermore, parents usually defined AT more with low-technology items that were suggested by family and friends, whereas professionals thought of high-technology systems and often avoided recommending them due to the exorbitant cost of acquiring such a device (Dugan et al., 2004; Mistrett, 2004). Therefore, AT for young children with disabilities tends to remain on the periphery of supports to employ that encourages overall development.

The major factors creating a gap between AT availability and AT implementation include parent and professional lack of understanding about the effectiveness of its use, minimal prospects of learning more about the advantages of AT in supporting inclusive learning environments, variations in parent and professional perceptions regarding what constitutes AT tools for young children, and a solid grasp of the possibilities for enhancing a young child's learning and growth by using AT supports. Wilcox et al. (2006) reported, however, that training appears to increase AT consideration in early intervention settings. Focusing on creating training opportunities for both parents and professionals is the most powerful strategy for decreasing the gap between AT options and actual AT interventions (Parette & Stoner, 2008; Stowitschek & Guest, 2006; Wilcox et al., 2006). This book offers a way to bridge the chasm between the wealth of technology currently available and the minimal implementation in early intervention practice. Having a comprehensive, centralized source for AT service delivery in early learning settings puts the information into the hands of families and practitioners. Here is where it will make the most difference for young children with disabilities by increasing opportunities to gain access to multiple inclusive environments in their home, school, and community.

OVERVIEW OF BOOK CONTENTS

The following chapters provide problems and solutions for using AT for young children under 5 years old. The format of each chapter includes the following items.

- Rationale
- Child considerations

- Topic-specific technology considerations
- The Functional Evaluation for Early Technology (FEET) case examples
- Questions
- Tips

Each chapter reviews the pertinent research supporting the functional domains addressed. A problem-solving technique is presented that helps the reader to follow a step-by-step approach in determining the appropriate AT tools to consider. Each content chapter focuses on a particular functional area for young children including communication, play, computer access, and emergent literacy. The FEET assessment system is provided as a way to evaluate potential AT considerations for the child. In addition, a variety of daily routines are considered in each chapter to apply various AT strategies across settings. Infant, toddler, and preschool learning foundations are referenced for each developmental area presented to provide a foundation for learning goals. AT applications are included for sample children using the FEET process. FEET forms are also included on the CD-ROM. Questions, tips, and other resources are included at the end of the book to provide readers with additional information on where to access resources via the Internet. References are also listed at the end of the book for works cited within the chapters.

REVIEWING THE CONTENTS OF EACH CHAPTER

The first chapter provides a brief overview of the field of AT and the format of the book. Chapter 2 addresses the guiding principles, laws, and funding options for AT. Chapter 3 introduces activity-based learning theories and recommended practices for young children with disabilities. Chapter 4 introduces the FEET assessment tool and process for AT considerations. Chapter 5 begins the focus on AT learning strategies within daily routines. Communication and AT is the first content area connecting language development and AT supports. Next, Chapter 6 focuses on play and learning, providing an in-depth look at play theory and application with young children. This chapter emphasizes the developmental and functional concerns for play and AT's role in creating access to play environments and promoting friendships and other social capabilities. Chapter 7 provides a thorough review of literacy issues concerning young children and discusses a plethora of theories on learning to read. The chapter encompasses both low- and high-technology possibilities to formulate a literacy-rich environment through enhancing books and other reading materials with a variety of adaptations and supports. Chapter 8 introduces the reader to computer considerations, including both hardware and software enhancements. A section is included that provides a list of child considerations and developmental skills for learning how to use the computer. Finally, Chapter 9 presents background information on how to design AT toolkits to use in assessment and intervention. The toolkits are divided into the four content areas presented in the earlier chapters. Each toolkit contains an AT map that helps the user navigate through AT assessment results, daily routines, potential child goals, and low-technology devices and materials that may support those outcomes. The columns list sample assessment items; possible natural environments such as home, school, or community; AT outcomes; and suggested toolkit items. Sample forms suggested in the various chapters are included on the CD-ROM for reproduction purposes.

SUMMARY

The book includes recommended practice in developing AT for young children with complex disabilities to gain access to and participate in natural environments and inclusive settings in early intervention and preschool services. The availability of technology to provide tools for development and learning for young children with disabilities in the birth to 5-year age range has expanded rapidly. The available technologies range from simple adaptations of typical activities and toys to more sophisticated technology solutions. Adaptations include adjustments of book pages to make them easier to turn and switch activation for battery-operated toys. Also available are a variety of low-tech voice output communication aids (VOCAs) and high-tech devices with computerized voices known as speech-generating devices (SGDs) to increase communication options. A host of computer hardware modifications such as touchscreens and switch interfaces, along with a plethora of cause-and-effect software for young children, exist to provide opportunities to explore computerized games and learning environments. The proliferation of technology to assist in the growth and learning of young children encompasses items for typically developing children and those with disabilities. The presence of technology is continuing to expand exponentially and with it comes a merging of AT devices specifically crafted for young children with disabilities to more universally designed tools that will soon become accessible to all. The book provides users with technologies and links the tools to existing curricular trends and teaching methodologies to increase the exposure of young children with disabilities to play and learning experiences that were previously unobtainable. AT is one answer to influencing full inclusion in schools and communities.

SUMMARY OF THE BENEFITS OF ASSISTIVE TECHNOLOGY

As technology for the general population becomes increasingly efficient, affordable, and available, the separation between technology and specialized supports for people with disabilities is shrinking. This movement from parallel technological systems to integrated options for everyone simplifies AT considerations by making them easily obtainable by all. Children who once were confined to limited choices to play and learn with others are now beginning to reap the benefits that technology offers. As will be demonstrated in the chapters to follow, scenarios of children before and after technology adaptations provide a glimpse at how simple classroom modifications increase access to general education curriculum and promote learning and development within an inclusive environment. A child who once was confined to a wheelchair now can be settled in a corner chair to enjoy circle time with the other children in the class or placed in a walker with a single message voice output device on the playground to direct classmates to "go" when it is their turn to slide. Simple modifications such as a binder covered with Velcro-friendly material that angles books in such a way that children can now view them are readily obtainable in home and school situations. Books placed on a slant board offer the child with limited use of reach and grasp and difficulty maintaining postural control while sitting a way to turn the pages of a book or view pictures that previously were not accessible. A software program with an animated edition of a story helps a child learn to attend to pictures on a screen and understand the auditory sequence of the story that he might not be able to focus on in a typical play setting where distractions are high and visual range is confined to his immediate environment. More costly technologies such as complex communication systems or adapted computer hardware are becoming more numerous and reasonably priced, such as a touchscreen built into the computer frame. The universal design of toys and games has ushered in a new trend of battery-operated and electronic versions that are easier to access by children with disabilities. In addition, toys have increased in their infant comfort with modifications to lights, color, texture, size, sound, and appeal that allow easier viewing, grasping, and manipulating to occur. Web sites geared for play and learning ideas that typically catered to typically developing children now provide sections on adapted toys and games focused on young children with disabilities. The resources are many for identifying potential AT tools to consider in home and school environments.

There is also a noted increase in the number and types of AT training materials appearing on web sites developed by various educational and health agencies across the country as well as internationally. A select few national and state technical assistance programs are carrying out research on AT use with infants, toddlers, and preschoolers and post results on AT effectiveness and recommendations for AT devices on their web sites. The advances in information acquisition via the computer including networking tools such as list serves, video streaming and conferencing, online communication, and multiple search engines multiply the impact of technology with the touch of a mouse. More online training programs focused on AT are springing up across the nation. With this book as a guide, all teachers, staff, and therapists providing services to young children, including those with disabilities, and their parents are now equipped with the tools to be successful in supporting AT considerations in their programs and locales.

2

Legal Foundations and Funding Options for Early Assistive Technology

Sean is a 2-year-old boy with multiple physical, sensorimotor, and communication challenges. His single mother works part time and does not have private insurance. Sean receives medical coverage under Medicaid and early intervention services from the county infant/toddler program. The coordinator of the program is well versed in the myriad of laws that support Sean's access to educational and community services. Sean communicates with definitive eye movements, head turning, facial expressions, and reaching with his right arm. His cognitive abilities are difficult for the specialists to determine due to his significant physical disabilities. He is using a small button switch attached to his adapted chair for activating toys and can demonstrate understanding of cause and effect. His teacher and therapists use an eye-gaze board with pictures from his environment for Sean to communicate with yes/no answers and request participation with family members, staff, toys, and other familiar activities. The early intervention coordinator recognizes Sean's potential and need for more sophisticated AT options to encourage further communication development. His mother has enrolled him in an Early Head Start onsite child care program and hopes that a computer with a touchscreen can be purchased so he can begin to use cause-and-effect software and advance to an SGD to make choices by selecting words that represent, activities and toys he enjoys. The early intervention coordinator asked the county AT specialist about assessing Sean to determine if he qualifies for high-tech AT such as an adapted computer and/or communication system. The AT specialist has already indicated she has no experience with younger children. Her recommendation is for Sean to continue to use the simple switches and communication boards until he reaches his third birthday, when special education will conduct an assessment of his learning needs. The early intervention coordinator does not want to wait and is worried that he will regress in his communication skills. She does not know where to turn to find other assessment and funding sources.

The story presented here is a familiar one echoed in early intervention programs across the nation. Often, children with more significant disabilities experience limited access to learning environments during the most critical learning years of their lives. This chapter discusses three categories of AT information that families and service providers must consider in order to find appropriate AT supports for young children with disabilities. The chapter reviews the legal requirements for AT consideration, guiding principles for AT use, and potential funding sources to obtain AT materials and devices.

Families and professionals must be knowledgeable regarding the legal parameters defining AT and AT services in their quest to identify appropriate devices and systems for young children with disabilities. In addition to the laws supporting AT use with young children, administrators and service providers must be able to provide justification for purchasing AT devices, which are often costly, by adhering to sound guiding principles supported in the early intervention literature. In addition, once review of the applicable laws and written justification are completed, funding sources for acquiring AT devices must be identified. Judge (2000) indicated that funding is the major barrier to successfully acquiring and using AT devices and services. In surveying 282 Part C providers across the nation, Milbourne and Campbell (2008) found that the prominent barriers to using AT with young children with disabilities are: 1) the availability of funding, 2) knowledge of early intervention staff regarding the potential of AT, 3) lack or use of lending libraries, and 4) provider or family access to training. Information gathering is the first step to consider in using AT with young children. Families and professionals alike need knowledge of three major areas of AT, including laws, rationale, and funding sources as a prerequisite to advocate and procure the appropriate AT device and/or services for a young child. Competence in these areas of AT is needed to provide the foundation for professionals to build sound partnerships with families in the process of collaborative assessment and determining the child's functional skills and accompanying AT supports to enhance access to multiple learning environments.

ASSISTIVE TECHNOLOGY LAWS

Returning to the story about Sean, the early intervention coordinator was familiar with the laws that supported considering AT to enable children to gain access to multiple learning environments. There are four federal laws that include the requirements for AT for people with disabilities: IDEA 2004 (PL 108-446), the Technology-Related Assistance for Individuals with Disabilities Act of 1988 (PL 100-407), Section 504 of the Rehabilitation Act of 1973 (PL 93-112), and the Americans with Disabilities Act (ADA) of 1990 (PL 101-336). These laws are reauthorized or amended every 5 years and accompanying regulations usually follow, so it is important that families and service providers stay abreast of the changes through training events, conferences, and monitoring government-sponsored web sites. The primary law covering early childhood special education is the IDEA 2004. This special education law was created in 1975 as the Education for All Handicapped Children Act (PL 94-142) to ensure that children with disabilities ages 3–21 received their education at no cost and within the least restrictive environment (LRE). Free appropriate public education (FAPE) has become the underlying principle to support the educational rights of children with disabilities and their families. FAPE requires school districts to offer appropriate educational services to any child deemed eligible for special education services through a team-based assessment process. The services must be specifically designed to meet the individual needs of the student. Special education law provided the foundation to serving children in the communities where they reside by providing a comprehensive assessment and diagnosis of their needs and developing an IEP that outlines how they will be educated through a variety of community, school, and specialized supports.

Although AT has been included in the landmark legislation since its inception in 1975, AT devices and services were not defined under the law until the IDEA 1991 amendments (PL 102-119). IDEA 1991 included considering AT when reviewing appropriate services for children who qualified under the law. Since 1997, IDEA has required considering AT devices and services when developing plans for infants and toddlers under Part C. During the 1997 reauthorization and the 1999 regulations, AT devices and services became required for districts to consider when developing each child's IEP. In the Part C, birth-to-3 programs, AT devices and/or services may be indicated as a component of the child's IFSP. Part C is a discretionary federal grant that requires states that receive Part C funds to provide a comprehensive, multidisciplinary system of early intervention services. The Part C system must offer an evaluation at no cost to the family that includes both family and child assessments and developing an IFSP that specifies family and child strengths and needs. Due to the discretionary nature of the funding source, Part C programs differ from Part B special education programs in their provision of FAPE. Families may be required to share the costs of early intervention services, including the purchasing of an AT device or service, if they are covered under public or private insurance options. Part C becomes the payor of last resort when the family has explored all potential avenues of funding sources.

> For children under three, if assistive technology is identified as part of a child's (IFSP) and if the family has exhausted all other possible sources of funding, such as Medicaid or health insurance, it must be provided at 'no cost' under Part C of IDEA (34 C.F.R. §303.527). No eligible child can be denied an assistive technology device or service because of a family's inability to pay. (Hanline et al., 2007, p. 5)

Table 2.1 provides a summary, focus, and definition of laws that require consideration of AT for young children with disabilities.

Beginning in 1988, the Technology-Related Assistance for Individuals with Disabilities Act (PL 100-407) provided state grants to increase availability and access to AT devices and services. Individuals who do not qualify under IDEA 2004 may be protected under the ADA and receive the necessary AT devices and services to improve their daily lives. The Assistive Technologies Act (ATA) of 1998 (PL 105-394) first defined an AT device that was similar to and adopted by IDEA 2004, except for the exclusion of surgically implanted devices. ATA services include evaluating potential users, purchasing and servicing devices, and training families and professionals on using the devices. Under provisions of the ATA, each state operates an AT center to provide information about potential AT resources and services. The Association of Assistive Technology Act Programs (ATAP), a national association of AT centers, serves as a member-based organization of AT centers across the United States to coordinate AT services at a national level. By visiting their web site (http://www.ataporg.org/atap/index.php), users can find AT resources at both the state and local level. For instance, in California, ATA funds are managed by the State Department of Rehabilitation Office supporting a State AT Network of services and training, as well as a lending library, through a contract with AT Network. In Pennsylvania, the Institute on Disabilities at Temple University oversees the Pennsylvania Initiative on Assistive Technology (PIAT).

Whether based within a public agency, private agency, or university program, parents and professionals interested in AT funding and technical assistance supports may want to familiarize themselves with their state program. The law specifies that each state must promote interagency coordination when considering using AT devices to capitalize on existing funding sources and build capacity across programs serving people

Table 2.1. AT laws

Focus	Definition	Law
AT	"Each public agency must ensure that assistive technology devices or assistive technology services, or both, as those terms are defined in 300/5 and 300/6 respectively, are made available to a child as required as a part of the child's special education under Sec. 300.36, related services under sec. 300.34 or supplementary aids and services under Sec. 300.38 and 300/114(a)(2)(ii). On a case-by-case basis, the use of school-purchased assistive technology devices in a child's home or in other settings is required if the IEP team determines that the child needs access to those devices in order to receive FAPE."	IDEA 2004 regulations authority (20 U.S.C. §§ 1412[a][1], 1412[a][12][B][i]
AT device	An assistive technology *device* is defined as "any item, piece of equipment, or product system, whether acquired commercially off the shelf, modified, or customized, that is used to increase, maintain, or improve the functional capabilities of a child with a disability. The term does not include a medical device that is surgically implanted, or the replacement of such device."	IDEA 2004 (34 C.F.R. § 300.5)
AT device	"Any item, piece of equipment, or product system, whether acquired commercially off the shelf, modified, or customized, that is used to increase, maintain, or improve functional capabilities of individuals with disabilities."	Assistive Technology Act (ATA; S2432, Section 3, 3)
AT service	"Any service that directly assists a child with a disability in the selection, acquisition, or use of an assistive technology device. The term includes: a. The evaluation of the needs of a child with a disability, including a functional evaluation of the child in the child's customary environment; b. Purchasing, leasing, or otherwise providing for the acquisition of assistive technology devices by children with disabilities; c. Selecting, designing, fitting, customizing, adapting, applying, maintaining, repairing, or replacing assistive technology devices; d. Coordinating and using other therapies, interventions, or services with assistive technology devices, such as those associated with existing education and rehabilitation plans and programs; e. Training or technical assistance for a child with a disability or, if appropriate, that child's family; and f. Training or technical assistance for professionals (including individuals providing education or rehabilitation services), employers, or other individuals who provide services to, employ, or are otherwise substantially involved in the major life functions of that child."	IDEA 2004 (34 C.F.R. § 300.6)

with disabilities and their families. The purpose of the law is to increase access to and availability of funding resources and information concerning AT devices and services.

Other laws that support individuals' rights to have AT considered include the Rehabilitation Act of 1973 and the ADA. Under section 504 of the Rehabilitation Act, programs receiving federal monies cannot discriminate against individuals due to their disability. Accommodations including AT devices and services may be required for students to increase their opportunities for participation in the general education setting. The ADA is a more comprehensive law concerning people with disabilities and includes provisions for children that may not qualify under IDEA 2004 but may benefit from accommodations due to their disabilities.

ASSISTIVE TECHNOLOGY PRINCIPLES

Recall that Sean's IFSP team documented the intended outcome to increase his communication skills through the support of AT devices and materials. The team met difficulties, however, when attempting to engage the district-level AT personnel to explore using a computer and the appropriate AT to provide access needed to support Sean to communicate and learn with his peers. In order to move forward, identifying a rationale for recommending AT is the next step for the IFSP team. Funding for educational purposes is likely to be available when administrators and other personnel understand and identify the benefits of considering AT for young children. Under pressure for educational accountability, district approval for funding an expensive device is more feasible when the assessment team for AT completes thorough diagnostics, observations, and AT trials through individual child and family assessment. The team must also be aware of the rationale of AT benefits for the entire population of young children with disabilities. The precursors to purchasing a high-technology device must include a discussion of the benefits of such a device for a young child. Without a well-informed team, the risk for device discontinuation and limited cost benefit is high. Judge (2000) indicated that discontinued use of AT devices typically occurs when professionals do not seek the advice of families concerning the particular reasons for device selection. Discontinuation of AT devices results from lack of team consensus, lack of access to repair for the device, and lack of motivation to use the device for the reasons specified originally by the family in the IFSP. In order to prevent device discontinuation, adequate parent and professional awareness and knowledge of AT devices and services are essential. To avoid the pitfalls of selecting, purchasing, and implementing AT devices, teams should adhere to sound AT guiding principles that are known to all members, including the family, administrators, and other personnel.

The most comprehensive listing of guiding principles for early childhood special education is reviewed in the *DEC Recommended Practices* (Sandall, Hemmeter, Smith, & McLean, 2005). Furthermore, a chapter by Stremel (2005) is dedicated to AT applications and includes recommended practices that help educational teams consider AT use by providing a researched-based rationale for AT devices and services. The overarching principles focus on families and professionals staying abreast of technology applications available in the field and working together in formulating and following through on plans for AT use in both the home and classroom environments. Training opportunities for families, staff, and others must be ongoing to ensure the device supports the growth and development of young children in multiple situations and activities. Selecting AT devices must be based on family preference and be accessible across multiple learning settings. In addition to the *DEC Recommended Practices*, a California training and technical assistance workgroup focused on AT developed a set of guiding principles supported in the early childhood special education AT literature (Sadao, 2008). Table 2.2 identifies nine guiding AT principles with supports from the literature and corresponding recommended practices for technology. Each principle must be acknowledged by the IEP/IFSP team and made applicable to local resources when considering AT for a young child with a disability. Each of the guiding principles shown in Table 2.2 is defined further in the following section, with suggestions for implementation. Readers are encouraged to consider each principle when determining the need for AT to support inclusive practices for young children with disabilities.

Principle 1

Families are involved in developing and implementing AT devices for young children.
IEP/IFSP teams are responsible for fostering positive working relationships with the families that they serve. In order to fulfill this commitment, ongoing communication between

Table 2.2.   Guiding principles for AT training and technical assistance

Guiding principle	Supporting literature	Division for Early Childhood recommended practices
1. Families are involved in developing and implementing AT devices for young children.	Parette and Brotherson (1996)	Families and professionals collaborate in planning and implementing the use of AT.
2. AT devices are infused in the child's daily routines across the home, child care, and other settings.	Dugan et al. (2004); Judge (2002); Lane and Mistrett (2002); Mistrett (2001, 2004); Stremel (2005)	Professionals utilize AT in intervention programs for children.
3. AT tools are easy to use and can be adapted to the environments of the child and family.	Judge (1998); Sadao et al. (2009)	Service programs and professionals consider the least intrusive, least expensive, yet effective low-tech devices in making decisions about AT for individual children.
4. Families are able to obtain AT devices from providers or a lending library or receive directions for using the equipment or activity.	Milbourne and Campbell (2008)	Families and professionals use technology to access information and support.
5. AT assessment and intervention is addressed in a team-based collaborative manner with the family as an integral member of the decision-making team.	Judge (2002); Long et al. (2003); Mistrett (2004)	Professionals' use and selection of AT is based on a family's preferences within assessment, implementation, and evaluation activities.
6. AT is a consideration for every child during the development of the IFSP/IEP.	Hanline et al. (2007); Stremel (2005)	Training and technical support programs are available to support technology applications.
7. AT is a strategy to foster learning and independence.	Long et al. (2003); Sullivan and Lewis (1995)	Service programs and professionals consider AT applications to increase children's ability to function and participate in diverse and less restrictive environments.
8. Families and professionals have access to ongoing training opportunities to increase their knowledge and awareness of AT use and benefits.	Sadao et al. (2009)	State agencies, service programs, and personnel training programs infuse technology at the preservice and in-service levels to increase competencies of service providers, families, and administrators in assistive, instructional, and informational technologies.
9. Families and professionals have information on potential funding sources for AT devices.	Judge (2000)	Service programs and professionals have knowledge of sources for funding and consider procedures to coordinate resources for funding and reuse.

Sources: Hemmeter et al. (2005); Sadao, Robinson, and Grant (2008).
Key: IFSP, individualized family service plan; IEP, individualized education program.

families and professional must be a priority in early intervention programs. In addition to the required meetings, programs may hold weekly or monthly parent meetings in which AT solutions are presented. Fact sheets about various low-, middle-, and high-technology devices can be made available in program waiting areas. A list of annotated links concerning AT use with young children can be provided to parents who indicate access and use of computers in the home setting. Program web sites can include a section on resources for more information about AT. Programs can create blogs about AT and what particular devices have been used by other parents in the program. Parents can be included in professional workshops and vendor demonstrations about various AT devices and services.

Principle 2

AT devices are infused in the child's daily routines across the home, child care, and other settings.
Simple AT tools such as adapted books and toys with switches can be experimented with in various learning environments. Professionals can create or gain access to lending libraries to explore different types of AT devices and determine utility in various educational settings. Allowing all personnel involved in the child's daily activities to try out various devices will result in the most appropriate device selection and continued use.

Principle 3

AT tools are easy to use and can be adapted to the environments of the child and family.
Special education professionals can demonstrate simple devices for families and other educational staff and conduct make-and-take workshops on simple adaptations to use in home and school settings. Professionals can organize a basic AT toolkit including one-page fact sheets on different tools that can be lent out to families and educational staff. There are resources available online for creating simple toolkits that including communication boards, adapted toys and games, and adapted books.

Principle 4

Families are able to obtain AT devices from providers or a lending library or receive directions for using the equipment or activity.
If families are to fully participate as active members in selecting and implementing AT, then trial equipment with accompanying information on its use must be readily available from the program. Creating basic lending libraries of an assortment of AT devices that can be checked out for short periods of time allows families to experiment with different supports such as an SGD that offers several categories of requests for the child to create requests for favorite foods, toys, and activities. Service providers need to stay abreast of commercially offered AT tools by subscribing to list serves of various AT companies and schedule regular visits to online sources for updates. Staff can assist parents in connecting with local and regional AT centers where devices may be on display and lent out for trial periods. Families need information on the benefits to utilizing AT supports through contacts with their local family organizations and national technical assistance web sites where information on AT use can be downloaded.

Principle 5

AT assessment and intervention is addressed in a team-based collaborative manner with the family as an integral member of the decision-making team.
This book emphasizes the importance of adhering to a team-based approach to service provision when considering AT for young children. Developing a relationship with family members who have primary roles to care for the child with special needs clearly may extend beyond a single initial visit. Identifying family perspectives, however, will provide direction in completing all stages of assessment and intervention.

Principle 6

AT is a consideration for every child during the development of the IFSP/IEP.
The program administrator provides an agenda for each IFSP/IEP team meeting that

includes considering AT for the young child. The assessment process for developing AT solutions with young children can be used to explore the types of AT tools the team may want to first consider on a trial basis (see Chapter 4). Using the basic assessment information gathered from the initial evaluation and each team member's particular expertise is the first step in determining whether AT supports might be advantageous for a particular child.

Principle 7

AT is a strategy to foster learning and independence.
Considering AT must be made in the context of how technological supports might enhance the child's access to learning environments and curriculum. When considering any outcome focused on nurturing the child's independence in home and school environments is the first indicator that some type of technology might bridge the child's connection with the world around him or her. The question to consider by the team is whether the child can gain access to learning environments readily available to other children. If the answer is "no," then AT may need to be considered.

Principle 8

Families and professionals have access to ongoing training opportunities to increase their knowledge and awareness of AT use and benefits.
There is a wealth of information available online to parents and professionals regarding AT use with young children. The team can create an AT binder that is shared with parents and updated frequently and includes lists of web links reviewing AT basics. Many state and federally funded training and technical assistance programs have included AT as a focus on their web sites. In addition, there are training modules available in individual and group formats that programs can easily obtain. Including a monthly AT workshop at a program or creating a monthly parent make-and-take activity can ensure that AT is reviewed in an ongoing way. Technology advances occur by the minute, so it is critical that programs stay abreast of changes in the field. State and local AT agencies are potential collaboration partners to hold annual AT trainings across agencies. In addition to sharing costs for the AT training, a collaborative effort encourages cross-fertilization among programs serving young children and increases the awareness level of AT possibilities in local communities. Programs can also take advantage of AT vendors' training resources. Vendors may provide training events at no cost to the program to advertise their particular merchandise.

Principle 9

Families and professionals have information on potential funding sources for AT devices.
At least one staff member needs to be knowledgeable about program and community-level resources concerning the funding of AT devices and services. Enlist the assistance of district-level grant writers to explore community resources for funding AT through minigrants and special projects. Include an AT subcommittee on the local early childhood interagency committee to investigate funding sources not readily available through public and private insurance programs. Early intervention and preschool program coordinators need to network with any staff involved in funding AT and other school-related projects. Lastly, get to know AT vendors and their representatives in the state. AT companies often provide products on a trial basis and free materials as part of their marketing efforts.

Programs serving young children with disabilities will benefit from following the guiding principles offered here by increasing the likelihood of success in garnering the support for AT consideration. Families and professionals who are knowledgeable about the benefits of AT are more likely to reduce program barriers that may include lack of administrative support, family dissatisfaction, and inevitably device discontinuation that becomes costly to all involved.

ASSISTIVE TECHNOLOGY FUNDING SOURCES

Once the IFSP/IEP team has determined the need to develop AT solutions for a particular child or children, identifying funding sources comes next. In Sean's case, the early intervention coordinator was familiar with applicable laws when considering AT for a young child, but was unsure how to complete an assessment for Sean that would justify the need for more sophisticated high-technology devices. The cost of a high-tech AT system that may include a computer-based program or SGD is often so expensive that administrators and staff avoid suggesting it. Similarly, families may hear about a particular system or company that they want the professionals to purchase without specific information about how the use of the device would enhance their child's learning potential and independence. Judge (2000) discussed the problems inherent in using traditional assessments to identify the specific functional skills of young children that would justify purchasing more expensive equipment. Information about how children experience multiple learning environments cannot be determined when professionals in contrived testing situations outside of their daily routines assess them. When children's physical and cognitive challenges pose difficulties in accurately measuring performance and progress, professionals may view the possibility of an AT device to increase access to learning environments as a premature consideration until such time the benefits can be clearly specified. Judge further recommended that professionals develop and follow assessment and intervention processes that involve families in all aspects of determining the need for AT. In addition, Judge and Parette (1998) indicated that professionals' lack of knowledge regarding funding policies is one of the main reasons AT is not purchased. IFSP/IEP team members, including administrative staff, need an awareness of potential AT funding sources once the assessment process reveals the need for exploring AT supports.

There are 12 steps in determining funding options for a particular AT device for a child during the assessment and intervention process. The IFSP/IEP team can use Figure 2.1 to help identify the funding actions that need to be accomplished in order to purchase an AT device, especially when considering high-technology systems.

Step 1: Child Data

In the first step of the funding process, the team completes a transdisciplinary assessment using applicable assessment tools for the child's age, developmental level, and specific disability conditions. The information about the child characteristics, learning potential, and functional skills in multiple learning environments is used to create learning outcomes that are linked to the general education curriculum and learning foundations for infants/toddlers and preschoolers. The team utilizes child data to determine the need for further AT assessment using the FEET assessment model. Once additional information is obtained about the child's functional skills, the team moves to the next step in the process.

Step 2: Individualized Family Service Plan/ Individualized Education Program Documentation

On the IFSP/IEP, the team records the child data determined from the preliminary and AT assessments. The team determines whether AT supports are critical to the child's overall

Funding consideration	Funding question	Funding action
Child data	What are the specific needs of the child?	
IFSP/IEP documentation	What is specified on the IFSP/IEP about assistive technology (AT)?	
Device determination	Are the devices a medical necessity? For communication purposes? Other?	
Child outcomes	What does the family hope to accomplish with the support of an AT device for their child?	
Learning environments	In what types of learning environments will the child use the device?	
Device utility	For what purpose?	
Device longevity	Is the device for a short-term goal or a long-term outcome?	
Device appropriateness	What types of devices have been considered?	
Device availability	What companies sell the device and at what cost?	
Device sources	What are the potential funding sources available based on the age and needs of the child?	
Funding application	What types of documents are required for the funding sources being investigated?	
Funding appeal	If denied, what appeals process is available to parents?	

Figure 2.1.   Funding action steps. (*Key:* IFSP, individualized family service plan; IEP, individualized education program.)

functioning and necessary for participation in daily routines. The team notes specific information about the types of AT tools, such as low-technology supports that will be explored during the implementation phase of the plan. The team considers and documents if more assessment and a device trial phase is needed. The team can agree to try a variety of AT supports, such as adapted books or simple switches, with a plan to meet again to measure the effectiveness of the initial adaptations. The team builds on the information gathered about AT use and considers other AT options if the simple and less costly AT strategies are ineffective. The team may want to note what resources they have for purchasing or obtaining the low-tech tools and materials, such as gaining access to the teacher supply budget to purchase self-adhesive foam to make book props or asking the PTA for foam and material to make adapted grips for toys, markers, and other play items.

Step 3: Child Outcomes

When the team has collected a variety of child data from the transdisciplinary assessment process, they need to record the child's next step on the IFSP/IEP. The team can refer to the learning foundations for infant/toddlers or preschoolers available in their state. In Chapter 9, examples are provided on how to connect foundations and curriculum to child outcomes and AT supports. The outcome is linked to the goals for individual children, rather than the intended device. The intended child outcomes must be functional and tied to the general curriculum. For example, the staff wanted Sean to be able to have a computer system for communicating in an Early Head Start child care program. The device cannot drive the development of goals for Sean. Rather, the staff records the outcomes they want him to accomplish in the learning setting and provides assessment data as the rationale for the intended outcome that is selected by the team. The child care teachers can share the learning foundations they are using with the rest of the children and talk about what universal design characteristics exist in the setting, such as an existing computer with some software. If the goals for Sean are to increase his requests for activities by making choices, then methods for communication may include indicating yes/no on a choice board or pointing to words on a touchscreen that provides auditory feedback. Following trial observations with alternative methods for communication, the team may then decide to use a software program on the existing computer with the addition of a touchscreen. Furthermore, the team may contact an AT lending library at the local or state level to try a basic 16-choice communication board when he is not at the computer. The child outcomes drive identifying and selecting AT devices.

Step 4: Device Determination

Step 4 involves determining whether there is a medical necessity for the device. If the AT device is determined through a physician's referral as a medical necessity, then the family may qualify for funds targeted for medical need, such as Medicaid or private insurance. If the child is diagnosed with a low-incidence disability, such as being deaf or hard of hearing, blind, or having orthopedic impairments, then the child may qualify for equipment purchased under low-incidence funding sources. If the team indicates that there is a specific need for AAC strategies, then the speech-language pathologist (SLP) can assist in creating simple communication boards and/or visual schedules. At this point in the funding process, the team needs to access web sites and their local AT center for more information about potential devices and applicable funding sources. If the team encounters funding barriers such as in the case of Sean's staff, then reaching out to AT centers may offer alternatives to purchasing expensive equipment. The team may also want to explore the availability of training and technical assistance to focus on the benefits to AT for all staff and parents.

Step 5: Learning Environments

The team discusses the multiple learning environments in which the child will use AT, including low- and high-tech tools. If the device is portable, such as the 16-choice communication board, then the stationary computer at the child care site may suffice for Sean's child care environmental needs. In the home environment, the team may want to consider VOCAs placed in rooms throughout the house for Sean to request or comment on activities located in that area when the communication board is not available. Sean's mom may enlist support of the regional parent center to submit a mini-grant through a private foundation for a home laptop computer as well. Other environments such as the car and the swimming pool need to be discussed for what communication tools may meet Sean's needs in those settings. All environments need to be considered when thinking about AT tools because all AT tools may not be effective in all environments.

Step 6: Device Utility

The utility of the device is the next step in the funding process. The team decides the rationale behind considering particular AT supports. The team must understand the purpose of the device and how it will support the child's functioning in multiple learning environments. Some devices may only be appropriate for use in certain activities, routines, and/or places. If child care offers the use of the desktop computer for the software programs purchased through the program funds, then how will Sean use the communication system in other routines and environments. The team discusses how the device is used and for what purpose, along with ways of supplementing the utility of the device outside of the primary learning environment of the child care setting.

Step 7: Device Longevity

If Sean demonstrates the need for further AT devices after significant trials are conducted on the software program at the child care program and the basic 16-choice communication tool is used around the house, then the team needs to evaluate how long the new and more expensive device will function before it breaks down or becomes obsolete. The team can explore multiple vendors' device suggestions prior to purchase and ask about the warranties and expected longevity of the equipment.

Step 8: Device Appropriateness

The more research conducted on device selection, the more assured the team will be in purchasing a tool that is appropriate to meet the needs of the child as determined in the IFSP/IEP. The team needs to consider the age of the child, how long the child will be able to use the device before needing a more complex system, the systems use in multiple learning environments, the adaptability of the device in various daily routines, and the cost of the device compared with its durability and longevity. The FEET assessment process described in Chapter 4 can help the team determine that the device has been matched to the needs of the child. The FEET covers all areas to consider when exploring the use of one or more AT supports for outcome attainment. Information is gathered about the parents concerns and understanding of AT, specific child characteristics—including positioning for AT, observations and AT trials, and AT action planning. Sample FEET charts have been included in Chapter 5 as models for identifying the functional outcomes of AT assessment and device selection.

Step 9: Device Availability

Many AT vendors have regional representatives that can provide product information to the team. The team can contact their AT center for more information about vendors in the vicinity. It is important to consider vendors with representatives available to provide technical support and maintenance after the device is purchased. Judge (2000) mentioned the lack of access to and information about equipment repair and replacement as one of the reasons for device discontinuation.

Step 10: Device Sources

Vendors often provide information about potential funding sources for their equipment. AT centers are a good resource for finding out about local grant opportunities and private/nonprofit organizations that may want to support the purchase of an AT device. Medicaid covers durable medical equipment that has been recommended by a licensed physician. AT services, such as speech-language therapy, physical therapy, and occupational therapy, may also be covered under Medicaid. State AT centers may have purchasing and/or loan programs available for families.

Step 11: Funding Application

Meeting the requirements of a funding application is the next step in purchasing an AT device. Each agency will provide directions for applying for funding or an equipment loan. Education staff can assist families in contacting the appropriate funding agencies and acquiring the paperwork necessary for obtaining financial support. Community parent resource centers (CPRCs) and the Parent Training and Information Centers (PTIs) help families navigate the various funders and complete funding applications. The IDEA requires the CPRCs and PTIs to offer guidance, assistance, and training to parents of children with disabilities, ages birth through 26. The Technical Assistance Alliance Center, funded by the Office of Special Education Programs, supports more than 100 CPRCs and PTIs in their provision of services to families. These centers can be found in states that serve young children with disabilities. (For more information, visit http://www.taalliance.org/index.asp)

Step 12: Funding Appeal

Many times the first attempt at gaining access to funds is denied through the various sources. The family needs to be familiar with the appeal process as outlined by the particular agency providing the funding. If families are not successful in securing funding through public sources or private insurance, then the education program as payor of last resort would need to cover the costs of the equipment if deemed necessary in meeting the child's IFSP/IEP outcomes. The better aware education staff members are of the funding process, the more likely they will be able to assist the family in securing other funding options or borrowing the equipment from a lending library.

Funding opportunities exist in both public and private sectors. Under IDEA 2004, the school district becomes the payor of last resort for children ages 3–21 who qualify for services. For the early intervention population of birth to 3, the lead agency is designated as the payor of last resort if the IFSP includes documentation that the child needs AT to participate in daily activities. Typically, the terminology means that other possible funding resources must be considered before relying on the school district or lead agency for Part C for the funding of AT devices and services. The following programs offer potential funds if the child qualifies under the particular funding organization's criteria.

Medicaid

The Medicaid program provides reimbursement for some SGDs. An SGD can be classified as durable medical equipment that is specified in the language of the program. The physician must prescribe the SGD based on the daily functional and communication needs of the child.

Early Periodic Screening, Diagnosis and Treatment Program

The Early Periodic Screening, Diagnosis and Treatment (EPSDT) program is run through the Medicaid system and provides regular physical checkups for children birth through 21 years of age who are income eligible. An AT service or durable medical equipment may qualify for funding under this program if it is determined to be medically necessary through the EPSDT examination.

Private Insurance

Some private health insurance carriers cover AT services including assessment and therapy. Typically, private insurance covers equipment that is medically necessary and recommended through a physician. Policies vary widely so families must call their individual insurance carrier to get information on what might be covered and for what duration. For instance, speech-language therapy for using an SGD might be covered for only six sessions.

Other Private Sources

Private organizations and foundations such as United Cerebral Palsy and United Way have funding options that may support the purchase of an AT device. In order to secure funding from a private organization, the family would have to follow the criteria for purchasing funding of AT devices and submit individual agency applications for consideration. Private sources usually ask that a parent exhaust other potential funding resources such as Medicaid or private insurance first. Often, there are other local private/nonprofit groups that seek community projects to fund. A list of local foundations and other private agencies can be obtained from the public library. In addition, parents may seek out support from small groups of people such as the PTA to sponsor fundraising events for the cost of the device.

Lending Library

Public school programs sometimes offer a small lending library of basic AT equipment such as switches to adapt toys, adapted toys and games, computer software, positioning supports, and simple communication devices. Directions for creating an AT lending library can be found at several online sources listed at the end of this book. AT centers may also have lending libraries where equipment can be checked out for longer periods of time and mailed directly from the center to the child's home location. This type of center-based library houses the actual equipment and maintains the functional aspects of the devices. Other types of lending libraries can be cyber linked through online communities such as Facebook or Twitter and contain access to vendors, fact sheets on various kinds of AT equipment available, ways to evaluate equipment and software, training opportunities, and other information resources. With the increased use of the Internet, a cyber-based lending library has advantages over a center-based program in which upkeep of the facility and equipment as well as mailing costs for the equipment can become cost prohibitive.

SUMMARY

This chapter reviewed the laws, guiding principles, and funding options for considering AT for young children with disabilities. The involvement of family in the assessment and intervention process is the hallmark of the legislation and guiding principles. AT is included in the legislation to ensure that all children with disabilities have a chance at participating in their daily routines. AT provides access to learning environments for children by supporting their outcomes for interaction and independence. Knowledge of funding sources is critical not only to obtaining the most appropriate AT devices, but also to ensuring that all potential funding options have been exhausted before gaining access to education funds.

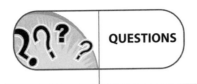

QUESTIONS

1. What are the four laws applicable to AT for young children with disabilities and their families?

2. What is the meaning of *payor of last resort?*

3. What are the guiding principles for considering AT with young children with disabilities?

4. Which guiding principle is the most important when considering AT for young children with disabilities? Provide support for your answer.

5. What are the funding sources applicable to AT purchase?

6. How does a lending library help with the purchase of an AT device?

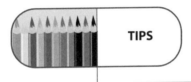

TIPS

❍ Be familiar with all applicable laws that guide AT consideration.

❍ Use guiding principles as a rationale for considering AT for young children with disabilities.

❍ Start with universal design concepts for home and classroom. AT can be useful and fun for all.

❍ Know all the applicable funding sources available in your community.

❍ Access the web links for more information on AT.

❍ Request annual training and technical assistance on AT use in the home and classroom through local, regional, and state programs.

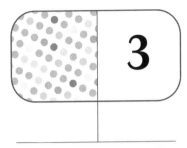

3

Assistive Technology for Inclusion in Early Childhood Environments

AT for young children with disabilities from birth to kindergarten offers a range of simple to sophisticated tools to enable children to participate with family members and typically developing peers. For example, the availability of inexpensive adaptations to toys, books, VOCAs, SGDs, and computer-based literacy tools brings AT within reach of families and early childhood practitioners. The preceding chapters provided definitions of AT devices, services, and legal considerations. The next phase to providing AT services for all children involves a series of informed decisions to enable children to participate in learning environments with families and peers.

This chapter demonstrates methods to apply AT with young children with disabilities to be a part of daily interactions with family members, other children, teachers, and key people across all potential childhood environments. The reader will find recommended practices to infuse AT strategies and services for children with complex disabilities in a naturalistic model that builds on daily routines and activities. In order to provide a framework for infusing AT throughout all childhood environments, a brief review of major perspectives that shaped early childhood services is provided and includes inclusion in natural environments, family partnerships, universal design for learning, and standards-based intervention. Within the context of these influences, the naturalistic approach to early childhood interventions and applications for AT will be discussed in some detail. The chapter concludes with examples of naturalistic approaches to infuse AT services and strategies in multiple settings. In particular, examples of applying AT to support inclusion of young children with disabilities in home, school, and community settings will be linked to curriculum content, early learning standards, and developmental goals.

INCLUSION AND NATURAL ENVIRONMENTS IN EARLY CHILDHOOD

General education and special education systems for young children with disabilities are increasingly intertwined, related to legislative, policy, and program development since 1980. The passage of the Education for All Handicapped Children Act in 1975 established a legal requirement to educate all students with disabilities in the LRE. The Education of the Handicapped Act Amendments of 1986 (PL 99-457) extended the principle of LRE to the youngest children with disabilities, using the term *natural environments* as the required setting for early intervention services. Part C of IDEA 2004 states that early intervention services, "to the maximum extent appropriate, are provided in natural environments, including the home, and community settings in which children without disabilities participate; and are provided in conformity with an individualized family service plan adopted in accordance with section 636" (§ 632[4][G][H]). The legislation provides the opportunity for services in other settings when the parents and the IFSP team determine that a child's needs cannot be satisfactorily met in natural environments as defined by IDEA 2004 (American Speech-Language-Hearing Association [ASHA], 2006).

Subsequently, the influence of these laws, regulations, and related policies can be seen in IDEA 2004. Over the decades, the requirement to educate students in the LRE has become known as inclusion. Furthermore, the emphasis on access to the general education curriculum for all children and youth from birth to 21 years has been significantly strengthened. Inclusion has become a central theme of service delivery in early intervention and early childhood special education settings. Although implementing inclusion for all children with disabilities is not fully realized, the U.S. Department of Education (1998) reported that nearly 50% of preschool children with disabilities experience some degree of inclusive education with typically developing peers.

Vohs (1993) addressed the issue of defining natural environments based on the progressive history of legal requirements for education in the LRE for students with disabilities. The term *natural environment* arose from the succession of laws and policies intended to require inclusion of people with disabilities in regular school, community, and home environments. Vohs pointed out the problems inherent in defining natural environments for young children with disabilities who may often be at home with family members and not necessarily included in community settings. Vohs posed several questions in her discussion.

- What are natural environments?
- How do concepts of integration, inclusion, and natural environments relate to each other?
- Who determines what the natural environments are for individual families?
- Is the natural environment the same for every child and family?
- What happens during a transition from services provided under Part C of IDEA 2004 to Part B regarding the natural environment and LRE?

Based on a review of literature focused on these questions, Vohs concluded that natural environments for individual children vary and require consideration of the range of environments that are available to each child and family. The intent of the legislation, although clearly focused on increasing participation for young children with disabilities in typical settings with peers, remains difficult to implement due to variability of early intervention services across communities, regions, and states in the United States.

Chai, Zhang, and Bisberg (2006) challenged the original concept of natural environments based on the reasoning that intervention settings are narrowly defined under IDEA 2004, and, in fact, families with young children may participate in a range of settings that are not restricted to school settings. Chai et al. proposed a conceptual model of natural environment practice that includes providing natural settings for infants and toddlers, involving caregivers and other children in typical daily routines, and offering naturalistic specialized intervention. Dunst et al. (2001) also contributed a broader perspective to consider multiple environments where children with and without disabilities may participate with their families, such as family gatherings, parks, malls, public transportation, and homeless shelters. The expanded view of natural environments challenges the thinking about early intervention and early childhood services for children with disabilities, particularly regarding the application of AT devices and services to support their participation in multiple settings. We advocate a broad view of natural environments for all children, specifically in the design of AT services to be embedded within the daily lives of children, their families, and early childhood teams.

Parallel but related developments in early childhood education for typically developing children have resulted in an educational movement to eliminate barriers for children of diverse learning abilities, including those with disabilities. Saracho and Spodek (2003) described trends in general early childhood education for young children from birth to 5 years of age as follows.

- Educating all children in inclusive classes
- Managing vertical and horizontal transitions
- Emerging educational and early child care programs
- Developing school, family, and community partnerships
- Emphasizing language learning and emergent literacy
- Integrating classroom learning
- Applying technology in early childhood education

Although these trends were described in relation to early education for typically developing children, they overlap significantly with trends in special education services for infants, toddlers, and preschool children with disabilities. Since the early 2000s, research in early intervention and early childhood special education has focused on effective methods for including children with disabilities with typically developing peers through adapting curricular approaches to accommodate diverse learners (Odom, 2000).

Family Partnerships

The need to involve family members and address cultural and linguistic diversity is central to the delivery of AT services in early intervention with young children. The roles of family members and children who use AT and AAC are core to all phases of assessment, development, and implementation of AT services (Beukelman & Mirenda, 2005; Glennen & DeCoste, 1997; Lloyd, Fuller, & Arvidson, 1997). Although family participation is identified as a necessary component of effective AT and AAC services, the methods to support family members on collaborative AT teams are just beginning to be understood and implemented in practice (Bailey, Parette, Stoner, Angell, & Carroll, 2006; Judge, 2002; Judge & Parette, 1998; Parette, 1998; Parette & Angelo, 1996; Parette, Brotherson, & Huer, 2000; Parette & VanBiervliet, 2000).

Research literature provides recommended professional practices to involve family members in all phases of AT service delivery. Research by Angelo (2000), Parette and VanBiervliet (2000), and Parette, Brotherson, et al. (2000) emphasized the need for professionals to provide family-focused and culturally sensitive interventions in response to the increasing diversity among student populations. Parette and VanBiervliet provided seven recommendations for professional practice that are adopted in this chapter as guidelines for AT teams in early childhood settings.

1. Recognize that families have many demands placed on them from both outside and within the family unit.
2. Understand that the presence of a disability in the family affects all family members within the immediate family.

3. Recognize that each child with a disability has unique needs.

4. Identify the child's communication needs in the home, school, and community.

5. Recognize differences and strengths in families.

6. Spend time with each family member before discussing the AT intervention.

7. Develop competence to provide culturally responsive assessment and intervention services.

Each of the recommendations provides the foundation for implementing AT services described in this chapter and those to follow.

Universal Design for Learning

The convergence of programmatic trends and issues in early intervention, early childhood special education, and early childhood education are a result of separate and related developments in legislation, policy, and program development. The universal design for learning initiative promotes access, participation, and progress for all learners of diverse needs and abilities (Hitchcock, Meyer, Rose, & Jackson, 2002). At the same time, IDEA 2004 states that access to the general curriculum is the key to successful education for children with disabilities, meaning that inclusion of children with disabilities in general education is more than physical placement in regular education. Access to the general curriculum requires accessible curriculum for all learners. Grisham-Brown, Hemmeter, and Pretti-Frontczak (2005) developed the concept of *blended practices*, which is defined as integrating teaching practices that can be used to address the needs of children with disabilities and their typically developing peers in inclusive settings so that all students benefit from the activities and routines of the classroom.

This book's major premise is that implementing AT services provides tools for children with disabilities to increase their participation in social and learning environments. Because AT is a bridge to enhance developmental opportunities for children with complex disabilities, the context of where children learn and interact with peers is a critical component in the delivery of AT services. Trends in early intervention, early childhood special education, and early childhood education are based on the philosophy of inclusion for all children to participate together, reinforced by law and recommended practices since the 1980s.

Universal design for learning is defined as a research-based framework for designing curricula—that is, educational goals, methods, materials, and assessments—that enable all individuals to gain knowledge, skills, and enthusiasm for learning. This is accomplished by simultaneously providing rich supports for learning and reducing barriers to the curriculum while maintaining high achievement standards for all students (Hitchcock et al., 2002). Furthermore, universal design for learning is based on the idea that the needs of all learners are accommodated during the design, implementation, and evaluation of a curriculum framework (Grisham-Brown et al., 2005). This approach contrasts to adapting curriculum after the fact because considering diverse learning needs is part of the initial curriculum planning. Three key principles define the goal of universal design for learning: access, participation, and progress for each child in a given learning environment (Hitchcock et al., 2002).

In practice, implementing universal design for learning aims to provide a flexible, customizable learning environment for all children through three primary strategies: multiple means of representation, multiple means of engagement, and multiple means of expression (Grisham-Brown et al., 2005). The compatibility of universal design for learning with AT is immediately clear because AT has the potential to provide a range of tools to enable students with complex needs to gain access to, participate in, and progress in the general

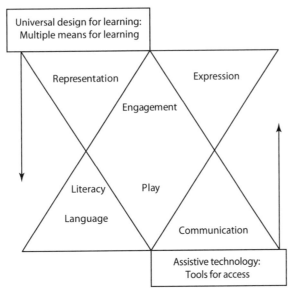

Figure 3.1.   Universal design for learning and assistive technology services in early childhood education.

curriculum. Indeed, as AT is a required consideration in IFSP and IEP planning in the provisions of IDEA 2004, the relationship between universal design for learning and AT is dynamic and reciprocal.

Lieber, Horn, Palmer, and Fleming (2008) emphasized two principles in IDEA 2004 that reinforce applying universal design for learning with children with disabilities in general education settings: 1) access to the context in which instruction is presented and 2) active engagement with the curriculum. Universal design for learning reaches beyond IDEA 2004 with the goal to eliminate barriers to learning as an integral part of educational planning. Individual accommodation supported by AT services is certainly part of universal design for learning. Universal design for learning, however, is founded on the concept of "preparedness" by teachers to meet the diverse learning styles among children and pushes the concept of inclusion to a proactive stance. For example, Horn, Lieber, Li, Sandall, and Schwartz (2000) pointed out that the primary means to include children with disabilities in early childhood education settings is traditionally through specialized services defined in the IEP, such as physical therapy, occupational therapy, speech-language therapy, and AT services that focus on adapting the setting for individual children. Although special education and related services in inclusive settings are essential, the anticipatory planning component of universal design for learning and its relationship to special education services has the potential to improve access to learning for all children. Figure 3.1 illustrates the potential dynamic and reciprocal influence of universal design for learning to create opportunities for access, participation, and progress for all learners in inclusive early childhood education settings.

AT services are traditionally implemented as adaptations to existing environments for young children. Universal design for learning offers a window for AT to become part of initial planning and design of early learning settings. Furthermore, existing AT resources provide the means to expand universal design for learning planning to develop learning tools based on research-based practice in a wider perspective that includes specialized technology for learning and development. For example, rather than adding AT elements such as pictures to increase communication tools for children with limited speech, picture symbols can be placed in all learning centers to emphasize key vocabulary and concepts that are *core* (words to use all the time) and words that are *fringe* (activity specific). Access to learning for all children can be achieved through planning, designing, and implementing AT tools.

Standards-Based Development and Learning for Young Children

Learning standards for young children appear to have their basis in legislative initiatives such as the No Child Left Behind (NCLB) Act of 2001 (PL 107-110), which emphasized all children need to be ready to learn by the time they enter kindergarten and first grade. In response to NCLB, progress measures and assessments for young children are implemented by many organizations responsible for early education including Head Start, the National Association for the Education of Young Children, Division for Early Childhood, the U.S. Department of Education/Office of Special Education Programs (OSEP), and special education systems in individual states. In order to create meaningful assessment measures, general learning outcomes expected for typically developing children provided the benchmarks for curriculum standards that can accommodate the diverse learning needs of children with disabilities. Two program initiatives in California that developed learning standards for young children with disabilities include the Desired Results for Development Progress (DRDP) project and the Preschool Learning Foundations.

Desired Results for Development Progress
Assessment System for Preschool Special Education

The DRDP initiative in California was developed to provide a greater focus on standards, assessment, and accountability. Furthermore, in accordance with IDEA 2004, each state is required to have a 6-year performance plan that 1) evaluates the state's efforts to implement the requirements and purposes of IDEA 2004 and 2) describes how the state will improve such implementation—the State Performance Plan (SPP). Each state is required to submit data on child progress to OSEP by reporting the percentage of preschool children with IEPs who demonstrate annual improvement in the following preschool assessment indicators.

- Positive social-emotional skills (including social relationships)
- Acquisition and use of knowledge and skills (including early language/communication and early literacy)
- Use of appropriate behaviors to meet their needs

DRDP Access was developed for preschool children served with IEPs. DRDP Access meets the SPP requirement for preschool assessment in special education programs. DRDP Access enables California to report progress toward OSEP's three child outcomes for preschool-age children with IEPs and to meet statewide assessment requirements under IDEA 2004. A crosswalk of the OSEP preschool assessment indicators and the DRDP Access tool is found at http://www.draccess.org/administrators/OSEPCrosswalk.html

Preschool Learning Foundations

As stated on the California Department of Education (CDE; 2009) web site:

> The purpose of California's Preschool Learning Foundations is to provide the child development field with research-based competencies—knowledge and skills—that we can expect most children to exhibit in a quality program as they complete their first or second year of preschool.

California's Preschool Learning Foundations are developed in the following areas: social-emotional development, language and literacy, English language development, and mathematics. Examples of specific skills expected in each of these areas are shown in Table 3.1.

Table 3.1. California Preschool Learning Foundations: examples of developmental areas and standards at 4 and 5 years of age

Social-emotional relationships		
Self	4 years of age	5 years of age
1.0 Self-awareness	1.1 Describe their physical characteristics, behavior, and abilities positively	1.1 Compare their characteristics with those of others and display a growing awareness of their psychological characteristics, such as thoughts and feelings
2.0 Self-regulation	2.1 Need adult guidance in managing their attention, feelings, and impulses and show some effort at self-control	2.1 Regulate their attention, thoughts, feelings, and impulses more consistently, although adult guidance is sometimes necessary
5.0 Initiative in learning	5.1 Enjoy learning and are confident in their abilities to make new discoveries, although they may not persist at solving difficult problems	5.1 Take greater initiative in making new discoveries, identifying new solutions, and persisting in trying to figure things out

Language and literacy		
Listening and speaking	4 years of age	5 years of age
1.0 Language use and conventions	1.1 Use language to communicate with others in familiar social situations for a variety of basic purposes, including describing, requesting, commenting, acknowledging, greeting, and rejecting	1.1 Use language to communicate with others in both familiar and unfamiliar social situations for a variety of basic and advanced purposes, including reasoning, predicting, problem solving, and seeking new information
2.0 Vocabulary	2.1 Understand and use accepted words for objects, actions, and attributes encountered frequently in both real and symbolic contexts	2.1 Understand and use an increasing variety and specificity of accepted words for objects, actions, and attributes encountered in both real and symbolic contexts
3.0 Grammar	3.1 Understand and use increasingly complex and longer sentences, including sentences that combine two phrases or two to three concepts to communicate ideas	3.1 Understand and use increasingly complex and longer sentences, including sentences that combine two to three phrases or three to four concepts to communicate ideas

Reading	4 years of age	5 years of age
1.0 Concepts about print	1.1 Begin to display appropriate book-handling behaviors and begin to recognize print conventions	1.1 Display appropriate book-handling behaviors and knowledge of print conventions
2.0 Phonological awareness	2.1 Orally blend and delete words and syllables without the support of pictures or objects	

English language development			
Listening	Beginning	Middle	Later
1.0 Children listen with understanding Focus: Beginning words	1.1 Attend to English oral language in both real and pretend activities, relying on intonation, facial expressions, or the gestures of the speaker	1.1 Demonstrate understanding of words in English for objects and actions as well as phrases encountered frequently in both real and pretend activities	1.1 Begin to demonstrate an understanding of a larger set of words in English (objects and actions, personal pronouns, and possessives) in both real and pretend activities

(continued)

Table 3.1. *(continued)*

English language development			
Listening	Beginning	Middle	Later
1.0 Children use non-verbal and verbal strategies to communicate with others. Focus: Communication of needs	1.1 Use nonverbal communication, such as gestures or behaviors, to seek attention, request objects, or initiate a response from others	1.1 Combine nonverbal and some verbal communication to be understood by others (may code-switch—that is, use the home language and English—and use telegraphic and/or formulaic speech)	1.1 Show increasing reliance on verbal communication in English to be understood by others
3.0 Children use language to create oral narratives about their personal experiences. Focus: Narrative development	3.1 Create a narrative in the home language (as reported by parents, teachers, assistants, or others, with the assistance of an interpreter, if necessary)	3.1 Begin to use English to talk about personal experiences; may complete a narrative in the home language while using some English (i.e., code-switching)	3.1 Produce simple narratives in English that are real or fictional

Mathematics		
Self	4 years of age	5 years of age
Number sense	1.0 Children begin to understand numbers and quantities in their everyday environment	1.0 Children expand their understanding of numbers and quantities in their everyday environment
Algebra and functions	1.0 Children begin to sort and classify objects in their everyday environment	1.0 Children expand their understanding of sorting and classifying objects in their everyday environment
Measurement	1.0 Children begin to compare and order objects	1.0 Children expand their understanding of comparing, ordering, and measuring objects

From California Department of Education. (2008). *The California preschool learning foundations* (Vol. 1) Sacramento: CDE Press. Available at http://www.cde.ca.gov/sp/cd/re/psfoundation.asp; reprinted by permission.

NATURALISTIC INTERVENTION

Several curriculum approaches and models have been researched and established to support inclusion of children with disabilities with typically developing peers. Applications for implementing AT will be discussed in relation to the following: developmentally appropriate practice, naturalistic intervention, activity-based intervention, universal design for learning for all children, and standards-based curriculum in preschool settings.

Throughout early childhood education, a guiding philosophy of developmentally appropriate practice and developmentally and culturally appropriate practice provides a theoretical and applied recommendation that provides a context for early intervention and early childhood special education (Bredekamp & Copple, 1997; Hyun 1996, 1998). Hyun and Marshall (2003) provided a background and qualitative review of the concept of teachable moments and learnable moments from the perspectives of teachers and learning needs of young children. Historical foundations of teachable moments and definitions are attributed to Rousseau in the 1760s and extend to contributions by Piaget, Gesell and Gesell, Froebel, and others (as cited in Hyun & Marshall, 2003). The notion of responding to children's interests to promote learning in the moment, thus bringing both adult teaching skills and child-initiated attention together in a transformative experience for the learner and teacher, provides a common thread for both early childhood education and early childhood special education. Hyun and Marshall referred to developmentally and culturally appropriate practice in early childhood education and a pedagogy that takes the processes involved in teachable moments into account from multiple perspectives. The crux of capitalizing on teachable moments in implementing developmentally and culturally appropriate practice is found in the natural opportunities for learning based on the individual, developmental, and cultural needs and settings for each child (Hyun & Marshall, 2003). Hyun and Marshall recognized and identified the limitations for effective implementation of teachable and learnable moments throughout the child's daily learning environments. The skills of the teacher to immediately respond to the child's perspective (developmental needs, focus of attention, cultural and linguistic needs, and learning needs) and the child's ability to respond in the moment affect learning outcomes. Understanding multiple perspectives in the learning environment allows the teacher to manipulate teaching events to provide access for all children to participate. According to Hyun and Marshall,

> Teachable moments arise when teachers observe, recognize and interpret the spontaneously occurring interests of diverse learners. As curricular opportunities, these spontaneous moments represent a confluence of students' unique cultural identities, developmental growth and change patterns, together with their particular needs, interests and curiosities. Teachers' careful observation, recognition and interpretation of these opportunities (from the students' perspective) help to form an emerging purposeful instructional action (curriculum practice) that is equal to or relevant as a 'learnable moment'. Once this kind of emerging and purposeful instructional action becomes an inherent and pervasive daily practice within teachers' continuous consciousness of what they are doing, teachable-moment-oriented curriculum practice has taken root. (2003, p. 113)

In early intervention and early childhood special education with children with disabilities, the concept of the teachable moment has a sibling term, *incidental teaching*. Approaches to incidental teaching with preschool children with disabilities arose from the work of Hart and Risley (1975) who introduced a systematic approach to hierarchical prompting within daily routines and in response to the child's focus of attention. Hart and Rogers-Warren (1978) further developed and researched milieu teaching approaches to support language development. Milieu teaching is based on methods of incidental teaching and includes applying a least-to-most prompting hierarchy that includes a mand, requirement for a response; time delay, wait for the child's response; model of the desired response; and mand-model, request for response and model of the desired response. Various configurations of milieu language teaching are found related to the learning and developmental needs of individual children. The primary principle involved in milieu approaches is to base teaching in the natural environment in response to the child's immediate focus of attention—otherwise known as the teachable moment/incidental teaching. Adjustments in prompting and timing are provided by the adult in direct relation to the child's needs for success. Prompting is provided quickly and, to the best extent that the child's intent can be determined, the apparent intent of the child's communication is provided on the adult's judgment of the child's best effort to communicate in that given moment.

Activity-Based Intervention

In a related vein, curricular approaches to support effective inclusion have been studied and analyzed from several perspectives including the efficacy of specific methods regarding outcomes for children with disabilities. Naturalistic, embedded approaches to intervention with young children with disabilities are generally recommended in daily routines and preschool environments (Odom, 2000). According to Macy and Bricker,

> Intervention strategies are needed that can be quickly learned and easily used, be integrated into or mapped onto daily activities and routines, and produce desired child progress. (2007, p. 108)

Specific approaches that are described include activity-based intervention, embedding intervention/instruction, routines-based instruction/intervention, and integrated therapy (Pretti-Frontczak, Barr, Macy, & Carter, 2003). Activity-based intervention is attributed to Diane Bricker and her colleagues at the University of Oregon (Bricker, Pretti-Frontczak, & McComas, 1998). Due to the significant overlap in the approaches listed, the general term *activity-based intervention* will be used to include methods of early intervention and early education that are based on the principle of naturalistic instruction with embedded learning opportunities within daily routines for infants, toddlers, and preschool children. See Wolery (2000) for a more extensive discussion of naturalistic intervention. The development of activity-based intervention as an approach to provide specialized services for young children with disabilities is based on the premise that meaningful learning and development occurs within typical daily routines (Bricker et al., 1998).

Several studies have demonstrated increased generalization of skills when instruction is provided in an activity-based or naturalistic approach rather than a direct instruction approach (Chiara, Schuster, Bell, & Wolery, 1995; Losardo & Bricker, 1994). Rather than pulling children aside and delivering instruction in a one-to-one approach, embedded instruction in daily routines with learning trials distributed throughout the day contributed to increased generalization of learning. The effectiveness of using a distributed trial approach gained increasing evidence-based support to teach specific skills including a range of communication, social, and preacademic skills (Brigman, Lane, Switzer, Lane, & Lawrence, 1999; Chiara et al., 1995; Dunst et al., 2001; Malmskog & McDonnell, 1999). Activity-based intervention with young children with disabilities changed the design and delivery of early intervention and early childhood special education by focusing specifically on the context of typical daily routines as the appropriate venue for services (Pretti-Frontczak & Bricker, 2004).

Implementing activity-based intervention aims to provide distributed opportunities for learning and engagement throughout the child's day rather than in specific intervention sessions with specialized professionals. For children with various types of disabilities, AT can be part of daily activities, such as the use of a picture placemat for snack and art activities. AT can also be infused into family routines by beginning interactions with a single-message VOCA that says, HOW WAS YOUR DAY? Others in the child's environment, including teachers, assistant teachers, parents, siblings, and peers, can be intervention agents. For example, Grisham-Brown, Schuster, Hemmeter, and Collins (2000) found that paraprofessionals were able to consistently and correctly implement response-prompting to teach specific skills to preschool children throughout the day. Further evidence for the efficacy of teacher-implemented activity-based intervention is reported in two separate studies. Kohler, Anthony, Steighner, and Hoyson (1998) reported that two teachers were trained and successfully used a naturalistic teaching approach to encourage children to engage in peer play, make choices through implementing incidental strategies, and provide comments and questions to prompt responses and expansions on childrens' communicative attempts. These researchers also identified the importance of regular contact and support for teachers with the researchers to consistently implement the naturalistic strategies. Horn et al. (2000) demonstrated that teachers and assistant teachers successfully implemented embedded learning strategies with preschool children. Studies such as these demonstrate the effectiveness of intervention conducted by educators and assistant teachers. Teachers trained to implement activity-based intervention are able to identify specific methods to be used in the classroom. Although activity-based intervention is to be implemented in naturalistic settings such as daily environments at home and preschool, the strategies are specific and direct. The embedded nature of instruction within daily routines is actually highly structured, yet integrated with natural opportunities for teaching and responsive to child-initiated behavior.

The science of early intervention and early childhood special education is articulated in the research literature; however, widespread practice is still developing (Odom, 2000). The quality of services for children with disabilities included in early childhood education programs is compromised due to lack of systematic instruction by teachers who lack specialized skills to implement IEP goals and objectives for children with disabilities (Odom, Wolery, Lieber, & Horn, 2002). The process of embedding instruction for children with disabilities into typical daily routines can take many forms and, at its simplest, requires the teacher to connect learning experiences by taking advantage of each activity to increase access to learning. For example, Macy and Bricker (2007) provided the example of play with a large, multicolored parachute to increase opportunities to experience and learn about spatial relationships such as up and down, in and out, and over and under. Additional prompting and repetition of these concepts within the parachute activity may be an appropriate strategy to embed specialized focus on these concepts for specific children with disabilities who are included in the early childhood classroom.

In order to link AT tools to daily routines and learning experiences, children with a range of disabilities may require additional adaptations to participate and learn in the parachute activity. For example, for a child who does not use speech to communicate, a photograph of the activity attached to a single-message VOCA that says PARACHUTE TIME, GET READY! may be provided to the child just before starting so that he can "announce" the activity that is coming up. This type of AT application is embedded in a typical activity and gives the child who does not use speech an opportunity to initiate communication with peers. Multiple opportunities throughout the parachute activity and ensuing routines in the day can be structured so that children with even significant challenges have a meaningful role to make choices, comment, take turns, and demonstrate understanding of concepts addressed. The applications of AT as additional tools for children with disabilities to learn along with typically developing peers through embedded teaching is relatively unexamined. In theory, applying AT tools to enable children to be part of play, communication, socialization, literacy, and preacademic programs with their peers is consistent with legal and recommended practice in the field. Specific methodology can be derived from early childhood and AT resources in the field, with attention to evidence-based approaches.

ASSISTIVE TECHNOLOGY WITH INFANTS AND TODDLERS IN NATURAL ENVIRONMENTS

Multiple perspectives and approaches exist in curricular methods implemented in early intervention, early childhood special education, and early childhood education. The diversity and variability of these methods to support young children with and without disabilities to learn and flourish present challenges for integrating AT strategies. The degree of structure in learning environment ranges from highly structured to play-based approaches. In addition, the setting of early education and care clearly influences the degree of structure in intervention. For example, a young child with attention and behavioral needs may prosper and learn more easily in a highly structured, tightly scheduled preschool. In the after-school program, however, this same child may not have the benefit of highly structured child care, and the success of recommended AT strategies and tools hinges on the difference in setting variables that include the degree of structure. Thus, the intensity of intervention and curriculum approaches will likewise vary. From their work in transition to inclusive preschool and kindergarten environments, Noonan and McCormick (2006) demonstrated the importance of preparing children with skills to meet the expectation of the "receiving" educational environment.

A parallel to this is the understanding that the expectations of each child's daily environments affect the recommended AT strategies. For example, a computer-based literacy
activity may be more successful in a highly structured early childhood education setting,
and a low-tech adapted book may be more successful in a less-structured after-school
care program.

The specific goals in each child's intervention plan is foremost in determining the
scope and type of AT services and strategies to be provided for individual children. In
early intervention, the IFSP and the IEP will guide the nature of AT services needed and
required. The role of the IFSP and IEP team and family members in considering AT tools
is a critical one that must be informed by assessment results. Chapter 4 provides a structure and process for early intervention and early childhood education/early childhood
special education teams to determine the extent of AT services needed for individual children. General developmental goals may not specifically identify how AT can be utilized
to provide access to typical childhood settings with peers and family members. For example, a developmental goal on the IFSP for 2-year-old Sina, a highly social girl born with
Down syndrome, is to increase expressive vocabulary as follows.

Sina will request one of two favorite toys by reaching toward the desired object
when presented with a choice of two toys by an adult during floor play with other
children at the child care center.

The previous goal provides a developmental focus on increasing communicative intent in
a play activity with Sina. When her assessment results were further reviewed by the early
intervention team (including Sina's mother), however, significant motor limitations were
identified due to Sina's generally low muscle tone. The effort associated with Sina's ability to reach directly toward her desired toy appeared to reduce the frequency of her gestures and interaction around making choices in routines. Sina's mother asked the team
how reaching toward her selected toy so infrequently would help her daughter to communicate more. Together, Sina's team listed all of her communicative strengths that included making facial expressions, looking directly at her toys, making eye contact with adults,
producing whole body movements, and focusing attention on photographs/pictures in
books. Photographs of her favorite toys were introduced into play routines so that Sina
could simply look at a photograph and then obtain her toy. This simple adaptation helped
to support Sina to progress beyond the effort of gestures alone and use all of her communication skills to indicate her preferences while also introducing symbol use through photographs. This example demonstrated the importance of establishing goals and assessing
further to determine the types of AT support that increase access and participation in
functional contexts.

The process to determine appropriate levels of AT intervention is one of individualization. In addition, more general guidelines to provide AT options for consideration by
IFSP and IEP teams are needed to ensure that all children are provided appropriate opportunities to access AT for learning and development in childhood settings. Grisham-Brown
et al. (2005) demonstrated the need to "crosswalk" the curriculum content, standards, and
developmental goals, connecting expectations in general early childhood programs with
specialized interventions in early childhood special education intervention planning.
Crosswalks provide links between general early childhood standards and methods for children with disabilities to participate. Tables 3.2 and 3.3 demonstrate examples of goals for

Table 3.2. Ecological model to implement AT in early intervention

IFSP goals	Snack and mealtime	Bath time	Storybook reading	Circle/music
Increase participation and build social interaction/turn taking	Use sign language or gesture to request MORE	Talking picture frame with picture of child in bath and simple message to bathe	Adapted story with Velcro-attached pictures or objects to remove	Record message on a VOCA to enable child to say MY TURN in circle time
Express range of communication functions	Laminated picture placemat provides choices for food	Basket with suction cups filled with pictures of bath toys for choices	Familiar story with predictable phrases such as, "goodnight moon"; allow child to complete the phrase and give picture to hold	Record three to four messages on Tech 4 for child to choose favorite songs in circle time
Develop breadth of semantic concepts to support more diverse communication	Expand use of picture placemat to describe foods and textures	Expand use of pictures of bath toys to describe actions (wash, swim, float, wet, dry)	Record favorite story on sequenced voice output device, such as Step-by-Step, and take turns "telling the story" as child hits the switch	Prepare object board to go with songs in circle time; have child choose object to go with song and child can choose object from board to feel and touch
Build greater complexity of language structure to support more complex communication	Use picture board at mealtime to build sentences ("I want more juice." "Tommy likes fish crackers.")	Laminated picture board near bathtub to model phrases about bath ("more water," "blow bubbles," "wash toes")	Provide story overlay from favorite book (see web sites for prepared overlays); take turns pointing to pictures to tell the story and build short sentences	Record song or other group activity on voice output device such as Go Talk or Tech 4 with sequenced steps; provide turns for child to "say" parts of song or activity
Build phonological awareness/foundations for literacy development	Use pictures of foods that begin with same sound—emphasize /p/ (popcorn, pizza, punch)	Foam letter shapes to play with in bathtub—emphasize sounds of bath time (pop, bubble, hot, boat)	Read repeated line stories with sounds and record on Tech 4; allow child to hit switches and make sounds	Record animal sounds in songs; allow child to "say" sounds of animals at appropriate points in song

Source: Light (2005).
Key: IFSP, individualized family service plan; VOCA, voice output communication aid.

Table 3.3. Ecological model to implement AT in preschool

IEP goal	Circle	Art	Play centers	Storytime	Snack	Closing
Develop vocabulary	Greet each child using VOCA message	Request art supplies using VOCA	Request favorite toys in play with VOCA	Place props from story on Velcro strip when named in story	Provide visual placemat for choosing foods	Pull off photos of children on Velcro strip
Develop early phrases and sentence development	Complete routine phrase on Velcro strip with each child's picture	Describe artwork using adjective phrases with VOCA	Complete phrase on Velcro strip, "I want to play with ___," with picture of favorite toy	Select two to three pictures to answer questions about story	Point to one or two pictures to talk about snack (using American Sign Language [ASL]), such as "Cookie yummy," "More juice"	Complete routine closing phrase with Velcro strip and each child's photo
Develop phonological awareness and literacy skills	Target a specific sound each week, and find an object that begins with that sound	Provide VOCA with repeated sounds as part of art activity	Provide picture and printed word for each center and toy to build word awareness	"Read" target sounds such as /p/ with VOCA	Provide picture and word placemats for child to choose, interact with, and take turns at snack time	Use printed names with photos in closing circle
Oral narrative development	Choose pictures to "tell story" about weather, yesterday, and so forth	Describe art projects to peers using picture board or VOCA	Provide VOCA for child to take turns in centers (dress-up, store)	Repeat foods eaten by the *Very Hungry Caterpillar*	Review sequence of activities from the day during snack time, using pictures or VOCA	Sing "good-bye" song using VOCA
Social interaction skills	Provide VOCA near classroom door for morning greeting	Provide communication board to socialize	Express turns, reactions in play with VOCA	Program VOCA with sequence of story for child to "read"	Provide communication board to socialize; program VOCA or AAC device with "small talk"	Provide VOCA near classroom door for closing activities

Key: IEP, individualized education program; VOCA, voice output communication aid; AAC, augmentative and alternative communication.

young children and sample activities within the context of daily activities for infants, toddlers, and preschool children.

Embedding Assistive Technology in Childhood Environments and Routines

Implementing AT in the home requires that family and professional partnerships are well established. The design and use of AT in daily routines can begin simply and include family input on the development of adaptations and tools to enhance child-focused developmental goals and family priorities. McCormick (2003, 2006) described ecological assessment as a functional approach to develop IFSP and IEP goals and to determine how goals can be embedded in daily routines across many settings for young children. The ecological assessment approach requires several steps as follows.

1. List daily activities and routines.

2. List major developmental expectations.

3. Identify what the child "can do" or "needs to learn."

4. Formulate goals and objectives.

5. Plan instruction.

6. Plan data collection.

Mistrett, Ruffino, et al. (2004) developed an ecological approach to assist early child teams to implement AT in a number of routines and settings. By determining what the child needs to learn within daily environments and routines, considering a range of possible AT adaptations and devices is conducted. Mistrett et al. developed the Every Kid Can AT Wheel, a tool that enables families and providers to systematically identify potential AT solutions for increased participation and access to inclusive activities with families and peers. Now available commercially through TAM Technology (Mistrett et al., 2006), the AT Wheel provides a menu of AT options for early childhood providers and family members to support increased independence for young children with disabilities across daily activities. Table 3.4 demonstrates the range of AT devices that can be considered to meet IFSP and IEP goals for increased participation through the day for children with complex disabilities.

In addition to an ecological perspective on AT, Mistrett, Ruffino, et al. (2004) listed AT adaptations and devices for general consideration (see Table 3.5). Mistrett et al. further recommend the following beginning steps for early childhood teams to identify appropriate AT for individual children.

1. Start with a single routine and ask, "Could the child be participating more or more independently?"

2. Include all team members in technology decision making.

3. Consider a range of technology options.

4. Ask if the technology is helping the child "do more" in the routine.

Mistrett et al. also recommend the following guidelines in selecting AT devices.

• Less may be more. Ask, "Is there something simpler or easier to use that we could select?"

• Start with what the child can and wants to do best.

Table 3.4. Considering AT devices within natural routines for young children

Meals/snacks	Bath/grooming	Changing/bedtime	Playtime	Book reading	Expressive arts	Early writing	Early math
Adaptive bottles/cups (special nipple, cup cut-out)	Adaptive tub seating (chair; inflatable tub)	Dressing aid (zipper pulls, Velcro closures, elastic shoelaces)	Toys with large buttons, knobs, dials, multi-sensory features	Apron/vest with story pictures, symbols	*Drawing*	Variety of large crayons, markers, pencils	Large beads and counters, blocks (Velcro, magnetic), pegboards and puzzles
Adaptive utensil (curved handle and dish guard) (plate guard)	Adaptive bathing aid (mitt, scrub brush)	Room adaptation (single touch/clapper light, dresser pull grip, labeled drawers)	Toys adapted with Velcro, suction cups, magnets	Book: cardboard, tactile, scented object books, audiobooks	Variety of large crayons, markers, brushes, rollers	Adaptive writing tool (grips, weights)	Adapted measuring tool
Sandwich holder	Toys: floating, suction cups	Adaptive bedding (sleep positioner, weighted blanket)	Toy/game adapted for single-switch use	Book adapted with page turner, texture, text label (symbols, braille)	Adapted grips, weights	Hand wrap/universal cuff for holding, arm support	Abacus
Hand wrap/universal cuff for holding	Adaptive hair and tooth brush (curved, enlarged handle)	Mounted CS: notify, "I'm up," family routines	Switch interface (timer, appliance, latch)	Book holder	Adapted easel, spill-proof paint	Adaptive paper/outlines (raised, color lines)	Large-button/display talking calculator
Switch-operated feeding device	Switch-adapted toothbrush		Adaptive toy (beeping balls, glitter roll)	Switch-operated recordable device (book, single phrase)	Adapted scissors	Tracing template	Interactive television program
Communication system (CS): food choices, manners, and "blessing"	Adaptive toothpaste dispenser		Adaptive riding toy, swing	Portable touch-activated reading and learning system	Switch spin art, electronic scissors	Slantboard/clipboard, easel	Computer
	Adaptive stool, potty chair		Software: cause and effect, drawing, games	Interactive television software	Software: drawing, stamps, graphics	Adaptive rubber stamp	Play set: kitchen, building
	Laminated CS: body parts and play choices		CS: play choices, comments and interactions	Software: nursery rhymes, stories	*Music*	Software: word and picture, large letters, create books	Software: building, sorting, counting
				CS: choosing story, retelling, participating	Adapted instruments	CS: requests and comments	CS: counts, requests, and comments
					Switch-adapted music player		
					Software: music, songs with slow rate		
					Dramatic play		
					Accessible toy, puppet, environment		
					Adaptive dress-up clothing: Velcro closure		
					CS: choices, sequences, and comments		

40

From Mistrett S., Ruffino, A., Lane, S. Robinson, L. Reed., P., & Milbourne, S. (2004). *Every kid can: Technology supports for young children.* Available at http://letsplay.buffalo.edu/AT/EKC-wheel.pdf; reprinted by permission.

Table 3.5. General considerations of options for AT devices for young children

Positioning	Mobility	Communication	Going places	Computer use	Hearing	Vision	Adaptive materials
On back: mat, wedge, beanbag chair	Crawling; padded, textured flooring; crawling support frame	Visual schedule, calendar, lists	Adaptive carrier, car seat, bed, tray	Keyboard: pointing aid, key guard, key labels (large, braille letters), play set, alternate and customized keyboard, keyboard overlay with objects/pictures/ words, switch and switch interface	Materials with visual and tactile features	Magnifying glass, sheet Glasses, tinted glasses	Attach: links, cuff with Velcro to pick items up, colored
On tummy: wedge, round pillows	Walking: walkers/gait device, wheeled stander; weighted vest, ankle or foot brace	Boards with objects, photos, pictures, symbols	Adaptive stroller (lightweight, all terrain)		Headphones, speakers at computer	Materials with large print, lights, sound, and texture	Velcro strap, shoelace, magnet
On side: wedge, rolled towel, sidelier		Wallet, vest, eye-gaze frame	Wheelchair lift, ramp		Television, telephone amplifier	Backgrounds for high contrast	Confine: box top, basket, tray, hula hoop
Sitting up: booster chair, adaptive chair, floor table; foam, nonslip material, foot block	Riding: stroller, manual and electric wheelchair, switch-controlled motorized scooter, adaptive bicycle	Auditory listening device	Accessible book, toy for car play	Mouse: adapted mouse, touchscreen, trackball, joystick, mouse, keyboard	Assistive listening device; hearing aid	Easels (stand, desktop)	Enlarge: adapted page turner, cylindrical foam tubing, puzzle knob
Standing up: exersaucer, stander, custom fitted chair		Voice output devices	Mounting system for bottle, cup, switch, device		FM or loop system	Adaptive precane mobility (push cart)	Label: textures, colors, pictures, picture symbols, words
		Single-message device; recordable picture frame	Portable communication system for comments, questions, songs	Large monitor, speakers, microphone, color printer, graphic/braille embosser		Audiobooks	Stabilize:
Adjustable aids: neck/head rest, lap belt, foot strap, chest harness	Switch-adapted rider/scooter	Multimessage device for choice making, activity specific		Digital microscope		Labeled item; tactile materials and braille labeler	Velcro/showloop, Dycem, nonslip shelf liner, clamp, suction cup
		Device with levels		Child and computer positioning aids		Light box	
		Device with dynamic screen, direct and scanning				Raised line drawings	
		Software: develop communication overlays, systems				Video magnifier	

From Mistrett S., Ruffino, A., Lane, S., Robinson, L., Reed, P., & Milbourne, S. (2004). *Every kid can: Technology supports for young children.* Available at http://letsplay.buffalo.edu/AT/EKC-wheel.pdf; reprinted by permission.

- Technology use enhances, not hinders, development.
- Technology can be used for other purposes across routines.
- Technology use is a dynamic process. Children, technology, and life routines are constantly changing. General AT devices that are planned to meet specific developmental needs for individual children are listed in Table 3.5.

Considering AT options for young children with disabilities requires input from the entire team, beginning with the family. Based on family priorities, team assessment results, and development of IFSP and/or IEP goals, there are several key determinants that guide the selection, implementation, and further evaluation for the success of AT devices for individual children including: the specific goal for the child, the philosophy and resulting expectations of the selected environments, the degree of structure that is feasible in the given environment, the specific routine and activity, the individuals responsible for implementation, and follow-up evaluation procedures.

Table 3.6 demonstrates an example for Sammy, a young boy who uses a range of gestures and limited vocalizations to communicate. In addition, Sammy experiences significant vision difficulties, wearing thick glasses to be able to see toys and large color photographs at close range. His motor abilities are characterized by emerging independence in walking with a child-size walker across even floor surfaces. His IFSP goals and related activities using AT adaptations and low-tech devices are highlighted in Table 3.6 based on input from his mother and early intervention team, who provide home-based services and weekly consultations to his child care setting.

SUMMARY

This chapter examined a number of perspectives that form the initiatives, policy, and program directions for early services for young children in early intervention, early childhood special education, and early childhood education services. Since the 1980s, the field of early childhood special education, although having its roots in general early childhood education, came into its own. After becoming an independent field, the relationship between early childhood special education and early childhood education is turning toward a more collaborative and integrated one, largely related to the focus on inclusion since the passage of the Education for All Handicapped Children Act of 1975 and subsequent reauthorizations of that law.

The influence of inclusion and knowledge base regarding the importance of naturalistic methods for early intervention and early childhood education with young children with disabilities continues to draw educational programs together around the needs of young children. The advances and proliferation of technology further increase opportunities for children with disabilities to be part of typical environments to learn and develop with their peers. This chapter provided a rationale and methodology to incorporate teacher-made and commercial products to bring access for learners who might be denied or barred from participation, even while legislation and recommended practices say otherwise. AT devices and services are within reach of all children. The process and strategies discussed in this chapter provide a method to embed AT within the lives of children to communicate, play, and learn more completely and independently.

Table 3.6. AT planning for 2-year-old Sammy at home and in child care settings

Child-focused IFSP goal	Home/routine	People responsible and data keeping	Child care/routine	People responsible and data keeping
Make clear choices with field of two	Meals: *Picture placemat with clear plastic pockets to put photos of food choices available on one side, comments on top edge to indicate likes, turns, more, all done, and so forth.*	Mom, Dad, 7-year-old sister, Auntie, Grandma Sally (SLP) from the early intervention program visits the home weekly Data keeping: discuss progress with SLP provider weekly	Outdoor play: *Pocket page from photo album placed on clipboard near door with photos/icons of two to three play choices outside. SAL approach (make choice and point to photo; wait for child to imitate)*	Anita (teacher) Louellen (aide) Maria (volunteer) Data keeping: All staff make checkmarks for successful trials on Sammy's Activity Chart
Take turns in game with peer or adult	Playtime: *Adapted spinner to take turns in Candy Land made by early intervention staff and parent (http://www.adaptivation.com/Adaptivation_Website/Adaptivation_Games_Puzzles_and.html)*		Playtime: *Adapted bubble blower with switch interface to allow for two switches, taking turns with peer to turn on (http://enablingdevices.com/catalog/toys_for_disabled_children/bubble-blowers/bubble-mania)*	
Move independently to get favorite toys and books	Bath time: *Suction cups on clear container of sponge or rubber bath toys just out of reach. Provide cotton rug to move across floor and prevent slipping.*		Naptime: *Using child's walker, encourage child to get favorite stuffed toy and blanket to put in basket on walker and bring to nap area*	
Turn pages of book and show understanding of pictures named by adult	Storytime: *Adapted book with sponge curlers glued to edges of cardboard book. Adult uses time delay to name a picture and waits for Sammy to touch, look, or point.*		Storytime: *Computer area with One More Story (http://www.onemorestory.com/) with adapted switch to "turn pages" and find characters named by adult or peer.*	

Key: IFSP, individualized family service plan; SLP, speech-language pathologist; SAL, System for Augmenting Language.

43

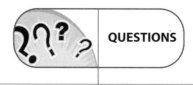

QUESTIONS

1. Identify at least three different contexts of natural environments in the daily lives of infants and toddlers with disabilities. Describe adaptations with basic types of AT that would enable children with disabilities to participate in each of the environments that you identified.

2. Compare the concept of natural environments for infants and toddlers to the concept of inclusion for preschool children. What are the similarities and what are the differences in the settings and types of AT that may be needed in these settings?

3. Define the major components of universal design for learning. How might universal design for learning and AT complement and interact in providing services for preschool children with complex disabilities?

4. Compare milieu intervention and activity-based intervention. What are the key practices of each? How are these approaches to intervention with young children complementary to support using AT in daily activities with young children?

5. Think of a young child you know with special needs. What low-tech AT tools might you select to support that child to play, communicate, and experience books? What high-tech AT tools might you apply to support the same functional skills?

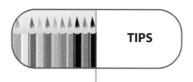

TIPS

○ Observe daily routines with young children and note the children's responses to activities such as mealtime, bath time, storytime, and music circle time.

○ Within the daily routines that you observe, identify the ways that typically developing children might respond in the same activity. Compare the child with a disability in his or her response and list the potential barriers to participation.

○ Problem solve with family members and professional team members to identify adaptations that can be made from what is available in the home to overcome barriers that were identified from observation.

○ Consult preschool teachers in general early childhood settings to identify expectations they might have for typically developing children in daily routines such as greeting, morning circle, art activities, playground time, dress-up, and dramatic play.

○ Plan low-tech, inexpensive adaptations to create physical access to activities for children with disabilities. Consider physical, cognitive, communication, vision, and hearing avenues to gain access to in planning AT solutions.

○ Spend time in discount stores looking at materials differently and thinking of ways to use sponges, plastic clothespins, photograph albums, and more. For example, pieces of sponge or clothespins can be attached the pages of children's books to make them easier to turn. Photo albums can become communication books, and microfiber dust mitts can be a place to attach pictures with Velcro backing.

○ Attend AT and AAC vendor trainings in your area to be aware of changing high-tech AAC that may provide access to communication and learning for young children.

○ Review the success of AT solutions that you implement periodically and be open and ready to change and to improve what is put in place.

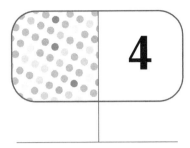

Dynamic Assessment and Intervention in Early Assistive Technology

Assessment to develop AT solutions and tools for individual children builds on established practices in early childhood programs. In this chapter, practitioners working with young children with disabilities will find tools that map onto existing assessment procedures that are in use, with additional components to identify AT strategies for individual children. Assessment to determine appropriate AT devices and services for young children with disabilities is an ongoing process, not a one time event. Furthermore, as a process, AT assessment is connected to the comprehensive assessment that is conducted as part of required early intervention and early childhood special education services, rather than a stand-alone process. Prior to embarking on AT assessment, a team needs to be established, and this requires support from administrative levels of programs serving young children.

This chapter begins with a discussion of AT services from a team-based perspective, followed by principles of family-centered practice in AT assessment. Major components of AT assessment approaches will then be reviewed and applied to young children (Mistrett, 2004; Zabala, 1995). A discussion of the application of AT assessment processes with young children will complete the chapter, based on six phases of assessment adopted from Mistrett. AT assessment for young children, as demonstrated in this chapter, draws on research-based practices to problem solve, develop, implement, and evaluate potential AT solutions for young children with disabilities. The authors developed FEET, a functional and dynamic approach to provide AT systems for young children to participate with peers in natural environments. The FEET is available on the CD-ROM.

ASSISTIVE TECHNOLOGY SERVICES AND COLLABORATIVE TEAMS

Providing sustainable AT services, including assessment, program planning, implementation, and follow-up evaluation, requires locally available resources. Limited professional resources regarding personnel with AT specialization are reported throughout the United States (Lesar, 1998). Often, a particular community or school district may depend on only one individual with the required expertise to conduct assessments and provide AT service delivery. This situation creates a backlog of referrals and dependency on one specialist and limits local capacity to effectively meet the needs of individual families and children throughout a community, district, county, or region. Although conducting AT assessment is the focus of this chapter, it is important to establish a foundation of AT services and a team of AT providers in order to provide ongoing services. A functioning AT system requires program development on at least two levels that include 1) leadership and 2) service implementation functions. Both administrative leadership and professional service delivery by a team are necessary components and will be described in the following section.

Administrative Leadership and Support

The best trained AT professionals cannot effectively meet the needs of children who may benefit from AT services without resources, and leadership and support at the administrative level are the most critical resources. Those responsible for program funding and organization need to understand the importance of AT as a necessary and required consideration for all children with disabilities to have opportunities to overcome barriers to interacting, learning, and developing with other children. Some of the major foundations to create a functioning AT service delivery program in a given community are gaining support from administrators to dedicate adequate professional resources to AT services, securing initial and ongoing training, developing funding for equipment and materials, and sanctioning adequate planning time for teamwork and collaboration across agencies involved in serving young children (Hunt, Doering, Hirose-Hatae, Maier, & Goetz, 2001). In programs serving young children in the birth-to-5 age range, multiple agencies are potentially involved, including health, education, family support agencies, social services, vocational training programs for parents, and Head Start. Interagency collaboration requires that administrative leadership in all key agencies involved work together in providing AT services. Consider the following example.

> In one rural community, a 2-year old girl and her family in an early intervention program who needed AT and AAC services were initially referred by a social worker in a county developmental disabilities agency to an occupational therapist in a public children's health agency. Specialists in these two agencies contacted a local university clinic where speech-language services were available for young children to plan an AT assessment. A physical therapist from the local hospital was contacted to participate in the assessment, and early interventionists from the local child development program also were involved. Initially, the team of professionals met to conduct an assessment with the child and her family who requested AT services. Following the assessment, the newly formed team approached their respective administrators to develop formal agreements across their four agencies to jointly fund assessment sessions and planning time to complete the report and funding request for a range of low- and high-tech AT devices that included a walker, a beginning AAC device, and adapted toys for the child. The process of developing a team and forming interagency agreements took several months, delaying the process for the child to receive AT services. Following this initial developmental process, however, the team was in place and able to perform in a more timely manner with subsequent referrals.

Assistive Technology Team Development and Collaboration

AT services are most effective in a team-based model, as illustrated by the previous example and repeatedly documented in research (Copely & Ziviani, 2007). The degree of expertise and the complexities in determining the physical, developmental, language, learning, and cultural needs for individual children and their families in the process of developing an AT system of services extends beyond the scope of a single profession (Beukelman & Mirenda, 2005; Glennen & DeCoste, 1997). There are many challenges for teams to conduct AT services, including limited time, training, and resources (Lesar, 1998). Support at the administrative level is needed for AT services to become established in a given community or district, particularly when multiple agencies are involved. Often, early intervention and early childhood services for children with disabilities are conducted by several agencies. In addition to administrative approval and funding for professional time dedicated to team processes, teamwork at the provider level is a critical process.

Team building requires that each professional understands the goals for the team and makes a commitment to follow through on agreed-on plans and activities. AT services, in particular, require specific expertise among team members to address multiple needs of individuals and families, and members of the AT team most often include representatives from physical therapy, social work, speech-language, vision specialists, occupational therapy, AT, education, health provider, and the family. Additional members may be child care providers, early intervention professionals, and others. The degree to which these individuals work together with a plan to conduct AT assessment and service provision, if warranted by assessment results, determines the outcomes for children and families shown in the preceeding example. Critical skills for effective teamwork are identified in the literature and include communication skills, understanding of diverse contributions, time management, group facilitation skills, record keeping, excellence in one's own discipline, willingness to teach others, and openness to learning new skills (Glennen & DeCoste, 1997; Hunt, Soto, Maier, Liboiron, & Bae, 2004; Sadao & Robinson, 2007; Soto, Müller, Hunt, & Goetz, 2001a, 2001b; Thousand & Villa, 1992).

Although general understanding of the importance of teamwork and the complexity of the collaborative process in AT service delivery is well known, systematic guidelines for AT teams to provide assessment, programming, implementation, and follow-up evaluation are more recent. Since the early 2000s, resources to guide AT team practice became available through several approaches to assessment that will be defined in more detail later in this chapter. Two types of resources are available and useful to AT team development—an initial self-assessment to establish a "baseline" knowledge for AT services and a guide for quality indicators for AT services. The Assistive Technology Confidence Scale (Weintraub, Bacon & Wilcox, 2004; Wilcox, Weintraub, & Aier, 2003) provides a nonjudgmental starting point for early childhood providers to gauge their current knowledge, skill, and training needs in the provision of AT services. The complete Assistive Technology Confidence Scale is included on the CD-ROM, providing a useful tool for early childhood teams to develop AT services within existing program options for families and children.

Following discussion and development of team goals to conduct an initial AT assessment or related activity, the team may refer to the Quality Indicators in Assistive Technology (QIAT) to identify benchmarks for conducting AT services (QIAT Consortium, 2009; Zabala et al. 2000). The QIAT materials are referenced to curriculum standards for school-age students and can be adapted for use in early childhood settings.

Both tools are examples of research-based guidelines for recommended practices in developing and delivering team-based AT services. The QIAT resources include guides for administrators and teams in the planning of AT assessment and services. These are available at no
cost at the following website: http://natri.uky.edu/assoc_projects/qiat/resources.html.

FAMILY-CENTERED PERSPECTIVES

Since the 1990s, the practice of family-centered care has been required in implementing
early intervention services for young children with disabilities. The Education of the
Handicapped Act Amendments of 1986 expanded the scope of services to begin at birth
and to be implemented with family members as primary members of the early intervention
team. Principles of family-centered care originally arose from medical practice, calling for
family involvement in decisions about health care for young children with special needs.
The Maternal and Child Health Bureau (U.S. Department of Health and Human Services,
2008) issued guidelines for family-centered care based on nationwide discussion groups and
reflection on the practice of family-centered care in early intervention services.
Recommended practices included a revised definition of family-centered care, as follows.

> Family-Centered Care assures the health and well-being of children and their families
> through a respectful family-professional partnership. It honors the strengths, cultures,
> traditions and expertise that everyone brings to this relationship. Family-Centered
> Care is the standard of practice which results in high quality services. (American
> Academy of Pediatrics, 2003)

Furthermore, revised family-centered care principles were published, as shown in
Table 4.1.

Table 4.1.   Principles of family-centered care for children

The foundation of family-centered care is the partnership between families and professionals. The following
principles are key to this partnership.
- Families and professionals work together in the best interest of the child and the family. As the child
  grows, he or she assumes a partnership role.
- Everyone respects the skills and expertise brought to the relationship.
- Trust is acknowledged as fundamental.
- Communication and information sharing are open and objective.
- Participants make decisions together.
- There is a willingness to negotiate.

Based on this partnership, family-centered care
- Acknowledges the family as the constant in a child's life
- Builds on family strengths
- Supports the child in learning about and participating in his or her care and decision making
- Honors cultural diversity and family traditions
- Recognizes the importance of community-based services
- Promotes an individual and developmental approach
- Encourages family-to-family and peer support
- Supports youth as they transition to adulthood
- Develops policies, practices, and systems that are family friendly and family centered in all settings
- Celebrates successes

From U.S. Department of Health and Human Services, Health Resources and Services Administration, Maternal and Child
Health Bureau, Division of Services for Children with Special Health Needs. (2005). Definition of family-centered care and
principles of family-centered care for children. Rockville, MD: U.S. Department of Health and Human Services.

Family-Centered Practice and Assistive Technology

The practice of family-centered care is also the recommended standard in planning and delivering AT services, specifically with young children (Parette & Judge, 1998b). Judge (2002) reported a summary of studies that showed that rates of discontinued use of AT devices continues to be a significant problem, ranging from 8% to 75%. Judge attributed discontinuation of AT device use to several variables, including 1) a lack of training and team support to implement AT; 2) the degree of sophistication of AT devices that led to confusion for families, children, and providers; 3) lack of access to information regarding maintenance and repair of AT equipment; and 4) lack of motivation to use AT systems related to the preceding variables. The rationale for gaining family input and involvement from the beginning of the AT process is supported by the continued problem of discontinuation. The practice of AT teams that consists of providers who complete assessment processes and determine the appropriate level of AT services and devices without family involvement runs the risk of limited follow up and implementation. Judge outlined a family-centered approach to AT services in three phases to involve family members, thus ensuring that family members are part of the decision making and are given opportunities to build partnerships with AT service providers.

Phase 1: Setting the Stage

The initial stage establishes a relationship with family members who are involved in decision making and daily care for the child and builds awareness of AT services and devices that are potentially useful for the individual child. A meeting is held with family members at a time and in a location that is determined by the family to discuss the purpose and format of the AT assessment, including the team members involved and steps in the process. The outcome of this initial contact is to jointly develop an AT assessment plan with input of family members regarding the child's daily routines, preferred activities, and potential trial use of AT devices within daily routines.

Phase 2: Activity-Based Assessment

As follow up to the initial meeting, an assessment session(s) is conducted in a natural setting for the child such as home, child care, or other location where the child typically interacts. AT devices are demonstrated on a trial basis with family members and professionals taking an active role, responding to family preferences for play and involvement with the process. A facilitator from the team sets up situations for the child to try the AT devices within familiar routines and activities such as playtime, storytime, and mealtime. Following single or multiple sessions of assessment and observation by the team, the facilitator summarizes input from the team, including family members, to develop IFSP and/or IEP goals based on the application and demonstration of AT devices that provide increased participation and developmental support for the child.

Phase 3: Ongoing Intervention and Evaluation

Following the first phases of family-centered assessment, ongoing early intervention services may be provided in home- or center-based programs, based on the goals that are developed through the AT assessment process. IFSP and IEP goals continue to be evaluated and revised, based on regular formative input from family members and other team members. The opportunity for formative input is planned within each intervention session so that family members are encouraged and supported to take a lead role in evaluating

Table 4.2.   AT partnership-building questions

Are parents asked about the level of involvement they desire at all stages of the AT assessment process?

Are family members asked about their preferred methods of involvement and communication?

Does the decision-making process consider the changing needs of the family and allow for flexibility in the plan?

Are partnerships developed between the family and professionals that evolve from mutual trust, honesty, respect, and open communication?

Are there opportunities for the family to evaluate the progress made at various times during the process (evaluation of the entire process as well as individual goals)?

Does the family have the final decision regarding whether to accept or reject the advice?

Has professional help been offered that matches the family's appraisal of their needs?

Are professionals positive and proactive in all aspects of interactions with the family?

Does the process clearly show that the family's needs, resources, routines, and values drive the process with the collaborative support of professionals?

Are families asked about their preferences concerning times and locations for interactions and AT services?

Source: Judge (2002).

the effectiveness of particular AT devices and overall AT services to support their child in daily activities.

The previous phases for involving families throughout the steps of the AT assessment and intervention process are useful to guide AT teams in service delivery. Judge (2002) also provided guiding questions for AT teams to evaluate and periodically measure the effectiveness of family-centered practices in AT services (see Table 4.2).

Cultural and Linguistic Diversity in Families

In addition to the importance of including family members on the AT team, cultural and linguistic diversity among families introduces further issues for the AT team to address. Several researchers have examined the importance of considering cultural and language background among families and the potential impact on decision making about using AT with young children in the family (Huer & Saenz, 2002; Parette & Judge, 1998a). For example, some Native American and Asian families are reported to value and expect a certain degree of family dependence across family members (Hourcade, Parette, & Huer, 1997). In some cultures, using AT to increase independence may not be highly valued due to excessive attention being drawn to the child's disability (Parette, Brotherson et al., 2000). In order to effectively support family members from culturally diverse backgrounds to take an active role on the AT team, practitioners need to meet two primary goals: 1) prevent and break down barriers that may discourage families from becoming involved in using AT with their child, and 2) determine family members' comfort level of involvement to assist in implementing AT services in multiple family environments. Guidelines to assist teams include a process to determine familiarity with technology in each family. With families who do not have computers in the home, introduction of low-tech AT is often recommended to include families in developing simple adaptations for play, communication, and access to books. Parette and Brotherson (2004) described a four-step process adapted from Bevan-Brown (2001) and Kalyanpur and Harry (1999) to support cultural reciprocity in determining appropriate AT services with families of young children, which includes asking the right questions to the right person at the right time in the right place. Table 4.3 provides a discussion guide for early intervention and early childhood providers to identify areas for program development to meet the diverse cultural and linguistic needs of families in AT services.

Table 4.3. Discussion guide: Culturally responsive services in AT and augmentative and alternative communication

Self-assessment

How aware am I of my own cultural background, experiences, values, and beliefs?

How do my experiences, values, and beliefs affect my interactions with people from various cultures?

What is my comfort and experience level with the cultural communities that I serve?

Am I flexible when meeting with family members?

How will our program provide necessary assistance to the family members to ensure their participation in the AT/AAC process?

Cultural knowledge

Do I understand the family's attitude regarding disabilities?

Do I know who makes the key decisions for the family?

Do I understand the family's expectations of me as a professional?

Do I understand the importance of extended family?

Am I aware of the family's approach to discipline?

Do I understand the responsibilities of other siblings in the family setting?

Culturally responsive AT/AAC services

Am I aware of what the family expects in the AT/AAC assessment process?

Have I determined whether the family is willing to receive AT/AAC services?

Does the family accept the idea of AT/AAC as a tool to help their child?

Does the family's religious affiliation influence how they perceive AT/ACC?

Is it possible to meet with the family members in their home prior to the AT/AAC assessment?

How will our program provide information and printed materials related to the AT/AAC assessment process in language spoken by the family?

How might our program involve a community liaison who would be a contact between the family and me?

How will our program gain access to and provide translators to maintain communication with family members?

From Robinson, N., & Solomon-Rice, P. (2009). Supporting collaborative teams and families in AAC. In Gloria Soto & Carole Zangari (Eds.). *Practically Speaking: Language, Literacy and Academic Development for Students with AAC Needs.* Baltimore: Paul H. Brookes Publishing Co.; reprinted by permission.

ASSISTIVE TECHNOLOGY ASSESSMENT APPROACHES

Assessment approaches used in AT are primarily focused on school settings to determine appropriate technology adaptations to enable students with disabilities to participate in learning as part of the regular classroom and in self-contained special education classrooms. Copley and Ziviani (2007) reported on the effectiveness of AT to support children with disabilities to have increased opportunities to communicate and learn with their typically developing peers. Furthermore, Copley and Ziviani pointed out that although AT is shown to have positive learning outcomes for students with disabilities, limitations in the AT assessment process exist that may contribute to less integration of AT in the student's educational setting. Three areas of concern regarding AT assessment procedures for young elementary-age students with disabilities were identified by Copely and Ziviani: 1) lack of a comprehensive assessment profile for individual students who may require AT, 2) lack of teamwork or expertise among the team members who implement the AT assessment, and 3) limited attention to follow up and plans for training after the assessment process is completed in implementing AT devices and services with children who are determined by the team to be appropriate candidates for AT services. Recommended features of a comprehensive AT assessment that are identified in the literature include collaboration among team members, involving family members and the individual on the team, a clear and comprehensive process to determine the individual's strengths and needs, establishing goals for the IEP, and follow-up evaluation and feedback to the team and family (Edyburn, 2001).

Major approaches to AT assessment are described in the literature as a process that is needed to determine specific AT services and devices for individual students in order to support achievement of IEP goals in school settings (Reed & Bowser, 1998; Zabala, 1995). Although many prevalent approaches to AT assessment are focused on application in elementary school settings, there are foundation principles and practices that can be adapted for use with young children. The relevant aspects of well-known AT assessment approaches are discussed in the context of specific application with young children with disabilities. AT assessment approaches include common elements such as team-based approaches, observation in natural environments, data gathering, trial use of AT devices, and follow-up evaluation. The following sections describe process-based approaches to assessing AT.

Matching Person and Technology Model

The Matching Person and Technology (MPT) Model was developed for students over the age of 15, based on research by Scherer (1995, 2002), to determine effective methods to identify features of AT devices to meet individual needs in school, work, and community settings. The MPT Model has three components: 1) the milieu/environment(s) in which the user will interact with the technology; 2) the needs, preferences, and predisposition to use of the unique person; and 3) the functions and features of the most desirable and appropriate technology. The MPT Model has also been applied with infants, toddlers, and preschool children with specific attention to the environments (milieu) where children play and participate, child characteristics (person), and a range of low- and high-technology to match the needs of the child (technology; Scherer, 2008).

Lifespace Access Profile for Individuals with Severe or Multiple Disabilities

The Lifespace Access Profile (LAP) was designed to provide a tool for team members with differing areas of expertise to collect observations from differing perspectives in a systematic process (Williams, Stemach, Wolfe, & Stanger, 1995). Primarily intended for use with individuals with severe disabilities, the LAP assists team members to synthesize findings in developing IFSP/IEP goals to support and define AT services and devices for an individual child or student.

Wisconsin Assistive Technology Initiative

The Wisconsin Assistive Technology Initiative (WATI) is designed to provide a comprehensive AT assessment process and includes a resource manual for school-based teams (WATI, 2010). There are 10 sections of the WATI with specific guidelines for areas such as writing/computer access, communication, academics, recreation, leisure, activities of daily living, environmental control, positioning, seating, vision, and hearing. The WATI assessment process provides information to the IEP team regarding consideration of AT services and devices needed to meet IEP/IFSP goals and objectives.

Education Tech Points

The Education Tech Points (ETP) model provides a guide for AT teams at six points in the assessment, intervention and evaluation process for IFSPs and IEPs (Bowser & Reed, 2002; Reed & Bowser, 1998). Components of the ETP approach are as follows.

- Referral
- Evaluation
- Extended assessment

- Plan development
- Implementation
- Periodic review

The ETP model includes a manual that contains information on team building, components of effective AT service delivery, and systems change. Assessment forms are also provided. Results of the ETP are summarized at each point and provided to inform the development of AT services and plan for AT devices to meet IEP/IFSP goals and objectives.

Student, Environments, Tasks, and Tools

The Student, Environments, Tasks, and Tools (SETT) model is a process that arose from discussions described by Zabala (1995) with her colleagues regarding the need to provide a clear framework to make the AT assessment process understandable to school personnel. The process of evaluating individual students' needs for AT in particular school and other settings is highly individual and reportedly difficult to standardize in a specific tool. Thus, the SETT process became a method to explain a complex and flexible process in a repeatable manner, providing a systematic means to identify appropriate technology to support the individual needs of each student. Each of the components of the SETT model encompass a series of data-gathering questions as follows.

Student

1. What does the student need to do?
2. What are the student's special needs?
3. What are the student's current abilities?

Environment

1. What materials and equipment are currently available in the environment?
2. What is the physical arrangement? Are there special concerns?
3. What is the instructional arrangement? Are there likely to be changes?
4. What supports are available to the student?
5. What resources are available to the people supporting the student?

Tasks

1. What activities take place in the environment?
2. What activities support the student's curriculum?
3. What are the critical elements of the activities?
4. How might the activities be modified to accommodate the student's special needs?
5. How might technology support the student's active participation in those activities?

Tools

1. What strategies might be used to invite increased student performance? What no-tech, low-tech, and high-tech options should be considered when developing a system for a student with these needs and abilities doing these tasks in these environments?
2. How might the student try these tools out in the customary environments in which they will be used?

Guiding questions are used at each point in the SETT model to gather data from the team, individual, and family members toward the planning IEP goals and objectives that incorporate AT services (Bowser & Zabala, 2004; Zabala, 2005).

Six-Step Framework for Decision Making

Using an activity-based approach, Mistrett and colleagues (Mistrett, 2004; Mistrett, Lane & Ruffino, 2004) developed a six-step process for early intervention teams to follow as a guide to make informed decisions regarding using AT tools for young children to participate with peers.

1. Collect child/family information
2. Identify activities for participation
3. Identify observable targets for activity-based assessment and intervention
4. Brainstorm AT solutions and action plan
5. Conduct trials with AT supports
6. Identify what worked

Table 4.4 illustrates an application of the Six-Step Framework by Mistrett et al. regarding increased participation through AT in play activities.

Each of the AT assessment approaches previously reviewed have similar elements that can be applied to young children with disabilities and their families, including focusing on gathering a profile of individual strengths and needs, observing in daily environments, identifying activities and AT devices to reduce barriers and to increase participation, and following up with evaluation and modifications in AT services and devices. Furthermore, the steps described in each model are organized in a similar sequence. In general, AT assessment models developed for older students, including the MPT, LAP, and WATI, focus on more high-tech, computer-based technology than is typically needed with young children. The ETP and SETT approaches are developed specifically for alignment with general education curriculum and IEP implementation. As elementary and secondary students become more independent from family members, the membership of the AT team changes from family-centered to a self-determination perspective. The emphasis on making the transition to post-school settings is a key focal point of AT planning for students and youth in secondary settings. The Six-Step Framework draws on elements of models for school-age populations and increases the focus on family membership and activity-based AT solutions to support inclusion in natural settings.

FUNCTIONAL ASSISTIVE TECHNOLOGY ASSESSMENT WITH YOUNG CHILDREN

Drawing on the major AT assessment models reviewed in the previous section and guiding principles for family-centered approaches, this section brings all elements together in an applied process for AT assessment with young children with disabilities. The FEET follows the Six-Step Framework for Decision Making (Mistrett, 2004; Mistrett, Lane et al., 2004) and provides a format to build team consensus for AT services and devices in the all phases of the IFSP/IEP process: planning, implementation, and progress evaluation monitoring. FEET was developed as a guide for early intervention and early childhood professionals to incorporate literature and recommended practices in AT assessment and intervention. Furthermore, FEET is designed to enable early intervention and early childhood professionals to conduct AT assessment as an extension by building onto all

Table 4.4. Six-Step Framework for Decision Making

AT planning framework	Gabriel's participation
Step 1: Collect child/family information. This includes information about the child's strengths, abilities, preferences, and needs and the family's values, dynamics, activity levels, schedule, and culture.	Step 1: Gabriel is beginning to make choices by looking at his preferred toys when two choices are provided. He smiles and reaches toward other children in circle time when songs and story choices are provided with related objects/instruments/books.
Step 2: Identify routine activities for participation. What is preventing the child from participating more?	Step 2: Gabriel watches other children during music and storytime in the circle. Because he is nonverbal, he listens but does not respond vocally.
Step 3: What will indicate the intervention is successful? Level of independence now and anticipated?	Step 3: Gabriel will increase his participation in songs and stories as the "song leader" by activating single-message voice output communication aids (VOCAs) to repeat lines independently.
Step 4: Brainstorm AT solutions. Start with what is available and adaptations. Consider a full range of options, from low- to high-tech, and strategies to support their use.	Step 4: Record repeated lines for song/story on a single-message VOCA.
Step 5: Try it out. Create an observation form/plan. Record how the child participates with the AT supports.	Step 5: Tell the class that Gabriel is the song leader for today. Assist Gabriel initially to activate the VOCA when it is time for the repeated line. After a few turns, pause and wait for him to activate the VOCA independently.
Step 6: Identify what worked. Make modifications as needed and try again.	Step 6: Gabriel responded well to the first introduction of the VOCA and became more independent after several turns, activating the VOCA with a time-delay cue. Multiple message VOCAs are planned for trial use for Gabriel to "sing" and "say" a series of lines in songs and stories in response to questions during circle time with peers.

Sources: Mistrett (2004); Mistrett, Lane, and Ruffino (2004).

assessment tools that are used by the team. Components of the FEET approach include the following.

- Family concerns, priorities, and child characteristics
- Team assessment planning
- Observing activity-based participation
- AT action planning
- AT activity-based observation trials
- AT evaluation and modifications

A description of each step in the FEET process with related forms is provided in the following section.

Functional Evaluation for Early Technology Process

Each step in the FEET process enables the early intervention and early childhood team to organize prior assessment information and systematically plan for AT services that may include low-, mid-, and high-tech devices with individual children. Accompanying forms provide a method for documenting observations and decisions with family and all team

Table 4.5.   Steps in the FEET process

Steps	Forms
Step 1: Collect child/family information.	1, 2
• Identify child strengths and needs.	
• Include family perception of technology.	
• Identify cultural expectations and experiences.	
Step 2: Identify activities for participation.	3
• Identify environments and activities.	
• What activities are key for increased participation?	
• What are access barriers to participation?	
Step 3: Identify observable targets for activity-based assessment and intervention.	4
• Identify typical peer participation in activity.	
• What is current level for target child?	
• What changes are expected?	
Step 4: Brainstorm AT solutions and an action plan.	5
• What AT solutions are needed for increased participation (access, mobility, communication, vision, hearing)?	
• What can be adapted in the environment?	
• What resources (people, equipment, training) are needed?	
Step 5: Conduct trials with AT supports.	6
• Set time to begin AT intervention.	
• Observe and record child's participation in activity.	
Step 6: Identify what worked.	7
• Evaluate the AT intervention plan.	
• Discuss what worked and what did not.	
• Identify needs for change (equipment, training, modifications).	
• Complete documentation and reporting.	

members. Research-based procedures for AT assessment with young children are described in each step of the FEET process. Table 4.5 summarizes steps in the FEET process and lists the corresponding forms for each step.

Family Concerns, Priorities, and Child Characteristics

Identifying family concerns and priorities is the initial component of an effective AT assessment (Judge, 2002). The three-phase process developed by Judge applies to the first step in the FEET process in order to determine activities to demonstrate AT use in a manner that is consistent with family input to the team. In addition, collective family and team knowledge is gathered at this point based on backgrounds and prior assessments regarding the child's developmental strengths and needs for consideration in AT assessment.

The intervention team summarizes family perspectives related to their child's special needs and priorities for intervention. Two corresponding forms (1 and 2) are provided for this initial step to gain family perspectives and objective observations regarding the child's current developmental stage and functional characteristics, strengths, and needs. Defining family concerns provides a place to start for all assessment processes with young children with special needs. Family-centered care principles offer guidelines for providers of early intervention and early childhood services to respond to family concerns and priorities in planning steps in the assessment process. Furthermore, Dunst, Boyd and Trivette (2002) outlined recommended practices to determine family strengths and needs when planning comprehensive assessment with children with disabilities. Identifying family concerns allows the team to learn about family members' understanding of the child's needs, developmental history, health status, and functional abilities. When first meeting with family members to determine the resources available for the child with special needs, team members can also ascertain who the primary caregiver for the child is and who provides the income for the family's needs. In addition, cultural and linguistic backgrounds and preferences can be understood more readily by becoming acquainted with family members prior to conducting a child-focused assessment. Let the family know that AT and AAC can be integrated with other services that the child with a disability already receives. The family members may be able to accept AT and AAC services as part of the system of services that are already being provided for the child.

Developing a relationship with family members who have primary roles to care for the child with special needs may extend beyond an initial visit. Initial information gathered in the FEET process includes the family perspectives in the following areas.

Child's Strengths and Needs Regarding Hearing, Speech, Vision, and Motor Development

Obtaining a description of the family's views of the child's current needs regarding hearing, speech, vision, and motor development serves to gauge the extent of information that is available to the family members regarding the child's developmental and health history. More extensive assessment information may be needed following this initial interview. The family perspectives of the child's needs, however, helps establish how much assessment has already been done, location and availability of assessment records, and remaining gaps in the diagnostic and assessment profile for the child.

A number of existing tools and methods can be used to gather background information regarding child characteristics. Early intervention and early childhood programs may have an already established assessment process to build a profile of each child's abilities and needs upon referral to services. Summary information from administration of currently used assessment tools may be provided to describe child characteristics regarding speech-language, hearing, vision, motor abilities, and other developmental areas. Information from multiple tools may also be summarized in the FEET format (see Figure 4.1 for an example of Form 1, completed for Abby, age 4 years with physical disabilities). Form 2, not shown, can be used to gather further information on communication modalities for children with very limited expression.

Family Priorities for Child Participation in Daily Activities

This section of the FEET process is based on recommended practices by Judge (1998, 2002) and Judge and Parette (1998), who identified the importance of family-centered practice in providing a profile of a typical day for individual children. This practice is also aligned with a six-step process for using an ecological approach (McCormick, 2006) to describe daily routines for individual children and families and to prioritize specific environments for the purpose of targeting skill development in specific areas such as communication, mobility, and interactive play in the context of familiar and regular routines at home and school settings. Family perspectives regarding the child's current participation in daily routines provide possible strategies to adapt activities with AT tools for increased access and inclusion of the child within the context of daily life at home.

Family Use of Technology and Priorities

Judge (2002) included recommendations to determine the individual family's familiarity and comfort level with technology as a starting point for developing AT supports with each child. The degree to which family members are knowledgeable and at ease with technology use has a bearing on the outcome for implementing AT services and devices with their children.

Family concerns	
Child's name: Abby Age: 4 Parent's name: Naomi Address: 123 B Street Telephone: 888-666-4444	Agency name: Our Town Early Intervention Center Referral source: Hospital social worker Date of assessment: March 1 Team members: Early intervention team (social worker, nurse, PT, OT, SLP, early intervention specialist) Dominant language in home: English

AREAS ADDRESSED	FAMILY COMMENTS
Child strengths/needs 　Vision 　Hearing 　Communication 　Motor	Abby smiles when familiar people enter into her field of vision, which appears quite strong. She uses her eyes to communicate often, and we have established a yes/no system with her to look up for yes and down for no. Her hearing seems normal because she responds to even faint noises inside and outside of our home. Due to her type of cerebral palsy, Abby does not move independently except to roll on the floor. Her arms, legs, and torso are quite stiff, yet often in a reflex pattern with constant movement. This makes it hard to hold her comfortably because she is always extending her legs and arms, which causes stiffening through her body. She does seem to understand much of what we say, smiling and looking at the people, toys, photographs, and even small drawings that we name with her.
Family daily routines and activities	Our days are so busy with getting the new infant up and getting Abby ready for the school bus to come. We often miss the bus and have to drive her to school and pick her up to get to extra therapy appointments. Her assessments are completed through the developmental services center in our county and are up to date. So most of our days are spent in the car, going to and from appointments. At home, we have some book/television time, meals, bathing, and bed. Sometimes, just relaxing on the sofa and floor with the whole family together is our only down time.
Child's preferred activities	Abby is playful and loves when her grandpa tickles her and plays with her. She is most comfortable playing on the floor, where she can reach for the ball or dolls to play with her older cousin.
Family priorities for child participation in daily activities	We need to have more toys and ways for her to play with her cousins and kids her age. I know there is more we can do to develop her communication beyond eye contact and facial expression. She fights her car seat and cries often when put into her wheelchair. I want to know what is going on in her head and how to help her be more comfortable physically.
Family use of technology and priorities	We bought a laptop computer for Abby to use on her third birthday. Our family is learning to use it, and several of the early intervention team members have put on different programs for her to use. She enjoys photographs of our family and books on the computer. She has a hard time reaching the switch to "click" on pictures and words.

Figure 4.1.　FEET Form 1: Family concerns for Abby.

Team Assessment Planning

Gathering team members' perspectives is adapted from the SETT model developed by Zabala (1995), an AT assessment process that provides an organizational framework to assess student, environmental, teaching, and technology solutions and strategies. In the FEET approach, current child characteristics and team perspectives are gathered in order to formulate assessment questions for further evaluation using AT tools with young children in daily environments. Child characteristics and family concerns form the basis of team problem solving and provide opportunities for team members to form a collaborative assessment plan.

After completing the first step of the FEET assessment process, the team can summarize all available information in order to plan the remainder of the AT assessment process. The team can focus specific assessment questions that inform the remaining steps in the assessment and intervention planning process to implement AT with individual children. At this point, the team meets to review the information presented by the family, using Form 3 in the FEET process. The four components shown in Form 3 include family concerns and child characteristics, environments, tasks/activities, and AT tools. Furthermore, the form provides a summary of what the team knows in each of the four components and what is yet to be learned. An exam-

Team assessment planning				
What we know	**Family concerns and child characteristics**	**Current environments**	**Current activities/tasks**	**Current tools**
Family concerns form provides family concerns and child characteristics	Abby's hearing and vision appear within normal limits Receptive language a strength Communicates with eyes upward to indicate "yes" Family wants to move beyond yes/no indication with eyes Positioning very challenging, high level of extension Family wants more help with positioning Abby	Abby and her family are often in transition. **Mornings at home** Dressing/breakfast, car, school bus, preschool classroom, early childhood therapy clinic **Evenings at home** Television time, book time, mealtime **Weekends** Family gatherings, swimming pool	Abby participates in home, school, therapy, and weekend activities with her family, teachers, and therapists Dressing, eating, riding in car seat, joint book reading, participating in circle time with class, doing art activities, going to therapy sessions, swimming, playing with family, having storytime, bathing at night	Communication is primarily done with no- and low-tech AT: Gestures Vocal sounds Eye gaze to yes/no choices Partner-assisted scanning with two choices Photograph albums of favorite activities to choose
What we need to know	**What are family's goals and the child's strengths and needs?**	**How is disability limiting environments?** **What are possible future environments?**	**What are desired activities and possible future activities?**	**What AT tools or strategies will increase participation in activities?**
Questions and concerns from family define assessment questions to be answered	Communication system Optimal positioning support for Abby in sitting Computer access to see digital photographs, software to play games, learn on computer Receptive language and sensory skills are strong	Environments are focused primarily on home, car, travel, school, and therapy Weekend environments are more flexible Team can seek more community environments Physical access is barrier to participation	Weekends have more possible activities with family and swimming Family wants Abby to have more peer interaction Team can identify choices for preferred activities in community settings and provide choices to Abby and her family	Abby responds readily to yes/no questions and choices Low-tech photograph/icon books for choices Activity boards with steps in task Single-message VOCA Multiple-message VOCA Transition to SGD with symbol set to build vocabulary

Figure 4.2.   FEET Form 3: Team assessment planning for Abby.

ple of a completed Form 3 is shown in Figure 4.2, summarizing the team planning process for Abby's team.

Observing Activity-Based Participation

The next step in the FEET process is identifying specific activities and targeted observation in order to determine appropriate AT tools based on the previous steps in the assessment process, using Form 4. Following the development of a team assessment plan, team and family members take the next step to conduct targeted observations of the child within activities in order to customize AT tools for child's needs.

Applying the FEET process is organized around four functional domains used to evaluate the child's participation in daily routines in an activity-based framework (Beukelman & Mirenda, 2005; Dowden & Marriner, 1995). Specific AT tools in the FEET assessment process are designed to observe and determine the child's degree of participation in a natural, unaided context and also with AT supports provided. More detail regarding specific AT tools recommended for use in the FEET assessment process are included in Chapter 9. Functional domains targeted in the FEET process and development of the AT toolkit include communication, play, computer access, and emergent literacy. Specific observations are conducted following the team meeting and are based on the functional domains. An example of the activity-based observation process is described in Figure 4.3, with Abby. Further examples of activity-based dynamic assess-

Observing activity-based participation

Child's name: Abby
Age: 4
Location/setting: Preschool classroom

Date of observation: March 5
Observer: Parent, SLP, OT, PT
Begin and end time: 9:00AM to 9:20AM

ACTIVITY/ROUTINE Art activity with peer

Child's physical position	Child's actions (what he or she does)	Child's communication behaviors (gestures, sounds, gaze directed toward another person)	Barriers for child's participation	Expectations of typically developing peer in same activity/routine	Discrepancy between child and typically developing peer expectations	Possible AT solutions to increase child's participation
Seated in supported seating system with wheelchair, trunk, and head supports Table surface easily accessible to chair and Abby pushed up to table	Looks at art supplies on table Reaches toward art items Watches peer complete pasting shapes on paper and shaking glitter Remains focused on activity for entire observation	Looks at art supplies on table and looks toward teacher repeatedly, to request Smiles at teacher in response to question about art activity Looks toward her preferred color of paper, markers, and paint when offered choice of two items including glue stick, glitter shaker, paintbrush, and sponges to stamp shapes	Physical barriers to manipulate art materials Reaching toward art items, but was not able to grasp Reliance on adult to provide choices of art supplies rather than independently gaining access Independent communication tools not available for Abby to indicate choices Adult responded to peer who was verbal, thus limiting turns for Abby to communicate	Peer reaches toward art supplies Peer verbally requests colors, paper, glue, and glitter when needed Peer offers items to Abby to choose Peer comments on location of shapes and what she is creating on paper Peer answers questions about her glue, shape, and glitter project when asked by teacher Peer shows her creation to Abby voluntarily	Abby's initiation of communication is limited; waits for teacher to offer choices Vocal and verbal use of vocabulary to talk about art project lacking Gestural and vocal communication only in response to teacher and peer questions Turn taking with peer limited to peer initiations toward Abby	Provide visual access to communication board with art activity items, actions, and place in visual proximity to use eye gaze VOCA device that allows Abby to choose art supplies and comment on peer's work Set up scanning on multimessage device with switch location for Abby to activate START and STOP with scanning to select colors

Figure 4.3. FEET Form 4: Observing activity-based participation for Abby.

ment are included in the following chapters and in supplemental materials included on the accompanying CD-ROM. Providers may also incorporate their own assessment tools in the process of determining the child's participation with various forms of early AT tools.

Assistive Technology Action Planning

A process for action planning, adapted from Mistrett, Lane, and Ruffino (2004), is provided for team decision making regarding introducing AT tools with individual children using Form 5. Figure 4.4 demonstrates the action planning process for Abby and her team. Following observation of the child in the context of familiar activities, the team and family members can summarize the relative effectiveness of one type of AT support over another and in combination with low-, mid-, and high-tech methods. Action planning includes identifying appropriate AT strategies, including low-, mid-, and high-tech tools. At this step in the FEET process, the team is ready to identify specific AT solutions, resources needed, time lines, and further specific plans to implement the AT supports identified in the previous steps.

Assistive Technology Observation Trials

Following action planning, designated team members (including family members) conduct additional trial observations in daily environments (Mistrett, Lane et al., 2004). Figure 4.5 illustrates the process of observation trials implemented for Abby to determine the appropriate selection of AT tools in her activities. The purpose of additional observa-

AT action plan					
AT access	AT solutions	Environmental adaptations	Resources needed (equipment, funding, training, personnel)	Timelines	Person responsible
Positioning	Maintain seating system; supports in car seat/customize form; tumble forms for floor play; adapt materials with Velcro and magnets for doll play	Position materials for access for wheelchair to position at table with other children in class	Review and consult with AT specialist regarding seating system at school; customize form for car seat; tumble forms for play; regional center funding	Within 2 weeks	Regional center (funding), OT, PT, parent
Mobility	Seating system Mobile standing system	Clear obstacles in classroom for ease of access to materials	Consult with OT and PT to evaluate access in classroom and home	Within 3 weeks	OT, PT, parent
Communication	Activity boards with large icons of core and fringe words to choose with eye gaze; single-message VOCAs and sequenced message VOCA; multiple-message VOCA with scanning access	Enlarged icons to represent activities placed throughout classroom on Velcro-friendly background; stabilize toys and switches with rubber mats	Create activity boards with static (core words) and removable icons (fringe words) in AT/AAC resource lab; single-message VOCA ($15); Ablenet Step-by-Step or Adaptivation Sequencer ($150–$175); seven-level communicator with sequencing ($700)	1 each week for 6 weeks; 6 weeks	SLP, teacher, regional center, parent
Vision	Recheck as needed	Position materials in visual field for eye gaze			School nurse, physician
Hearing	Recheck in regular physicals	Ensure attention when communicating with Abby			SLP, teacher, parent

Figure 4.4. FEET Form 5: AT action plan for Abby.

tions, as indicated in Form 6, is to evaluate AT tools in daily use and to further problem solve to provide optimal support for children to gain access to inclusive activities with peers.

The importance of observation trials with specific AT tools that have been identified by the team members is to determine the effectiveness and need for modification. This step is designed to reduce AT device discontinuation that often occurs when professionals and family members select an AT device without carefully considering the child's individual needs (Judge, 2002). Furthermore, implementing AT solutions across settings will support generalization and use of AT to increase participation and to gain access to learning in multiple activities. The initial focus on one type of activity can be expanded following initial evaluation and modification, as needed.

Assistive Technology Evaluation

Following observation trials, team members reconvene to evaluate the success of particular AT tools and further develop solutions for individual children, using Form 7.

Evaluating the relative success of specific AT strategies that are selected by the team and family members is finally conducted, based on the results of several observation trials. At this point, carefully selected AT tools have been implemented and observed by multiple team members including the intervention/education team and the family. Further recommendations can be developed based on the results of the evaluation and observation for each child's use of AT in specific activities, using Form 7. Figure 4.6 highlights the summary of all assessment information for Abby in a completed Form 7. At this step, the entire FEET process is summarized and reviewed. Although this may take several weeks to complete, AT support is demonstrated and evaluated throughout the process. Figure 4.7 illustrates the relationship and process in imple-

AT support	Activity 1: Art & pretend play Date/time: Monday/10AM	Activity 2: Storytime Date/time: Wednesday/2PM	Activity 3: Mealtime Date/time: Friday/11AM	AT effectiveness	Modifications needed
AT for communication access Activity boards at a minimum of three stations in classroom to choose and comment on activities with peer and teacher	Activity board with core vocabulary for greetings, comments, requests, and questions of peers and fringe vocabulary with art items; partner-assisted scanning with verbal cue; eye gaze to respond and choose item	Same as activity 1, with fringe vocabulary focused on books and story content	Same as activity 1, with fringe vocabulary focused on foods and mealtime words	Abby responded readily to pictures on board; difficult to "read" her choices because her gaze is brief; several repeated requests required; she became frustrated; improved Friday	Provide orientation time for Abby to look over the activity board before giving verbal cue to choose; limit choices initially; cover part of board to provide three to four choices maximally; encourage commenting during activity
AT for play access Switch-activated crayon holder for drawing; thematic play available in drama area	Switch-activated crayon holder to move crayon around the paper with peer assisting; thematic play activity with peer in drama area	Baggie books of pictures of peers during dress-up time; peer assists Abby to turn pages of book attached to a Velcro-friendly slantboard	Princess-themed cups and plates; all children wear king and queen hats during mealtime	Themed baskets helped the peers to select the already prepared Velcro-friendly equipment and Step-by-Step for the activity; labeling the play center with a voice-over helped to identify play item of choice	Provide emotion words on four-choice templates to use with seven-level communicator or Go Talk 4 to indicate how the doll is feeling; begin with child as agent of play with peer and proceed to doll as agent with props and communication device
AT for literacy access Provide adapted books with high-interest themes; reduce clutter in text and pictures; provide stable surface for books; select books with phonological targets for rhyming, alliteration, and sound awareness skills; provide eye-gaze method to select letter	Adapted books with princess themes; page turner that is soft and can be grasped easily (sponge roller, makeup sponge); repeated patterns in words with rhyming words, repeated lines, and fill-in words at end of phrases	Adapted books that teacher selects per curriculum theme with props; prop for Abby to handle and select to respond to specific word or line in book; VOCA activation to participate in repeated line in book/story; eye-gaze method to select letter to correspond with the sound the teacher names	Placemat for food items and choices during mealtime at home	Abby showed sustained attention and motivation to participate with adapted books, especially the princess theme; difficulty turning pages due to grasp and release problems; positioning difficult to maintain due to changing muscle tone; eye gaze to correct letter with sound required two to three prompts; accuracy improved quickly	Stabilize books on slantboard with Velcro backing on book; white-out tape on excess text; reduce clutter on page; highlighter tape on key text; large sponge rollers on edge of pages to grasp and turn; eye-gaze board with target words and letters for sound-awareness
AT for computer access Cause-and-effect computer software programs; switch and switch interface for activating software	My Face software by Marblesoft with a toggle switch and switch interface for activation			Two peers modeled software demonstration on the first day; Abby activated toggle switch after two attempts on software on the second day	Begin with two peers as models of action; Abby observes on first trial and participates on second, continuing in a turn-taking fashion

Figure 4.5.   FEET Form 6: AT observation trials for Abby.

menting the steps in the FEET approach to AT assessment and intervention planning with young children.

FEET Forms

FEET Forms are provided for each of the components of AT assessment and are on the CD-ROM. These forms provide an ongoing monitoring system for early intervention and early childhood providers to determine the effectiveness of AT strategies with young children.

SUMMARY

This chapter identified considerations and methods to establish a system for ongoing AT assessment and services with young children. At the programmatic level, policy and administrative support are foremost to provide the foundation for families and professionals to have operational AT services. Professionals who are trained in AT services and able to implement all phases of identification, referral, assessment, and service delivery can only perform effectively with ongoing resources at the administrative level. The complementary and reciprocal relationship between service delivery and administrative leadership requires continued focus and development at management and practitioner levels. Furthermore, interagency collaboration is required for comprehensive services for young children with disabilities and family members, particularly in the provision of AT services.

In the delivery of AT services, assessment methods can be integrated with established assessment procedures as an additional component to create improved access

AT evaluation plan

AT intervention goal	AT materials implemented	Effectiveness of intervention	Need for modifications	Person responsible
Communication Select preferred items with activity board to answer questions in activity/story; comment with classmates regarding feelings and greetings in activities at school; select specific vocabulary in PODD communication book	Activity boards in classroom activities with core and fringe vocabulary; multiple-message VOCA with scanning access to stop and start; select answer to question or ask questions of classmates; PODD book with topics she likes to talk about and specific vocabulary, including range of semantic functions	Abby focused her gaze on specific vocabulary when asked yes/no questions; Abby activated switch to start and stop scanning and needed physical support to do so; Abby responded with directed gaze to choice of topics and vocabulary	Provide orientation time for Abby to look over the activity board before giving verbal cue to choose; limit choices initially; cover part of board to provide three to four choices maximally; support switch on foam padding or part of "swim noodle" to stabilize VOCA for her to activate; explore looking up to choose picture in yes/no question rather than gaze directly at picture	SLP, teacher, parent
Play Select at least two play props; use props with peers in pretend play episode	Themed pretend play baskets with visual scenes of the theme and step-by-step directions of the pretend play event	Abby was able to select two out of six props to attach to her Velcro apron	Seating modifications still need to be examined; step-by-step directions with each themed basket would provide a way for Abby to lead the pretend play event	SLP, OT, teacher
Literacy Increase book handling with adapted access; increase language development regarding phrase complexity and length; increase print awareness; increase phonological awareness	Adapted books with page turners/fluffers using sponge materials; slantboard with 3-inch binder and microfiber to hold Velcro-adapted book; highlighter tape to focus on phrases in text; all reading curriculum to focus on initial phonological awareness and sound blending skills; computer-adapted books with MOB on favorite themes	Abby mastered eye gaze to appropriate letter targets to correspond to sounds with minimal prompting; physical access to turning pages is difficult	Alternative computer activation for book access with eye gaze or air-puff technology is recommended	SLP, teacher, parent
Computer Demonstrate understanding of cause and effect on a computer; move from single actions to two or more; provide two switches for choice making	My Face cause-and-effect software program with toggle switch and switch interface	Abby has mastered the basic one-switch activation and is now ready for listening to storybooks on the computer and attempting basic concept software	Provide peer models to orient Abby to task prior to introducing functions; increase difficulty level as Abby achieves single action; move to choice making, storybook reading, and basic concept software as successive trials indicate progress	SLP, teacher, parent

Follow-up needed

	RECOMMENDATIONS	WHO IS RESPONSIBLE
Health provider	Monitor well-child care	Physician
Vision/hearing		
SLP/AAC specialist	Review activity boards, PODD booklet, VOCA programming	SLP, teacher, parent
AT specialist	Provide computer access: switch activation	AT specialist, early intervention, early childhood special education, early childhood education team
Physical therapy	Review seating and positioning system with AT tools for communication	PT, SLP, parent
Occupational therapy	Consult on access with computer, AAC device, VOCA	OT, PT, SLP
Early intervention/early childhood	Consult with team on classroom implementation of AT/AAC	Early intervention, early childhood special education, early childhood education team

Figure 4.6. FEET Form 7: AT evaluation plan for Abby.

for learning and development. Children with complex communication, mobility, cognitive, and sensory needs may require AT services and devices to participate in typical activities with their peers in infant, toddler, and preschool settings. Considering AT services and devices is a process that builds onto existing early childhood services. Major approaches to AT assessment were reviewed and compared with applications for young children. Six steps in the AT assessment process were adapted from Mistrett (2004) and further developed in the FEET model. Steps in the FEET model were described as a series of activities for members of the team, including professionals and family members. Further application in key learning areas for young children, including communication, play, literacy, and technology applications, will be demonstrated in the following chapters.

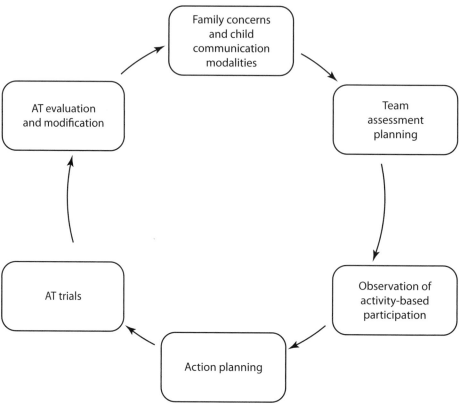

Figure 4.7. FEET assessment process.

1. Name and describe the six steps in the AT assessment process using the FEET model.

2. What are some cultural differences that need to be considered in AT assessment?

3. Which AT assessment processes used with school-age children and adults have been adapted for use with young children?

4. What are several reasons discussed in the literature that discontinuation of AT tools might occur?

5. What are typical functional domains to consider in AT assessment with young children?

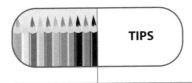

TIPS

○ Use the FEET process to identify potential applications and determine appropriate AT tools with individual children.

○ Consider team-based approaches when planning and implementing AT assessment.

○ Develop and implement steps to provide family-centered AT assessment, following recommendations by Judge (2002).

○ Observe the child's participation in typical activities with their peers. Compare participation without and with AT tools and strategies to identify successful approaches.

○ Conduct ongoing trials in several different settings at home, school, child care, and in community locations to identify AT tools and strategies that work and those that need to be modified.

Assistive Technology and Communication

At the moment of birth and possibly even before, tiny infants communicate with their mothers, fathers, and other caregivers. By 1 month of age, typically developing infants show a repretoire of communication skills that include making facial expressions, smiling, cooing, wriggling toes, grasping hands, squealing, and crying. Quickly, infants become adept at imitation and taking turns in favorite family games and routines that may include some version of Peekaboo or Pat-a-cake. Sounds and gestures evolve to first words somewhere near the first birthday, and a toddler expresses 100–200 words by the second birthday. These dramatic changes in communication and language provide the foundation for social relationships and learning in the preschool and early school years. Children who are born with disabilities that affect one or more developmental systems of hearing, vision, physical mobility, cognition, social interaction, attention, play, or other areas are at risk of delays in communication, speech, and language. For a smaller number of children with complex disabilities that involve multiple developmental challenges, early intervention with AT and AAC is needed to bridge the gap to communication and language development.

This chapter applies AT and AAC systems to support communication and language development with young children with complex communication needs. Initially, the overlap and distinction in definitions of AT and AAC are discussed. The rationale for including AT and AAC in early intervention is grounded in legislation, policy, and recommended practice based on research that demonstrates positive outcomes for children with complex disabilities when AT and AAC are provided early in life. The chapter then focuses on stages in communication and language development, AT, and AAC from developmental and functional perspectives. Language development strategies using AT and AAC, specifically explanding vocabulary and linguistic forms to support literacy and socialization, are reviewed. Furthermore, AT and AAC assessment and intervention planning will be demonstrated through specific examples with individual children using the FEET process. Finally, this chapter includes additional web and print resources related to AT, AAC, and communication.

DEFINING ASSISTIVE TECHNOLOGY AND AUGMENTATIVE AND ALTERNATIVE COMMUNICATION IN EARLY COMMUNICATION AND LANGUAGE DEVELOPMENT

Due to limited use of verbal speech, many children with disabilities require AT systems to support their communication and to acquire language skills. Past estimates of the prevalence of children with disabilities who were not able to use speech reliably ranged between 0.3%–0.6% of the total school-age population, and between 3%–6% of the students who were served in special education (Matas, Mathy-Laikko, Beukelman, & Legresley, 1985). Binger and Light (2006) found that 12% of preschool children enrolled in special education were in need of AAC. The population of children who may benefit from AT and AAC to support communication and language development is referred to as *children with complex communication needs* and may include children with a variety of diagnostic characteristics including autism, Down syndrome, cerebral palsy, apraxia of speech, delayed language development, and other types of disabilities.

AT and AAC to support communication, language, and literacy development among young children include a number of strategies and technologies designed to support infants and toddlers with physical disabilities and complex communication needs. Children with disabilities that affect communication development are at risk of limited social participation and development in all aspects of learning. AT for communication support includes low-, mid-, and high-tech devices from picture-based systems to computerized speech-output devices. For young children within the prelinguistic stage of language development, low-tech options are effective to begin building prelinguistic communication and emerging language skills. For children with emerging and developing language, making the transition to mid- and high-tech systems may be indicated. The development of appropriate AT solutions for each child is a process of matching individual needs and features of low and high-tech tools for communicating and learning. Most often, appropriate AT solutions involve a system of low-, mid- and high-tech strategies for each child. (Bowser & Reed, 2000).

AT is devoted to creating adaptations through a range of low- and high-tech equipment and devices that support children to participate in all areas of early play, communication, social, cognitive, and motor development. AAC includes the communication technology that is also part of AT and extends beyond technology to supplement communication in all forms of unaided and aided systems. AT also includes AAC in applying low-, mid-, and high-tech tools to support communication and language acquisition. One way to distinguish between the two areas is that AT covers all areas of child development through the formulation of accessible technologies and AAC focuses solely on communication and language skills.

AT is defined in the Assistive Technology Act Amendments of 2004 (PL 108-364) as any "product, device, or equipment, whether acquired commercially, modified or customized, that is used to maintain, increase, or improve the functional capabilities of individuals with disabilities" (Assistive Technology Act of 2004, Section 3). When AT supports early communication for young children with disabilities, Mistrett and Lane (2002) outlined types of AT to support early communication development in young children that includes gestures, picture-based tools, and VOCAs.

ASHA defined AAC as follows.

> AAC is, foremost, a set of procedures and processes by which an individual's communication skills (i.e., production as well as comprehension) can be maximized for functional and effective communication. It involves supplementing or replacing natural speech and/or writing with aided (e.g., picture communication symbols, line drawings,

Blissymbols, and tangible objects) and/or unaided symbols (e.g., manual signs, gestures, and finger spelling). Whereas aided symbols require some type of transmission device, unaided symbols require only the body to produce. Many individuals with severe communication and cognitive impairments can benefit from nonsymbolic forms of AAC such as gestures (reaching for a desired object) and vocalizations that convey different emotions. (2002, p. 2)

AT and AAC have considerable crossover when applied to supporting communication development in young children with disabilities. There are commonalities in creating tools and strategies, including picture-based systems and VOCAs. The two areas diverge, however, as language development becomes more complex and a system of AAC is needed to support vocabulary, phrase, syntax, narrative, and phonological skills. Figure 5.1 shows the commonalities and distinct differences of the two fields.

Rationale for Assistive Technology and Augmentative and Alternative Communication in Early Intervention

Increasingly, evidence shows the benefits of implementing AT with young children with complex communication needs early in life (Light, 2005; Romski & Sevcik, 2005). Recommended intervention practices using AT with young children are founded on established practice in early childhood special education. The field of early childhood special education established the research basis regarding the efficacy for early intervention with children with disabilities who are at risk of delayed development, specifically in the areas of communication and language (Iacono, 1999; Wolery, 2000). Recommended practices supported by research include early language intervention models, or milieu language intervention approaches, with specific steps to increase adult responsiveness to young children who are preverbal. Applying milieu principles that take advantage of the child's focus of attention and adult interpretation of possible child communicative intent are described as responsivity education or prelinguistic milieu intervention (Yoder & Warren, 2001, 2002). Applying prelinguistic milieu intervention with young children at risk of delayed speech-language development showed positive effects to increase intentional communication behavior and parental interpretation of their children's communicative acts.

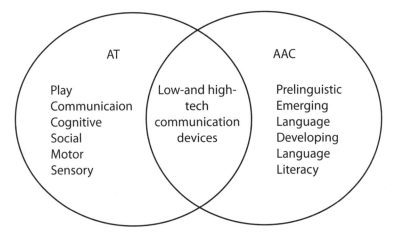

Figure 5.1. Relationship between AT and augmentative and alternative communication in early communication intervention.

Evidence from early language intervention research provides a naturalistic context and approach for implementing AT and AAC strategies to further support emerging communication and language development. For example, Cress and Marvin (2003) summarized research that supports early implementation and use of AT and AAC strategies with children with significant communication needs in order to provide support for further symbolic language development. A growing body of research demonstrated the efficacy of earlier use of AAC and introducing AT tools with young children who show delayed emergence of speech and verbal language. Rather than a "wait and see" approach to determine if speech-language may emerge, introducing AAC and AT approaches earlier is now recommended when signs of risk for speech-language delays become evident (Cress, 2002; Romski & Sevcik, 2005). AT and AAC tools for early communication and language include sign language, picture communication boards, adapted books, VOCAs, and high-tech SGDs (Skau & Cascella, 2006). Parents, other family members, and professionals can implement AT tools and AAC strategies with young children with complex disabilities to support communication at the prelinguistic, emerging, and developing language levels to assist children to establish a system for communication and links to symbolic language.

The rationale for implementing AT and AAC with young children at risk of communication delays gained research support by demonstrating the importance of prelinguistic communication with young children with disabilities. Cress and Marvin (2003), in particular, focused attention on the role of preintentional communication and adult intervention to scaffold and increase intentional communication acts with young children with significant disabilities. Cress (2002) introduced the "tools" model to guide the introduction of AT tools in developing the young child's transition from individualized gestural and preverbal communication gestures to symbolic forms of communicative acts. As Cress demonstrated, the effectiveness of introducing one tool at a time assists in building increasingly symbolic forms of communication. For example, initially, the child's own body forms a communication tool, and communicative acts are expressed through apparently fleeting gestures including eye gaze; reaching; and generalized excitement in arm, leg, head, and/or other movements. Following adult scaffolding to interpret possible communicative intentions from the child, AAC strategies such as objects, simple sign language, and photographs or AT tools such as single-message VOCAs can be introduced to assist in taking communicative turns within interactions. Light (2005) further demonstrated the effectiveness of using AAC in the form of computer-based visual scene displays to increase communicative acts and vocabulary development with young children with complex communication needs. Early AT tools and AAC strategies increase opportunities for communication and foster language and literacy development.

STAGES OF COMMUNICATION
AND LANGUAGE DEVELOPMENT IN YOUNG CHILDREN

Researchers characterize the emergence of language in developmental stages. These stages and the specific area of language that is being studied, such as vocalization, vocabulary or semantics, social or pragmatics, and sentence or syntax skills, differ by researchers. Child language literature, however, shows agreement among researchers regarding the general stages of early language, which include prelinguistic, emerging language, and developing language (Paul, 2007). At each of these stages, children show specific skills in the process of making a transition to the next stage. Table 5.1 highlights particular milestones in each stage of language and estimates of expected ages for typically developing children. Children with disabilities remain at some stages longer and often show scattered abilities. Although particular stages do not capture individual differences among children, the following progression provides a general framework. The three areas outlined in Table 5.1

Table 5.1. Early communication and language development stages in young children

Communication and language development stage	Typical age range	Vocal/verbal	Social/pragmatic	Vocabulary/semantics	Phrase/syntax
Prelinguistic	Birth to 1 year	Cooing, babbling, gesturing	Joint attention, turn taking, emerging communicative intent	Understands many words and routines	Not applicable
Emerging language	1–2 1/2years	First words with simplified forms; gestures continue	Clear communicative intent; requests, comments, greets, refuses, and interacts with words	Expands expressive vocabulary from 3 to 300 words; learns new words rapidly	Begins combining words in phrases and simple sentences
Developing language	2 1/2–5 years	Speech becomes clearly understandable; masters most sounds in primary language	Continues social interaction skills; tells events and narratives	Expands vocabulary from 50 to 5,000 words; deepens concepts	Develops complex sentence forms

are provided to guide early intervention teams in the process of supporting children at risk of communication and language delay with increased opportunities to strengthen and expand communication modalities.

The developmental stages outlined previously provide one method to characterize individual strengths and needs of individual children and to guide early intervention teams in selecting appropriate intervention goals. In addition to the developmental approach, a more functional view is the Continuum of Communication Independence or Communication Independence Model (Dowden, 2004), proposed as a means to support children and adults who use AAC to have appropriate communication tools and communication partner support at successive levels of communicative functioning. The continuum approach includes three stages—the emerging communicator, context-dependent communicator, and independent communicator. As Dowden explained, there are many barriers for individuals with complex communication needs for whom speech is not a reliable means of communication. The challenges for children with complex communication needs include possible misconceptions on the part of other communication partners who may think that the child with a disability may not understand or have the cognitive abilities to communicate. Misperceptions and stereotyping often create walls of silence and keep the child with complex communication needs confined within the misunderstandings and lack of methods to communicate. Through the Communication Independence Model, Dowden proposed a way to systematically identify communication needs and support individuals to develop reliable methods for communication with a wider circle of communication partners in a broad range of environments. Each of the stages of the Communication Independence Model is defined in Table 5.2.

The continuum approach is descriptive of children and adults across many ages and stages of development and serves a functional purpose to determine particular needs for an individual to reach a successive stage of independence. More specific descriptors of each type of communication stage were developed with input from leading researchers in the AAC field and published by DynaVox (2009) in the form of the AAC Goal Grid. Each of the three levels of communication independence is further described with a series

Table 5.2.   Communication Independence Model

Level of communication independence	Definition of communication independence levels
Emerging communicator	The individual does not have a reliable method of expressive communication through a system of symbolic language.
	This can apply to a young child with physical and developmental disabilities in addition to an adult with acquired disabilities. Each of these individuals may progress in their degree of independent communication at different rates.
Context-dependent communicator	This individual has a reliable method of communication that is symbolic and is limited to specific communication partners or contexts.
	Context-dependent communication is related to limitations that are challenges for the individual, such as physical access difficulties or dependence on communication partners to design vocabulary within communication systems.
Independent communicator	This individual has the ability and tools to communicate on any topic to anyone in any context.
	Individuals who are independent communicators have learned the ability to use a variety of communication tools that may include various forms of AT and AAC, natural methods of communication, and literacy skills in all settings where they may participate.

Source: Dowden (2004).

of indicators to help determine individual communication abilities. The AAC Goal Grid is a helpful resource for early childhood professionals, particularly regarding the emergent and context-dependent communicator levels, and is available at http://www.dynavoxtech.com/training/toolkit/paths.aspx?id=5

Developmental and functional perspectives are needed when considering the individual needs for each child. Initially, developmental stages of communication and language development were discussed as a framework to identify baseline skills and needs for communication support for individual children. In addition, the Communication Inde-pendence Model helps determine communication abilities and next steps to support more independence to communicate and use a symbol system in that process. Although the two approaches view the child differently, both are intended to identify current abilities and determine next steps in the intervention process. In order to align each perspective, it may be helpful for intervention teams to first identify developmental strengths and needs for an individual child prior to using the Communication Independence Model.

In the developmental model, determining the predominant characteristics of the child's communication abilities regarding the prelinguistic, emerging, and developmental language stages provides both family and intervention team members the background knowledge regarding the child's individual characteristics and leads to initial selection of potential AT tools and AAC strategies. Following a developmental assessment, the more functional approach using the Communication Independence Model is useful to determine specific AT and AAC intervention goals and strategies for intervention. As emphasized by Dowden (2004) and Gillette (2005), the goal of AT and AAC intervention is to support increasing independence in communication and language use across many settings and partners. The following poem provides the perspective from an individual who uses augmentative and alternative communication, drawing attention to the importance of communicating on all levels.

Speech Disorder

You and I are facing each other
The room is dark and silent
The only light I see is from your eyes and a burning candle
I have a speech disorder
You don't
Why are you so silent when your eyes say so much?
You wouldn't understand if my lips shaped
"I love you"
But I understand that your eyes say these words to me
Can you see it in my eyes?
Do we both have a speech disorder?

Carin Westerlund

The goal for early intervention with AT and AAC for communication and language development in the early childhood years is to establish a means for young children with disabilities to overcome the barriers to inclusion, independence, and participation with others.

Assistive Technology for Communication and Language Development

Research supports the effectiveness of early intervention to enhance language use with children at risk of delays. The earlier introduction of AT tools and AAC strategies also shows positive effects for the prelinguistic and early language skills with children in toddler and preschool settings. Cress (2006) reported the efficacy of early applications with AT tools to enhance prelinguistic skills; specifically, communicative intent with children with severe disabilities and subtle communication cues. Through increased opportunities and the introduction of a single AT tool, such as a photograph with a toy, and later, a VOCA with a toy, Cress showed an increase in frequency of child-initiated communication and adult response. These findings mirror the results of early language intervention research that demonstrated increased communicative interactions and vocabulary growth with toddlers when parents were taught to be more responsive and employ prelinguistic milieu techniques (Yoder & Warren, 2001, 2002).

Beyond the prelinguistic level, emphasizing naturalistic social interactions in early intervention supports communication and language development. However, the new element at this stage, however, is focusing on building vocabulary and language. Binger and Light (2007) raised awareness of the need to expand vocabulary rapidly with young children who rely on visual communication tools that include low- and high-tech AT and AAC systems. Often, interventionists may unintentionally limit children's exposure to words and opportunities to learn new words due to the need to preprogram vocabulary specific to each daily activity into an AAC device or to create a picture overlay. Adults' decisions about vocabulary for individual children to use in daily environments can thus limit opportunities for children to learn new words and to experience the rapid vocabulary expansion that occurs with children who develop verbal speech and language. Typically, at the emerging language stage, children are not required to practice and master vocabulary before being exposed to new words. Fast mapping, or the process of recognizing novel words and linking experience to possible word meanings, is thought to accelerate language with typically developing children. Wilkinson and Albert (2001) urged practitioners in early AAC intervention to adopt a fast mapping approach to vocabulary exposure. Sevcik (2006) also demonstrated the importance of focusing on vocabulary comprehension and expression in young children using picture-based AAC devices. A focus on vocabulary development, both comprehension and expression of words through alternative communicative modalities, is important because of the role that vocabulary plays in the next stage. An extensive vocabulary, even though not completely mastered, allows children to move forward to form word and concept combinations with increasingly complex forms of language expression.

Developing language includes formulating and expressing sentences in phrases, complex sentences, and narratives and continues through early preschool until early school years. AT and AAC interventions to support developing language require a series of tools and strategies to encourage independent and spontaneous utterances with young children with complex communication needs. Soto (2006) and Soto, Hartmann, and Wilkins (2006) demonstrated the effectiveness of co-construction in storytelling to support children in early elementary school years to build narratives using story maps and story starters. Their findings showed that AAC strategies to encourage narrative development included leading questions and strategic scaffolding from communication partners. Children need to be able to use AT tools and AAC systems effectively in social and school settings to create conversation and to express themselves creatively. Recommended practices to support higher level, independent language construction continue to be identified and described in ongoing research.

Assistive Technology and No-, Low-, and High-Tech Augmentative and Alternative Communication Systems

As discussed in detail in Chapter 4, using AT to support communication for infants, toddlers, and preschool children requires an assessment by a team that includes the family; early intervention/early childhood education professionals; related services professionals such as SLPs, physical therapists, occupational therapists, behavioral specialists, and health care professionals; and specialists in AT and AAC. Following assessment and decisions made by the team, adaptations for communication and language development can be developed to meet the individual physical, sensory, communication, and cognitive needs of each child. In addition, the family preferences that may include diverse cultural and language backgrounds and daily activities need to be considered when choosing and designing AT for communication and language development. The types of AT that are selected for each individual child are, of course, directly linked to the results of assessment to determine individual strengths and needs. The process for matching the type of technology to the needs of an individual child is referred to as *feature matching*, which enables the early intervention team to explore the extent of low-, mid-, and high-tech features of AT tools that best fit the needs of the individual child.

Knowing individual needs can only be gained through a process of dynamic assessment that allows trial use of various types of AT and AAC devices. Through a series of steps detailed in Chapter 4 regarding the AT assessment process, teams that include family members can determine and identify a number of strategies and tools that are effective. The resulting selections may include low-, mid-, and high-tech AT devices, all for the same child. In other words, a system of AT support results from feature matching between the AT tools available and individual needs with different communication partners in different environments. For example, a young child who does not use speech to communicate may use gestures and a low-tech picture book with photographs of favorite activities on the playground, a single-message VOCA to greet other children in the morning circle time, and a high-tech SGD to interact with peers and teachers in the classroom. Integrating the individualized AT tools into a customized system through daily environments and routines allows flexible use of AT tools that best fit each child. The following tables demonstrate a range of technology in selected examples of no- and low-tech (Table 5.3); low- and mid-tech (Table 5.4); and high-tech (Table 5.5) AT and AAC devices to support early communication and language development with young children with complex communication needs.

The examples included in Tables 5.3, 5.4, and 5.5 were selected to show a broad representation of AT to support communication and language development at prelinguistic, emerging, and developing language stages. Although the examples are not exhaustive, the features in the types of available technology in the field of AT and AAC with young children are the most critical elements in the examples provided. Changing technology will certainly outdate the specific devices in the previous examples. The examples, however, are provided as tools to inform decision making in the AT assessment process and selecting appropriate device features to meet the needs of individual children.

LANGUAGE AND COMMUNICATION INTERVENTION

Language and communication intervention using AT and AAC with young children follows the same approach as activity-based intervention. Meaningful communication

Table 5.3. Examples of no- and low-tech AT tools for communication and augmentative and alternative communication (AAC) intervention

AT tool	Features	Purpose	Example of implementation	Examples/source
Communication photographs	Individual photographs Direct select to point to or handle photographs Eye gaze when mounted on clear plastic eye-gaze tool	Includes individual photographs of child's familiar receptive vocabulary and novel words Links to objects in environment to build communicative intent	Select appropriate number and size of photographs for individual child Position photograph in front of object to link symbol to object	Digital photographs of actual items, people, actions, places, and feelings of child's environment Digital camera Color printer
Communication book	Photograph book Clear pages Velcro backing on photographs Adult assists in selecting photographs	Photograph communication aids in photograph album format or individual photographs with digital camera	Provide photograph in single or choice formats to support making the transition to symbolic language	Inexpensive photograph album with soft Velcro on each page to store photographs of child's relevant vocabulary
Visual scene	Large photograph of familiar environment Access with pointing or eye gaze Individual vocabulary on small, laminated squares with Velcro backing	Depicts relevant actions, people, and interactions as context to build vocabulary beyond nouns Individual vocabulary photographs/icons can be placed on photograph to "contextualize" vocabulary of nouns, actions, people, feelings, and attributes	Introduce photograph prior to activity Preview what the child will see, do, and experience Review after activity to create a "story" about the activity Cover elements that are relevant for child—who, what, where, how, why, and feelings	Digital photograph printed in page size Page protector or laminated Small photographs mounted on sticky-back foam and covered with contact paper or laminated Velcro backing on photographs
Communication icons with printed label	Individual icons on single cards/laminated Direct select to point or handle Eye gaze when mounted on clear plastic with Velcro backing	Represents objects, actions, people, and other vocabulary in higher level of symbolic representation	Select appropriate number and size of icon cards for individual child Position photograph in front of object to link symbol to object	Boardmaker Plus from DynaVox ($300) Overboard from Gus, Inc. ($200) Symbol Stix from Symbol Stix ($100 yearly subscription) Unity Symbols from Prentke Romich ($50)
Activity board	Various sizes and number of photographs/icons on board Direct access, eye gaze, or partner-assisted scanning	Show steps of activities in sequence with core words in same place on repeated boards Color code for core and activity or "fringe" vocabulary	Adult uses aided language stimulation (ALS) to highlight words, waits for child's response to support comprehension and expressive language	Pogo Boards from Talk to me Technologies ($70) Boardmaker Software
Storyboard/song board	Various sizes and number of photographs/icons on board to show key concepts in song or story Direct access, eye gaze, or partner-assisted scanning	Photograph/picture icon display with concepts/words from song or story	Adult highlights words in song or story using ALS to support comprehension and expressive language	Teacher-made materials Making Language Visible CD from Creative Communicating ($50)
Clock scanning communicators	Switch operation with "clock" face and choice of objects, photographs, and icons Scanning access with switch activation	Provides visual display of communication choices on clear plastic clock face Icons/objects can be changed Method for assessment and learning step scanning	Place selected object/photographs/icons on clock face as appropriate for individual child's needs and selected activity	Clock communicators available from Enablemart ($115–$130)

78

Table 5.4. Examples of selected low- and mid-tech AT tools for communication and augmentative and alternative communication (AAC) intervention

AT tool	Features	Purpose	Example of implementation	Examples/source
Single-message voice output communication aid (VOCA): photograph frame; Single-message VOCA: Velcro-backed photograph on switch	Battery operated; Re-recordable; Direct select to activate; No-touch version is movement activated	Display photograph or picture icon with single recorded message, approximately 10 seconds	Place in reach and visual field for child to activate with greetings, requests, and repeated lines in songs and books for turn taking	Talking photo frame: Various online sources; Express One talking photo frame from Attainment ($15–$20); LittleMack, BigMack from Able Net ($129); No Touch Talker from Attainment ($50)
Multiple-message VOCA with objects/and or pictures	Digitized voice; Battery operated; Direct select for voice output; Scanning on Choice 4 model	Re-recordable message selection; Four messages (up to 12 levels on the Choice 4 model); Object compartments for linking object to voice output messages	Record names of favorite activities in each message button; Place corresponding objects for child to choose and activate voice output	Base Trainer from AMDI ($200); Talkable III from Enabling Devices ($300); Choice 4 Communicator from Enabling Devices ($500)
Sequential-message VOCA	Battery operated; Multiple message with levels; Re-recordable; Direct select to activate	Stores series of quickly recorded messages such as jokes, stories, and conversation scripts; Up to 75 seconds total recording time; Promotes turn taking and social interaction	Record messages about different topics, jokes, conversations, songs, and stories for child to take turns expressing words	Step-by-Step with levels from Able Net ($150); Sequencer with levels from Adaptivation ($130)
Multiple-message VOCA	Battery operated; Re-recordable cards with memory strip; Direct selection to activate voice	Records sentences and concepts in stories, visual scenes, narratives, songs, and themes that can be stored on separate cards with recorded memory strip	Prerecord sequence of favorite songs, stories, and news events for child to tell others by placing appropriate pictures in device/or touching key points on pictures	Voice Pod from Attainment ($50); Boardmaker Activity Pad from DynaVox/Mayer-Johnson ($1,000)
Multiple-message communicator: beginning devices	Digitized speech; Battery operated; Direct select to activate voice; 4–16 messages; Changeable overlays	Has a range of recording time and number of selections; Provides topic communication with overlays organized by topic/theme	Record a series of messages in separate overlays by topic, stories, or environments for child to make choices, "say" parts of story, converse, or make a choice in an activity	Basic Talk 4 from Enabling Devices ($130)
Multiple-message communicator: beginning devices with multiple levels	Digitized speech; Battery operated; Direct select to activate voice; Multiple levels from 1 to 16 messages on each level	Has a range of recording time and number of selections; Provides topic communication by levels or overlays organized by topic/theme	Record a series of messages in separate overlays by topic, stories, or environments for child to make choices, "say" parts of story, converse, or make a choice in an activity	Bluebird from Satillo ($1,000); Go Talk Series from Attainment ($200–$400); Super Talker from Able Net ($300); Seven-Level Communication Builder from Enabling Devices ($400)
Multiple-message communicator with scanning and levels	Digitized speech; Multiple levels, some with bar code technology to recognize overlays; Direct access and scanning 4, 8, or 32 selections	Allows 1, 2, 4, 8, or 16 different messages per level; Has overlays for each level; Total recording time is 300 seconds	Record a series of messages in separate overlays by topic, stories, or environments for child to make choices, "say" parts of story, converse, or make a choice in an activity	LEO from Assistive Technology, Inc. ($800); Flash Scanning Communicator from Able Net ($1,000); Talk 8 with Scanning from Enabling Devices ($350); Tech Scan 32 from AMDI ($1,000); Smart Series, 8, 32, 128 Plus from AMDI ($800–$1,500)

Table 5.5. Examples of high-tech AT tools for communication and augmentative and alternative communication (AAC) intervention

AT tool	Features	Purpose	Example of implementation	Examples/source
Pocket-size speech-generating device (SGD)	Synthesized speech Touchscreen PC computer Dynamic display Visual scene Display Onscreen keyboard Built-in camera	Provides pocket- or purse-size AAC device with touchscreen Dynamic display and speaking software enables device to access many prestored messages and generate words and speech from text	Select prestored vocabulary set to use in specific activities Create customized home page with photograph for individual Customize topical page sets for individual	Say it Sam! from Words+ ($3,000) Cyrano Communicator from One Write ($1200) Proloquo Speaking Application for iPhone and iTouch from Proloquo ($190) Small Talk Application from Lingraphica, free application for iPhone or iTouch
Mini-SGD	Touchscreen PC computer Dynamic display Visual scene display	Has concrete scenes and symbols Contains extensive page sets to accommodate a user's vocabulary	Combine visual scenes and emerging vocabulary development to "grow" with individual Begin with favorite scenes, build vocabulary	DynaVox Express ($7500) DynaVox M3 ($4000) Mini-Merc from Assistive Technologies, Inc. ($7000)
Small SGD Unity Beginning System	Touchscreen PC computer Dynamic display Window and static display Visual scene display Wireless capability	Teaches Unity system gradually with 4, 8, 16, and 32 locations Builds core vocabulary with conceptual symbols that "grows" with individual Has recorded and synthesized speech	Use Unity system with Minspeak symbols and sequences	Springboard Lite and Springboard from Prentke Romich ($2,500)
Medium-size SGD	Six-button design Lightweight PC computer Dynamic display Visual scene Display camera (in Tango) Direct selection or scanning	Provides simple display with dynamic display structure to build communication and language.	Vocabulary can be used for individual child to use within activities Import customized photographs to create narratives about each child.	Tango from DynaVox ($8,000)

Device	Features	Function	Products
Full-size SGD	Touchscreen for direct selection or scanning with switch adaptation PC computer Dynamic display Visual scene display	Dynamic display AAC device with full computer capabilities Wireless, environmental control, Internet access, photo import, music, and customization possible	Select vocabulary set to use in specific activities Explore page sets that are preloaded in device for application and customization to individual	DynaVox V from DynaVox ($8,000) Vantage Lite from Prentke Romich ($7,500) ECO 14 from Prentke Romich ($8,000)
Head tracker module	Dedicated camera USB function connects with reflective dot worn on any part of face or glasses	For those with limited use of their hands Attaches to many dynamic display SGDs Creates mouse functions with head movement/reflective dot	Attach Tracker Pro to top of device with USB input Place reflective dot on forehead, glasses, or similar location that individual child can control reliably Access targets on the screen	Tracker Pro from Madentec ($1,000)
Full-size SGD Built-in eye tracker	Touchscreen PC computer Dynamic display Communication software of various types Visual scene display Built-in eye gaze calibration	Integrated eye tracking Dynamic display AAC device with full computer capabilities Wireless, environmental control, Internet access, photo import, music, and customization possible	Calibrate eye tracker for individual user Select vocabulary set to use in specific activities Explore page sets that are preloaded in device for application and customization to individual	My Tobii P10 from Assistive Technology, Inc. ($15,000) ECO 14 with Echopoint from Prentke Romich ($15,000) DynaVox V with EyeMax System from DynaVox ($15,000)

takes place within ongoing activities with peers, adults, and family members. In addition to determining the constellation of low-, mid-, and high-tech AT tools that are most appropriate for each child, AT goals must be developed as part of the IFSP or IEP. Light (2005) provided a helpful framework for early AT/AAC communication and language goals for young children that extend across the prelinguistic, emerging, and developing language stages.

- Increase participation and build social interaction/turn taking.
- Express range of communication functions.
- Develop vocabulary and breadth of semantic concepts to support more diverse communication.
- Build greater complexity of language structure to support more complex communication.
- Build phonological awareness/foundations for literacy development.

Light's framework was demonstrated in Chapter 3, in Table 3.2, showing examples of AT/AAC to support communication and language development opportunities in daily activities for children with complex communication needs and/or physical disabilities.

Aided Language Stimulation

In addition to embedding intervention into natural routines, the approach to implementing AT and AAC interventions with young children includes several evidence-based strategies. Goosens' (1989) initially demonstrated the effectiveness of visual supports to increase functional communication and language skills with a young child with severe disabilities in her groundbreaking work that included song boards, storyboards, communication boards, and picture symbols in an enlarged format. Goosens' approach is referred to as aided language stimulation (ALS), which included highlighting (gesturing or pointing to) salient photographs and icons while also modeling key words with children. Goosens', Crain, and Elder (1992) further developed the ALS method to expand to designing preschool environments with visual communication tools throughout daily activities. Cafiero (2001) extended and adapted the ALS approach within natural routines, using the term *natural aided language stimulation*, using picture-based communication boards for daily activities and gesturing toward pictured key words and actions while engaged in activities with young children with autism. Acheson (2006) replicated these findings with picture-based systems with children with autism, finding increased comprehension and expression.

System for Augmenting Language

Variations of the ALS approach are reported in the field of AAC with young children, implemented in individual and group intervention settings. Researchers including Binger and Light (2007) demonstrated the effectiveness of the ALS approach to model and prompt language and communication development with young children learning to use both low- and high-tech AAC systems. In their work, Binger and Light reported the effectiveness of ALS to expand core vocabulary expression and increase mean length of utterance with young children using AAC systems. Dada and Alant (2009) also reported positive results to accelerate vocabulary acquisition using the ALS approach with preschool children.

The System for Augmenting Language (SAL) is a more comprehensive curricular approach that developed in the field of AAC as a method to support children's multimodal communication tools. Developing the SAL approach to support communication is attributed primarily to Romski and Sevcik (2002). Modeling visual communication strategies along with the child is a primary component of the SAL approach. For example, two identical visual communication displays are provided, one for the adult and one for the child. As the adult asks questions of the child, she points to the pictured symbols that represent her verbal message to the child. As the child is encouraged to respond, the adult also models possible responses on her communication display. The modeling and imitation process is designed to demonstrate how to use visual communication tools in a parallel and least intrusive format.

The similar components in the work of Goosens', Crain, and Elder (1992) using ALS and the SAL model described by Romski and Sevcik (2005) are the extensive use of visual communication support and deliberate modeling that the adult provides for children who use AT and AAC tools to communicate and to participate in daily environments. The ALS approach is more focused on the preschool classroom environment. The SAL approach is more focused on individual communicative interaction. Both approaches are applicable in providing AT services for young children in natural environment and inclusive preschool settings.

ASSISTIVE TECHNOLOGY AND FUNCTIONAL EVALUATION FOR EARLY TECHNOLOGY: FOCUS ON COMMUNICATION AND LANGUAGE DEVELOPMENT

As discussed in Chapter 4, the FEET approach follows a series of steps to complete a comprehensive process that results in developing AT services and devices for individual children. In this section, the FEET process will be applied to two children in developing AT focused on communication development. Each of the FEET steps will be discussed as they apply to the AT assessment process with a focus on communication and language development for early AT and AAC intervention with individual children. Examples of completed portions of the FEET forms are included in order to demonstrate the steps in the AT assessment and intervention planning process. Additional case study material and completed FEET profiles are on the CD-ROM.

Scott: Prelinguistic Stage, Emerging Communicator

Scott, now 3 years old, was born full term and developed typically until 18 months, at which time he stopped speaking. He currently does not use words to communicate, but uses some sounds and brief gestures to indicate his wants and needs. He demonstrates extreme mood changes, frequent tantrums, perseverative behavior, limited eye contact, and interactions. During play, he often sits alone and bangs toys together or lines them up repetitively in the same order. He avoids most foods except for French fries and chicken nuggets. He loves his Barney video. The results of a recent assessment at the university medical center showed that Scott demonstrates characteristics of autism spectrum disorder.

Although Scott was beginning to develop some language prior to 18 months of age, he has not used language to communicate since that time. His communication development at this time meets many of the characteristics described in the prelinguistic stage of communication and language development. In particular, Scott does not demonstrate a consistent means to engage his parents or others in interactive communication for any sustained back-and-forth turns in games. In addition, when he appears to want or need something, he does not consistently communicate through gaze, gestures, vocalization, or other expression to convey his requests, known as communicative intent. Furthermore, although there are several opportunities to respond to his behavior that may be communicative, only his family members are able to identify and to interpret some of the cues that Scott gives through his behavior.

Family Concerns

As reported in FEET Form 1 (Figure 5.2) in the completed FEET profile, Scott's mother and father, Sheri and Tom, are very concerned regarding their son's lack of consistent communication and language development since he developed a fever and unknown illness at 18 months of age. Extensive diagnostic work with an interdisciplinary team in the local university medical center recently resulted in a diagnosis that his parents had been expecting, autism spectrum disorder. This confirmed his parents' fears, and now they are trying to figure out what this means for their son and their family. At present, the early childhood team and Scott's family are considering AT as a means to support Scott's communication development. With both parents working and seeking a more comprehensive program for their son, they report that their schedule is stressful and they have limited time at home with Scott.

Child Characteristics: Communication Modalities

When reviewing the description of Scott's communication forms and functions in the completed FEET Form 2 (Figure 5.3), a pattern is evident that shows Scott's gestures,

Family concerns	
Child's name: Scott Age: 3 Parent's name: Sheri Address: 123 First Street Telephone: 444-222-1111	Agency name: Roundtree Preschool Referral source: Physician Date of assessment: September 1 Team members: Early childhood teacher, OT, SLP, parent, behavior specialist Dominant language in home: English

AREAS ADDRESSED	FAMILY COMMENTS
Child strengths/needs Vision Hearing Communication Motor	We really had no concerns about Scott's development until he was around 18 months old. He had a slight fever, and our doctor could not really tell if it was anything serious. From that point on, Scott was different. He did not talk and appeared not to hear us. He looks at me briefly, but does not seem to understand what I am saying to him. His walking is okay, but he seems clumsier than other children his age.
Family daily routines and activities	Our days are pretty full. My husband and I work full time in computer programming. Our nanny comes at 8:00AM to get Scott's breakfast and get him to preschool. Scott goes to a child care center after preschool. I pick him up on my way home from work. Then it is dinner time, bath time, and bedtime.
Child's preferred activities	On weekends, when I have time, our family takes walks to the park, which makes Scott happy. He loves to feel the wind in his face and leans forward in his stroller. He loves watching television, especially Barney and Teletubbies.
Family priorities for child participation in daily activities	My hope is that we see Scott try to talk more soon because it has been over a year since he has said any real words. We want to find a way for him to communicate that does not involve crying or throwing tantrums. He seems so unhappy, and we are so stressed with him always crying and fighting us. We can still carry him, but it is getting harder to do.
Family use of technology and priorities	Because my husband and I are both computer programmers, we hope that we can use computers with Scott. I have put some simple picture books and photographs with music on the computer, and he seems to like that for a short time, but he gets bored and moves away or just wants to play with the keyboard.

Figure 5.2. FEET Form 1: Family concerns for Scott.

Child characteristics: Communication modalities				
Child signal	**Elicitation examples**	**Possible meaning**	**Adult response**	**Possible AT strategies**
Scott bangs toy repeatedly on floor and looks occasionally at Mom	Talk with parent, ignore child; parent reports regarding how child asks for hug	Request attention, affection	Reaches toward Scott with another toy	Imitate Scott's actions with toy; offer choices for a new toy
Scott pats bag briefly, shows frustration, fusses, and drops bag	Place toy in closed bag or container	Request help	Takes bag and opens to retrieve toy for Scott	Take bag from Scott and use prompt, time delay to elicit sign/vocal request from Scott
Scott reaches for Barney videotape on shelf, fusses when cannot reach it	Show two objects/pictures and wait for response	Request desired object/action	Provides Barney videotape for Scott	Hold toy, pair with photograph to transition to symbol request
Scott pushes food away when offered on a spoon	Parent reports regarding how child shows dislike of object/food; expresses "no" to parent; expresses "all done"	Refusal, protest, cessation	Encourages one more bite	Adult models sign/word for no with card symbol for no
Scott briefly looks at parent, smiles when seeing after school	Greet child when first arriving	Greetings	Responds with greeting	Provide VOCA to prompt greeting, HI, MOM with photograph
Scott smiles and briefly looks at Mom	Make puppet appear; stop and wait for response	Comment: Person/object/action	Activates puppet to entertain Scott	Provide VOCA for Scott to activate and say MORE
Scott vocalizes, smiles	Perform "silly" action with puppet and toy animal	Express humor	Performs action again with Scott	Show photograph of Scott smiling, say FUNNY with VOCA
Scott looks at missing wheel on toy car; briefly fusses	Parent reports regarding what child does to express difficulty with toy/task	Express frustration	Comforts Scott; tries to help	Show icon for visual help and wait for Scott to look at adult
Scott throws a tantrum on floor when television turned off or activity changed	Parent reports regarding what child does when required to stop favorite activity	Express anger	Takes Scott to bed; turns off television	Two-step visual schedule with television and next activity, such as bath time; remove television icon
Scott smiles and laughs when he likes an activity such as swinging	Parent reports regarding child is engaged in favorite activity	Express happiness	Repeats favorite actions	Provide VOCA for Scott to activate and say MORE
Scott gets mad, cries; not sure if he knows sad versus mad	Parent reports regarding child experiences something sad	Express sadness	Comforts Scott when possible	Show icon of happy/sad faces, match to Scott's expression and label

Figure 5.3. FEET Form 2: Communication modalities for Scott.

smiles, cries, and tantrums to be his primary methods of expression. His brief gaze at his parents and social smiling within specific interactions demonstrate opportunities for adults to respond and build on Scott's actions by introducing no- and low-tech AT tools including photographs and a single-message VOCA to create opportunities for more intentional communication.

Team Assessment Planning

Based on what the team has learned from the family thus far, FEET Form 3 (Figure 5.4) summarizes what the team already knows and needs to learn in the ongoing assessment process with Scott and his family. A summary of concerns and characteristics includes Scott's strengths and needs, including a range of potentially communicative behaviors; the need to further evaluate his hearing levels; and a focus on AT to support his communication. A look at Scott's current environments shows a full daily routine and identifies potential activities to target for building his communication, play, and literacy skills.

Team assessment planning				
What we know	**Family concerns and child characteristics**	**Current environments**	**Current activities/tasks**	**Current tools**
Family concerns form provides family concerns and child characteristics	Scott showed typical develop-ment until illness at 18 months old Vision appears within normal limits; difficult to assess; only brief eye contact Hearing may be affected; limited response to sounds and words Communicates with family members through vocalizing sounds, crying, fussing, some pointing; no words recognizable	Scott in preschool and child care all day **Mornings at home** Dressing/breakfast, car, pre-school **Evenings at home** Meal, bath, story (two to three times a week), bedtime **Weekends** Family outings to park and running errands	Scott requires help in all daily activities; often has a tantrum when transitioning to next activity **Difficulty/resists** Dressing, eating, riding in car seat, being a part of circle time with class, doing art activities, playing with family members **Enjoys** Television, music/musical toys, storytime with Mom, bathing at night	Communication is primarily done with no-tech AT: Gestures Vocal sounds Fusses Cries Looks briefly at adult in play activities
What we need to know	**What are family's goals and the child's strengths and needs?**	**How is disability limiting environments?** **What are possible future environments?**	**What are desired activities and possible future activities?**	**What AT tools or strategies will increase participation in activities?**
Questions and concerns from family define assess-ment questions to be answered	Support with behavior and tantrums Technology to help his communication Hearing assessment needed	Daily routines take all our time to get ready; go to and from school/child care; home routines Weekend environments are more flexible Scott's tantrum outbursts limit places family can take him More inclusion in preschool settings with other children	Scott enjoys being near other children his age; more opportu-nity for this Scott to have computer or electronic communication with music and sounds Family wants to be able to take Scott to library, zoo, beach, and other outings	Scott looks at adult and pho-tographs, use photographs of toys and activities in book Scott uses VOCA to take turns singing songs and being in circle time at school Provide visual schedule with current and next activity to support transitions Adapt computer with touch-screen and voice output

Figure 5.4.   FEET Form 3: Team assessment planning for Scott.

Observation of Activity-Based Participation

In the process of reviewing prior assessments, receiving family input, and observing Scott with his parents thus far, the team selects book reading as a favorite activity to further assess Scott's communication in the context of storytime. The presence of one adult and one other child enable the team to identify Scott's means of participation and communication in comparison to a typically developing peer. In this way, the team can implement participation assessment that helps to identify Scott's current communica-tive attempts, potential barriers to his participation, discrepancy in his participation compared with a peer, and potential AT tools to overcome individual and environmen-tal barriers. As summarized in the completed FEET Form 4 included in Figure 5.5, the team identified several instances of Scott's attempts to interact with the materials, the adult, and the peer during the storytime session. Due to his brief and fleeting attention, the team developed several low-tech strategies to implement AT with photographs, props, and a visual schedule to increase Scott's participation in the activity (Mirenda & Iacono, 2009).

Assistive Technology Action Plan

The next step in the FEET process helps the team and family summarize what they have learned and propose for implementing AT with Scott to support his development in a more comprehensive approach, shown in FEET Form 5 (Figure 5.6). AT solutions are

Observing activity-based participation

Child's name: Scott
Age: 3
Location/setting: Preschool

Date of observation: September 5
Observer: Parent, OT, SLP, early childhood education teacher
Begin and end time: 11:00AM to 11:30AM

ACTIVITY/ROUTINE Storytime with adult and one other child

Child's physical position	Child's actions (what he or she does)	Child's communication behaviors (gestures, sounds, gaze directed toward another person)	Barriers for child's participation	Expectations of typically developing peer in same activity/routine	Discrepancy between child and typically developing peer expectations	Possible AT solutions to increase child's participation
Seated on floor with adult Old MacDonald or similar book with large pictures of animals in visual range Animals to represent pictures in basket nearby VOCA programmed with "Old MacDonald" song	Looks toward adult briefly when asked to name animals Looks at book, reaches toward pages of book Looks at other child briefly, moves away to another part of room Returns to story, shows curiosity with book and stuffed animals Randomly hits VOCA with lines in Old MacDonald	Shows interest in book, adult, and peer with brief eye gaze Reaches toward book, adult, and stuffed animal as if to request interaction or more of activity Vocalizes occasionally when hearing VOCA with recorded lines in "Old MacDonald" song	Attention to story, book, pictures, props, and peer are very fleeting Turning pages of book not accessible to child Method to communicate requests for more of the book, song, and activity are not available Adult responds more often to peer who is verbal	Peer of same age responds verbally, naming animals when teacher asks questions about pictures Sings "Old MacDonald" with teacher when looking at pages in book Chooses animal from basket when pause in song, "On his farm, he had a..." and names animal Offers stuffed animal to peer independently	Scott listens and looks briefly at book, does not name animals or verbalize Scott reaches toward book when teacher reads/sings song Scott vocalizes in response to song when others sing and on VOCA—imitation only Scott requires support to choose animal from basket Scott does not offer toys to peer	Tempo loop display board with laminated photographs of animals, one at a time to gain attention Link stuffed animal to photograph with Scott Provide animal prop to keep Scott engaged Support Scott to activate VOCA, taking turns signing OLD MACDONALD Photograph of next activity to support transition Develop visual schedule

Figure 5.5. FEET Form 4: Observing activity-based participation for Scott.

identified to provide consideration of Scott's individual needs in the areas of positioning, mobility, communication, vision, and hearing to have optimal access. Furthermore, environmental access is also considered regarding adaptations for the classroom as a whole that will enhance access for Scott and all children. Resources needed are also considered based on currently available materials and AT tools that have yet to be acquired by the team and the program. Resource identification provides an opportunity for the team to consider AT support that will be required according to the IEP that may already in process, thus opening discussions with preschool administration regarding funding for AT resources at the child and program level. Time lines and people responsible are also identified as a means to follow up in implementing AT services. Although this form is not meant to supplant the IFSP or IEP forms, the FEET assessment tool may be useful to early intervention and early childhood teams for the purpose of developing IFSP and IEP goals and documentation.

Assistive Technology Observation Trials

Observation trials provide a means to evaluate the effectiveness of planned AT strategies, shown in FEET Form 6 (Figure 5.7). As consideration of Scott's needs focuses on communication at this point, three different activities are selected to implement planned AT tools and strategies. The purpose of multiple activities allows the team to identify the effectiveness of low-tech AT tools using photographs, icons, a single-message VOCA for

AT action plan					
AT access	**AT solutions**	**Environmental adaptations**	**Resources needed (equipment, funding, training, personnel)**	**Timelines**	**Person responsible**
Positioning	Photographs or icons of familiar objects, actions, people, and places to keep visual attention	Limit distractions; place tempo-loop display fabric boards at eye level to place photograph of activity	Evaluate classroom furniture to provide appropriate seating and positioning for play, communication, and book time in classroom areas	Immediately	Classroom teacher, OT, PT, behavior specialist
Mobility	Keep classroom open and free of potential obstacles to trip over	Regular preschool setting; open areas with specialized activity centers clearly marked with large photographs/icons	Place baskets with toys within reach and at eye level; digital photographs of toys; Velcro-backing for photographs	2 weeks	OT, PT, behavior specialist
Communication	Photograph communication book with minimal number of choices; add additional photographs slowly; Step-by-Step VOCA	Place photograph communication book in reach in class and in home environments; objects in baskets to provide choices; photograph attached to basket to indicate activity; visual schedule with prompting to look at schedule and photograph of next activity	Digital camera, printer, three-ring binders for photographs; two books, one for home and one for preschool; laptop with touchscreen; Soft Touch vocabulary software or other photograph-based vocabulary building programs; cause/effect software	1 week: photograph communication binders Photographs/tempo-loop display; 2 weeks: VOCA; 3 weeks: computer with touchscreen	SLP, behavior specialist, teacher, parent
Vision	Observe increase in length of visual attention to people, toys, and activities	Provide photograph or icon of activity to gain visual attention prior to beginning activity; visual schedule for all children in classroom	Photographs of activities	Annual checkups	Vision specialist, teacher, OT, parent
Hearing	Audiologist and ear, nose, and throat physician evaluate Scott to determine hearing levels	Use visual cues to engage attention; observe responses to sounds, songs, and words spoken to him	Amplification possible pending outcome of hearing evaluation	6-month checkups	SLP, teacher, parent

Figure 5.6. FEET Form 5: AT action plan for Scott.

AT observation trials					
AT support	**Activity 1:** Book corner **Date/time:** Monday/10AM	**Activity 2:** Outdoor play **Date/time:** Wednesday/9AM	**Activity 3:** Mealtime **Date/time:** Friday/11AM	**AT effectiveness**	**Modifications needed**
AT for communication access Provide photograph/icon communication tools in daily activities; place objects in baskets with photograph/icon cues	Photograph/icon communication tools of books and animals in book corner; VOCA with repeated lines and recorded story or song	Photograph/icon communication tools of outdoor activities such as swinging and going down the slide; VOCA with requests for different ways to say MORE when swinging, climbing, or riding bike	Photograph/icon communication tools of foods, snacks, requests, and actions; VOCA with sequence of activities at snack time and script for Scott to say TIME FOR SNACK, MMM GOOD, and WHAT IS YOUR FAVORITE? to the group	Scott's attention was brief at first introduction; maximal support and cuing needed early in the week to look at photograph and then to receive object in storytime; more response with outdoor play; activated VOCA to request MORE very quickly; showed brief interest in VOCA at mealtime	Provide only one photo for Scott to look at; provide object that corresponds with photo quickly; if he does not show response, then immediately provide next photo; if he gazes even briefly at photo, then provide object to play with briefly; move to two photo choices when he shows longer gaze to one photo

Figure 5.7. FEET Form 6: AT observation trials for Scott.

AT evaluation plan				
AT intervention goal	**AT materials implemented**	**Effectiveness of intervention**	**Need for modifications**	**Person responsible**
Communication Gaze at photograph; choose one of two photographs; transition to next activity with photograph; activate VOCA in turn taking	Velcro-backed communication photographs with corresponding icons in photo storage book for home and preschool; tempo-loop fabric boards throughout classroom; centers to post photos and visual schedule; VOCA to take turns in activities	Scott focused attention on photo briefly, looked toward corresponding objects infrequently, improved with maximal cueing; Scott's attention was increased when photo placed on tempo-loop fabric board near activity center (books, toys); Scott randomly hit VOCA at first and became more purposeful to take a turn in repeated line stories	Only one photo at a time; wait for Scott to look at photo or reach toward picture; Immediately provide object; if he does not look, then move on to next photo and object; provide physical cue by holding VOCA toward Scott and wait when it is time for repeated line	Teacher, SLP, behavior specialist, teacher's aide

Figure 5.8.   FEET Form 7: AT evaluation plan for Scott.

requesting MORE, and a sequential message VOCA to have a "conversation" to support Scott to communicate more. Reviewing activities at the end of a trial period enables the team to modify and adjust the AT interventions to be better matched to Scott's current needs.

Assistive Technology Evaluation Plan

The final step in the process, FEET Form 7 (Figure 5.8) is actually a link to developing specific goals for IFSP and IEP planning and intervention. By completing targeted observations in the previous step, the team and family are able to identify Scott's needs, goals, and AT supports more specifically. The evaluation phase provides a review and summary of the entire process to date. Furthermore, the summary of effectiveness, further modifications needed, and people responsible reinforce the dynamic and ongoing nature of the AT services that are needed for all children to progress in communication, language, play, literacy, and all forms of development. The evaluation plan also links back to the beginning of the FEET process to add new elements and accomplishments for Scott, leading to new AT solutions or other forms of intervention as his abilities and needs change.

Jorge: Emerging Language Stage, Emerging Communicator

Jorge is 2 years old and lives with his mother, who is a single parent attending nursing school, and his older brother. He attends the child care center on his mother's college campus daily where he receives services from an occupational therapist, physical therapist, and SLP. His diagnosis is a suspected genetic syndrome that includes multiple disabilities such as vision, motor, and communication delays. He is a happy child who moves in time to his favorite music on the floor or in his corner chair. He has just learned to crawl. He shows some understanding of many familiar words, expresses many speech sounds, and demonstrates a limited vocabulary that sounds like words for family members and favorite games, such as "mama," "papa," "tickle," "go outside," "swing," and "doggie."

Jorge demonstrates developmental skills that can be characterized by emerging language because he shows repeated attempts to communicate with his family members, even though gestures and vocalization remain his most frequent form of communication. His persistence in requesting favorite activities consists primarily of reaching and looking toward adults with some vocalizations that are repeated and sound like real words. Although he does show some foundation skills to maintain interaction and to take turns, Jorge requires others to interpret some of his behavior in the classroom when he chooses a particular activity or expresses his preferences other ways. For these reasons, both his language development stage and communication abilities are characterized as "emerging."

Each step of the FEET process was completed with Jorge's team and his mother, Adrienne, through a series of meetings and observations over a 2-week period at the child care center where his early intervention team provides weekly services. Because Jorge will be turning 3 years old within the next year, the team is concerned with his upcoming transition to preschool. After completing a series of developmental assessments by the SLP, early intervention specialist, physical therapist, and occupational therapist, the team met with Adrienne to summarize concerns and plan AT services to support Jorge in his current child care and future preschool settings. In addition, Adrienne recently attended a parent workshop at the local family support agency and learned about the use of AT with young children as a means to assist learning and communication development. As a result, Adrienne has been thinking that Jorge could benefit from more technology support and asked the team to explore possible AT that may help her son to communicate and learn with other children. The areas of concern that focused on Jorge's communication development and AT solutions to address his needs for communication and language development are the focus of the following discussion.

Family concerns	
Child's name: Jorge Age: 2 Parent's name: Adrienne Address: 123 Market Street Telephone: 999-777-6666	Agency name: Big City Child Care Referral source: Parent Date of assessment: June 1 Team members: Parent, child care teacher and early intervention team Dominant language in home: Spanish

AREAS ADDRESSED	FAMILY COMMENTS
Child strengths/needs Vision Hearing Communication Motor	Jorge was diagnosed with central vision problems early in life. His vision specialist has helped me get glasses for him that we need to fasten on or he takes them off. Large, high-contrast photographs are best for him to recognize, and we recently tried smaller photographs that worked pretty well. After clearing up ear infections, his hearing is normal. Jorge started walking with his walker about 6 months ago and is able to walk short distances by himself. His speech is really delayed, but I can understand what he means from his facial expressions.
Family daily routines and activities	I work full time and attend nursing classes two nights per week, so my sister has him those nights. He goes to child care where the early intervention team (SLP, OT, PT, and vision specialist) provides services two times a week. We have a long day, getting to the child care center, to home, and to bed. On weekends, Jorge goes with me to my sister's house and plays with his cousins and brother.
Child's preferred activities	Jorge likes music a lot. Whenever he is tired or fussy, I turn on his favorite CDs and DVDs. I really don't like him watching that much television, but he likes it. He is not that interested in books unless he is sitting on my lap when I read to him, which is mostly on the weekends.
Family priorities for child participation in daily activities	I would really like to see what Jorge could do with a computer. We don't have one at home, but he likes the computer at school and pays attention to some of the games for a long time. He likes to play around other kids, but does not really know how to play together with his cousins or kids at school. I would like him to have more friends. He is very slow to talk and maybe there is technology that could help him.
Family use of technology and priorities	I really do not know much about computers, but in my nursing classes we are learning about online research. I plan to get a computer this summer and would like to help Jorge get started with games that would help him to learn and to speak.

Figure 5.9. FEET Form 1: Family concerns for Jorge.

Family Concerns

The team completed the first step of the FEET profile using the results from their initial meeting. As demonstrated in FEET Form 1 (Figure 5.9), Adrienne is primarily concerned about Jorge's communication development and his play skills with other children. In addition, she identified her lack of knowledge about technology, but desire to learn and acquire tools to assist her son. The fact that the primary language at home is Spanish means that the team will need to provide bilingual materials when introducing words for Jorge to use in expressive communication tools. As a next step in the process, the SLP completed a second form with Adrienne to determine how Jorge communicates most often.

Child Characteristics: Communication Modalities

The summary of Jorge's communication modalities in FEET Form 2 (Figure 5.10) indicates that he uses multiple modalities to communicate, including gestures, facial expression, vocal/verbal approximations, crying, and fussing. Adult responsiveness is immediate and shows consistent interpretation of Jorge's possible communicative meanings. From this snapshot of Jorge's methods of communication, Adrienne and the early childhood

Child characteristics: Communication modalities				
Child signal	**Elicitation examples**	**Possible meaning**	**Adult response**	**Possible AT strategies**
Jorge fusses and reaches toward Mom	Talk with parent, ignore child; parent reports regarding how child asks for hug	Request attention, affection	Picks up Jorge to comfort	Photograph of Jorge "mad." Adult labels Jorge's feeling verbally, then comforts him
Jorge shakes clear bag briefly and looks at Mom	Place toy in closed bag or container	Request help	Takes bag and opens to retrieve toy	Take bag from Jorge and use prompt, time delay to elicit sign/vocal request from Jorge
Jorge reaches to favorite toy	Show two objects/pictures and wait for response	Request desired object/action	Provides toy that Jorge chooses	Hold toy, pair with photograph to transition to symbol request
Jorge turns head away to refuse carrots and meat or pushes it away	Parent reports regarding how child shows dislike of object/food; expresses "no" to parent; expresses "all done"	Refusal, protest, cessation	Encourages one more bite	Photograph of Jorge refusing Adult models "no more" Encourage Jorge to touch photograph
Jorge approximates "ah" as greeting most mornings when arriving at the child care center	Greet child when first arriving	Greetings	Responds with greeting	Provide VOCA that says GOOD MORNING for Jorge to activate
Jorge looks up at adult expectantly	Make puppet appear; stop and wait for response	Comment: Person/object/action	Activates puppet to entertain Jorge	Take advantage of teachable moment to elicit request for action with puppet
Jorge vocalizes, smiles	Perform "silly" action with puppet and toy animal	Express humor	Performs action again with Jorge	Show photograph of Jorge "happy," say "funny," repeat action
Jorge fusses, cries when toy does not work	Parent reports regarding what child does to express difficulty with toy/task	Express frustration	Comforts Jorge, tries to help	Take advantage of teachable moment to elicit request
Jorge fusses, cries when television is turned off before bed	Parent reports regarding what child does when required to stop favorite activity	Express anger	Takes Jorge to bed, turns off television	Provide 5-minute warning and picture icon of OFF before turning off television
Jorge repeats actions he likes, such as blowing bubbles and playing with musical toys	Parent reports regarding child is engaged in favorite activity	Express happiness	Repeats favorite actions	Take advantage of turn taking to elicit request for MORE with VOCA or sign language
Jorge gets mad, cries; not sure if he knows sad versus mad	Parent reports regarding child experiences something sad	Express sadness	Comforts Jorge when possible	Show photograph of Jorge "sad" when hurt; label verbally

Figure 5.10. FEET Form 2: Communication modalities for Jorge.

Team assessment planning				
What we know	**Family concerns and child characteristics**	**Current environments**	**Current activities/tasks**	**Current tools**
Family concerns form provides family concerns and child characteristics	Jorge has central vision impairment; improved with glasses Hearing within normal limits with monitoring of ear infections Communicates with family members by vocalizing sounds, crying, fussing, and some pointing Concerned that speech is delayed with only a few sounds such as "mama"	Jorge, his mom, and older brother have long days in these environments **Mornings at home** Dressing/breakfast, car, child care center **Evenings at home** Aunt's home two times a week, television time at home, book time at home, mealtime at home **Weekends** Visit aunt and cousins	Jorge participates in home, school, and weekend activities with his mom and family Dressing, eating, riding in car seat, being a part of circle time with class, doing art activities, playing with family members, watching television, listening to music/musical toys, having storytime with Mom, bathing at night	Communication is primarily done with no-tech AT: Gestures Vocal sounds approximate words Fusses Cries Looks and points to large photographs when linked to favorite activities
What we need to know	**What are family's goals and the child's strengths and needs?**	**How is disability limiting environments?** **What are possible future environments?**	**What are desired activities and possible future activities?**	**What AT tools or strategies will increase participation in activities?**
Questions and concerns from family define assessment questions to be answered	Technology to help his communication Walking independently Using a computer Vision support	Environments are focused primarily on home, car travel, early intervention program, and aunt's home Weekend environments are more flexible Team can seek more community environments for Jorge to participate Vision and communication are barriers to participation	Activities with family more possible on the weekends Mom wants Jorge to have more technology support to communicate Team can identify choices for preferred activities in community settings	Jorge responds to large photographs; expand use of photograph communication books with choices VOCA to take turns in school activities Transition photographs to symbols Computer use to build vocabulary and turn taking with peer

Figure 5.11. FEET Form 3: Team assessment planning for Jorge.

team identified several strengths and possible AT strategies to introduce to support Jorge's increased communication and expressive language development. There are many opportunities to introduce photographs and icons within the communicative interaction as a means to assist Jorge to connect symbols with his communicative attempts. Specific examples using photographs of favorite toys, activities, people, and feelings can be stored in a photograph communication book and inserted into the communicative interaction by the adult. In addition, introducing single-message VOCA devices to encourage verbal turn taking and participation will provide natural opportunities for Jorge to build on his repertoire of natural communication attempts.

Team Assessment Planning

FEET Form 3 (Figure 5.11) shows that Jorge's team summarized family and child needs, environments, tasks, and tools that are currently known. Furthermore, the result of this summary provides a basis for team consensus to determine what is not yet clear and areas of focus regarding family and child needs, environments, tasks, and tools to support further development with Jorge, his family, and his team. As Zabala (2002) recommended, these four areas of summarizing what is known and what is yet to be learned provide the basis for collaborative problem solving and partnership with families in developing and implementing AT with the child in a coordinated fashion.

Observation of Activity-Based Participation

The team and family selected "play with musical toys" as an activity that will most likely appeal to Jorge and provide multiple communication opportunities because of his positive response to music. An activity was developed with musical toys so that the team could

	Observing activity-based participation					

Child's name: Jorge
Age: 2
Location/setting: Early intervention center

Date of observation: June 5
Observer: Teacher, parent, SLP, OT
Begin and end time: 10:00AM to 10:20AM

ACTIVITY/ROUTINE Play with musical toys with peer

Child's physical position	Child's actions (what he or she does)	Child's communication behaviors (gestures, sounds, gaze directed toward another person)	Barriers for child's participation	Expectations of typically developing peer in same activity/routine	Discrepancy between child and typically developing peer expectations	Possible AT solutions to increase child's participation
Seated on floor with peer Musical toys placed nearby	Orients toward toys Reaches to toy tape recorder Attempts to push button on tape recorder to turn on; not successful Moves to another toy; finds bells and shakes bells two or three times before going to another toy	Shows excitement in body movements, waves hands, and pats toy Touches toy, attempts to operate Stops and fusses when it does not work Turns toward adult briefly Looks toward peer banging on drum Bangs on floor	Visual attention limited due to central vision limitations Jorge's fine motor skills limit his ability to operate small switches on musical toy Lack of speech and clear communication signals to elicit help from adult	Peer reaches toward favorite toy Seeks help from adult to operate Claps hands in time to music Requests more when music stops on toy recorder Reaches to adult when two items offered to choose for music Names item, sings with music Holds toy out to Jorge	Jorge shows limited communicative intent to request assistance with difficult items Chooses from objects provided; limited attention to toy Visual ability challenging to sustain attention Listens to musical patterns; does not clap or sing	Provide photograph communication book with favorite musical toys to choose VOCA with preprogrammed songs in steps to "sing" songs with peer Object board for visual/tactile cues Computer software, touchscreen

Figure 5.12. FEET Form 4: Observing activity-based participation for Jorge.

gain more information regarding Jorge's positioning, specific actions, communication behaviors, possible barriers, typical peer participation, discrepancies between Jorge and typical peer participation, and customized AT solutions. FEET Form 4 (Figure 5.12) shows the specific focal points of the observation for the team members who were present. Although not all team members were present, videotaping the observation was completed in order to involve all team members.

By completing a targeted observation, specific data was gathered to further support Jorge to participate in his favorite activities with musical toys and experience multiple communication opportunities. Based on the observation, the team and family gathered further information regarding Jorge's actions and communication when playing with musical instruments with a peer. Jorge did not vocalize or express words in this observation setting, although he reportedly does this at home. He showed interactive communication briefly, looking toward adult and peer and reaching toward toys. Considering the discrepancy between Jorge and his peer's participation, Jorge's use of communicative intent, verbal requesting, vocalizing in singing, and gesturing toward toys and peer were clear limitations for Jorge. In order to overcome both individual barriers shown within Jorge's own development, teacher response was more geared toward verbal speech, another communication barrier for Jorge. AT solutions identified to bridge these barriers for Jorge included a photograph communication book of musical items, a VOCA programmed with a favorite song, tactile cues on an object board, and a computer with touchscreen access.

Assistive Technology Action Plan

After identifying potential AT tools that may support Jorge to expand his communication and language development, the team and family met to complete FEET Form 5, which is on the CD-ROM. The AT action plan for Jorge included physical, mobility,

AT observation trials					
AT support	**Activity 1:** Music **Date/time:** Monday/10AM	**Activity 2:** Playtime **Date/time:** Wednesday/11AM	**Activity 3:** Outdoor play **Date/time:** Friday/9AM	**AT effectiveness**	**Modifications needed**
AT for communication access Provide object board for choices in activities throughout the day with four to five objects on foam core board with black background	Object board with items representing musical instruments attached; encourage reaching and exploring objects; verbal cue to choose	Object board with items representing favorite toys attached; encourage reaching and exploring objects; verbal cue to choose	Object board with items representing slide, ball, sandbox, and tricycle attached; encourage reaching and exploring objects; verbal cue to choose	Jorge's attention was brief when introduced to object board on Monday but increased by Friday; more interested in music items; unclear choices	Provide maximum of three choices on each object board; use time delay with verbal cue to gain attention; wait for gaze, reach, or vocal response from Jorge and provide choice quickly; engage with object

Figure 5.13. FEET Form 6: AT observation trials for Jorge.

communication, visual, and hearing access. Steps in each area were identified to follow up on issues in each of the areas. Environmental adaptations to assist Jorge and all children in the child care center included oversized and high-contrast visual aids.

Assisive Technology Observation Trials

Observation trials using AT in three different settings involved object boards to address Jorge's low vision needs. Association of actual objects and activities to objects was conducted by using object boards to choose items within an activity. Effectiveness of the trials in this situation was reviewed at the end of the week and further modifications were made to simplify the choices and provide more time for Jorge to respond and play with objects of his choosing. The FEET process at this point is demonstrated in FEET Form 6 (Figure 5.13).

Assistive Technology Evaluation Plan

As the final step in the process, FEET Form 7 (Figure 5.14) is completed to evaluate the entire process and determine next steps in implementing AT tools and strategies with Jorge. Throughout the process, Jorge's team focused on establishing more consistent communicative intent and links between concrete objects and visual symbols (photographs). Using a VOCA was planned to support Jorge to take turns with peers in purposeful interactions including games, stories, and songs. As his abilities change, so will his needs for AT support. Expanded vocabulary, the potential for mid- and high-tech communication tools, and sustained interaction with peers are within sight for Jorge with appropriate AT intervention and evaluation.

AT evaluation plan				
AT intervention goal	**AT materials implemented**	**Effectiveness of intervention**	**Need for modifications**	**Person responsible**
Communication Communicative intent, refer to symbol; choose favorite musical toy or other items from board; activate VOCA in turns with peers	Communication photographs enlarged in early intervention center and home; object board with individual VOCA for each item; VOCA to take turns in activities	Jorge focused attention on photograph briefly, looked toward objects that corresponded infrequently; Jorge's attention was brief when introduced to object board on Monday, but it increased by Friday; Jorge randomly hit VOCA in group music activity	Place photograph in line of vision; move object close and extend for Jorge to touch; provide maximum of three choices on each object board; use time delay with verbal cue to gain attention and wait for gaze, reach, or vocal response from Jorge and provide choice quickly; provide physical cue by holding VOCA toward Jorge and wait	Teacher, SLP, vision specialist, teacher's aide

Figure 5.14. FEET Form 7: AT evaluation plan for Jorge.

SUMMARY

AT and AAC are difficult to separate in the support of early communication and language development with young children. This chapter explored the foundations of communication and language development and the importance of AT to provide the bridge to language development for children with complex communication needs. The extent of the population of children who may benefit from using technology has expanded. The importance of early communication support to establish the foundations of emerging language development through technology is becoming increasingly well established in research. Rather than wait until children demonstrate that verbal speech is significantly challenged, earlier intervention with technology support is advocated by research that identifies the effectiveness of low-tech visual supports, low- and mid-tech VOCA devices, and high-tech SGDs. The process of making decisions and developing a system of technology support for communication and language development is a complex one that requires a team and family members working together to identify priorities, activities, and customized tools that are implemented in daily routines. Through a step-by-step process to build consensus and problem solving, access to affordable and sustainable solutions for each child with complex communication needs is achievable.

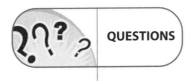

QUESTIONS

1. Identify a child whom you are concerned about with developmental delays that specifically affect the ability to communicate. What are the specific communicative strengths and needs of this child regarding developmental skills in the prelinguistic, emerging, or developing language stages?

2. Now think of the same child in a different way, considering the Continuum of Communication Independence. When considering this child's communicative abilities, where would you consider him or her to be regarding the stages of emerging communicator, context-dependent communicator, and independent communicator?

3. When thinking about the communicative stages and level of communication independence for the same child, what might your initial goals be to support increased communication and language development for this child?

4. What types of communication tools might you apply for a child who is considered to be at the prelinguistic stage of communication and language development?

5. What types of tools might be more appropriate to support social interaction and communicative intent with a child who is considered to be in the emerging language stage of development?

6. Consider a child in the developing language stage of development, what AT tools for communication may be most appropriate to support vocabulary expansion, phrase development, and storytelling skills?

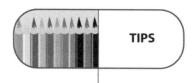

TIPS

As you embark on the AT assessment and intervention process to support the communication and language development of a young child with complex communication needs, consider the following guidelines.

○ Complete the AT self-assessment guide as a team. Identify your individual interests and areas where you want to learn more about AT support and services with young children.

○ Consider children in your programs who may demonstrate significant risk for developing communication and language skills in the toddler and preschool years.

○ Complete developmental assessments as a team to determine general developmental levels and stages of communication and language development.

○ Meet with family members to determine their concerns and priorities for communication, language, and overall developmental progress for their children.

○ Identify family interest and awareness of AT supports and services. Provide resources in the appropriate language with translation support, as needed.

○ Based on family concerns and priorities, identify activities that are of interest and plan an observation of the child with peers in a designated activity.

○ Identify potential AT solutions based on developmental level and functional abilities of child.

○ Conduct trial AT solutions for communication in several different settings.

○ Evaluate and modify as needed to support the child to use AT tools for communication to include gestural, sign language, object based, photograph based, icon based, visual schedule, story overlays, activity overlays, computer-based communication software, VOCAs, and SGDs in daily routines.

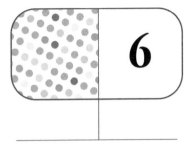

Assistive Technology and Play

Children enter the world equipped with sensorimotor processes that will enable them to explore their surroundings. Young children are capable of gaining access to their vision, hearing, smell, taste, and movement to learn about the new things they may come into contact with in their everyday routines. The growth of sensorimotor skills progresses along typical developmental trajectories that are imprinted in newborns through introducing and repeating daily events such as bathing, dressing, eating, and playing. Play is the vehicle for all children to experiment with the multitude of home and community environments they experience on a daily basis. Banerjee and Horn (2005) identified the hallmark of play as the focus on the means over the ends. In their summary of researchers definitions of play, Banerjee and Horn highlighted the following characteristics: positive affect, active engagement, intrinsic motivation, limited external rules, and nonliterality. Play is a unique developmental domain because it provides a way for children to learn about the various sensory experiences offered to them through daily routines. Play is learning, and play is all about enjoyment, satisfaction, and fun.

Typically, play is characterized by its unscripted and undirected attributes. Children construct meaning through predictions of what may happen while exploring multiple interactive situations involving toys, props, peers, and other objects surrounding them. Play is the avenue for young children to formulate multiple pathways of neurological connections that build the capacity for communication, thinking, social-emotional skills, and self-help competencies that are integral to their later school achievement. Not only does play teach problem-solving skills, language development, fine and gross motor coordination, and social-emotional relationships, but it also is a construct that includes a developmental progression of skills that children formulate through repeated experiences with their environments (Lifter, Ellis, Cannon, & Anderson, 2005; Piaget, 1962). The hallmark of play is that it is usually child directed and not something that is taught or developed by others.

Children move through stages of play and, in the process, they garner the capabilities necessary to create scenarios of their world to help them interpret meaning. In order to play to learn, young children need to learn to play. The progression of play begins with early environmental exploration through children's senses to later sociodramatic play events. Therefore, play is critical to children's overall learning because of the multiple contexts it provides for experimentation with other developmental domains such as language and cognition. In addition, play as a content-rich progression of techniques for relating to multiple environments through unscripted, creative, and self-initiated acts of interacting with toys and with others in make-believe events offers young learners a series of skills to enjoy and the chance to participate in the world around them.

For a few children, the multiple opportunities for play are often difficult to access due to delays in developing cognition, physical strength and coordination, and fine motor skills and having sensory impairments in sight, sound, smell, and taste. Participating in play routines becomes limited and difficult when children are diagnosed with disabilities such as blindness, deafness and hard of hearing, cognitive delays, and physical-motor challenges. Key developmental pathways are interrupted when early learning experiences through play are significantly compromised. Children may not move smoothly from typical benchmarks such as walking, talking, making friends, and thinking, and overall growth and development are inhibited. The creative, self-initiated nature of play is significantly challenged.

Since the 2000s, researchers in the field of early childhood special education have identified AT devices and services as a way to assist young children with disabilities to gain access to play (Campbell et al., 2006; Langone et al., 1999; Mistrett, 2004; Sadao, 2008; Sadao et al., 2009; Sullivan & Louis; 1995). As promoted by Buysse and Hollingsworth (2009), technology offers young children with diverse needs and capabilities to be involved in a multitude of inclusive environments. AT devices can offer a methodology for increasing opportunities for play and thus improve communication, cognition, motor, and overall development. AT acts as a bridge to participating in daily routines such as communicating with peers during a block-building activity or requesting assistance in the dress up area. In addition, due to the need for children to learn how to use AT, the self-directed nature of play is compromised. Instruction becomes a necessary component of exposing children with disabilities to various components of play, which complicates the process for experiencing play as a creative and spontaneous venture. For children with disabilities, play intervention becomes a way to learn play-related behaviors within the context of play. Malone and Langone (1999) recommended guidelines to increase young children's knowledge of how to play with toys. AT supports may provide the means for increasing access to toys and play settings accompanied by play intervention techniques that result in meaningful interactions with toys and enhancement of play skill repertoires.

Mistrett (2004) reviewed three components of AT supports that encourage the child's involvement in routines that include moving, communicating, and using appropriate materials that children are exposed to throughout their day. Judge (2006) designed a toolkit approach to play and learning and provided user-friendly low- to midtechnology ideas separated into three sections: communication, movement, and learning. Sadao et al. (2007) created a variety of training modules that are organized under assessment, communication, early literacy, play, and computers. The efforts on examining AT as a resource for exposing young children with disabilities to typical play events offers ideas for adjusting the item, activity, direction, location, position, and overall environmental design to assure better access to play opportunities that are contextually relevant.

This chapter provides readers with an overview of the developmental stages of play and describes general characteristics of play at each phase. In addition, a section provides a process for considering and selecting toys for young children. The chapter also covers the process for adapting toys and identifying toys that are already adapted. Readers will learn about the variety of switches available on the market for adjusting the access to a toy as well as how to position a child to assure that fun and games are within his or her individual reach. The FEET will be explored for assessing and intervening with examples of toys and game modifications to address play outcomes. The FEET approach will be applied to reflect the two play stages presented. In the latter part of the chapter, information about web sites will be annotated, and tips for play will be provided. A sample cross-walk between the HELP, an early education assessment tool, and OSEP child outcomes will be matched to AT devices that promote play.

STAGES OF PLAY

Play is both developmental and functional—it expands over time and increases other developmental domains. Lifter et al. (2005) affirmed the importance of play to overall learning and development. They described the two facets of play development—learning to play and playing to learn. The aspects of play as a developmental domain as well as a vehicle toward learning, communicating, and socializing attest to the complexities of conceptualizing play and play stages. Theoretical considerations tend to focus on the two distinct categories of play: developmental and functional. The developmental aspects of play correspond to constructs concerning cognition or learning to play. Other theorists relate play to socialization or playing to learn.

Understanding the development stages of play helps determine appropriate play activities for young children with disabilities. Play tends to develop sequentially along age-level trajectories for a typically developing child. Children experience their learning environments through motor exploration and communication with others. If a child is not achieving regular developmental benchmarks, however, then play skills are jeopardized. As highlighted by Mastrangelo (2009), children with autism spectrum disorder exhibit fragmented skill development in communicating and socializing with others, behavioral maturation, gross and fine motor skill development, and cognition and problem solving. With the global developmental delays associated with the diagnosis of autism spectrum disorder, learning to play is difficult because of the gaps in other areas of performance. In turn, later academic success is compromised. A functional approach is more appropriate for young children to enjoy play when their skills may not follow a typical path from simple understanding of cause and effect to more sophisticated sociodramatic play scenarios. Targeted play skills can be easily identified and modified when approaching the activity within a daily routine. For instance, a child with autism or other developmental disabilities possessing difficulties in communication, socialization, and cognitive skill acquisition may be unable to manipulate toys in a purposeful way. Their play tends to be more limited to a basic exploration of a particular toy feature. To increase meaningful play exchanges with a toy and later with peers, AT supports need to be considered to increase the visual cues needed to understand the functional dynamics of the toy. For the child with a disability, developmental progression of play may continue to be inhibited by the disability, but the functional capacity of play can be modified through direct instruction techniques. Incorporating a functional model of play allows for this type of intervention to occur in the child's daily routines and activities. Mastrangelo (2009) emphasized a functional definition of play to increase opportunities for increasing play skills with young children with autism. Because children with autism may not move through all the developmental stages of play, socialization, and learning, a functional approach allows for actual skill acquisition to occur.

For the purposes of this book, play will be considered as a variety of functional activities that enhance learning in all the various developmental domains. Play as a developmental sequence will be compared with functional play categories to assist the reader in understanding the two distinct ways of thinking about play for young children. The stages will be defined and examples provided of what play might entail at a particular functional level. A section will be devoted to reviewing individual case studies targeted at the four distinct play levels that follow the FEET assessment process for AT and play. The chart in Table 6.1 reviews the four developmental categories of play and functional play stages to offer a comparison of play as learning (socialization) and learning from play (cognition). Each of the stages is further reviewed in the following sections.

Sensory Play

During the sensorimotor period, play involves experimenting with objects to initiate some type of action or response. An infant grasps and shakes a rattle to listen to the sound and see the object move repetitively. The motor patterns become solidified neurologically as the infant repeats the activity. Increased engagement in the outcome of the play activity results when the infant accidently touches his or her body with the toy and startles in response to the connection. In addition to using vision and hearing senses, the infant might bring the object to his or her mouth to further explore the object through touch and taste. As the infant examines the toy features, the investigation of the property of the toys paves the way for creating meaning from their distinct attributes. Manipulating the objects allows the infant to begin categorizing toys as large or small, soft or hard, or colorful or plain. This period of time involves toy use for investigating the cause-and-effect relationships between toys and the environment. Developmentally, the stage is considered solitary due to the individual nature of the actions.

Functional Play

As children grow into the toddler years, their play begins to evolve from manipulating objects to using them for their intended purpose. The function, not the form of the object, becomes critical during this period of play development. During this time, parents and caregivers assist the child in exploring a toy's function by showing the toddler how to make the car go or the top spin. In addition, the child learns the names and labels of toys and objects he or she is manipulating. The social aspects of play are labeled parallel because the young child engages in actions to examine the function of the toy alongside another child without communicating with one another. An example of functional play is when two children play with the same train set stationed at a play center but do not talk about their play to one another.

Table 6.1.   Play stages

Play stage: socialization	Description	Play stage: cognition	Description
Solitary	Exploring the world Using their own senses Playing alone	Sensory exploration (experiencing) (Mistrett & Lane, 2002)	Using senses to explore objects in the same way in a repetitive fashion
Parallel	Playing alongside another child but not interacting	Functional (discovering) (Mastrangelo, 2009; Mistrett & Lane, 2002)	Manipulating objects in a functional manner, such as stacking blocks or rings
Associative	Playing with another child during the same activity and talking but not working together	Constructive (building) (Mistrett & Lane, 2002)	Symbolic organization of materials to sort and build objects
Cooperative	Playing with another child in an interactive way, including talking, interacting, and problem solving together	Pretend (expanding imagination) (Barton & Wolery, 2009; Mistrett & Lane, 2002; Piaget, 1962)	Object purpose is adjusted and used with a different intent, such as a cup becomes a car

Constructive Play

At this level of play, children begin building, creating, and exploring objects in new and unique ways. Blocks become a lane of cars, boxes become a spaceship, and cups and plates become filled with replicas of real food items. Objects and toys generate symbols of real-life events. Children engage in conversations about their toys with others, and they learn how to describe the characteristics of their toys, such as the dolly with black hair and brown eyes. Children construct elaborate scenarios of activities they participate in, such as going out to eat or shopping in a grocery store, using toys and objects to represent items they have been exposed to in various community settings. During this time, children are making associations about their world through imitation. They might use a cup to take an imaginary sip and share it with their stuffed animal. They are learning the difference between concrete objects and symbols for those objects. Real objects can be offered in a pictorial form, and children are able to recognize that the actual banana is the same as the photograph version in the book. Children also recognize the emotional aspects of the play activity, such as action figures being afraid of each other or the doll that is hungry and is crying for her food. They can discriminate between the fantasies they are constructing during the play event and what actually happens in real life. Children also offer predictions for what might happen next during their construction of a play occurrence. For instance, the train is heading into the tunnel and will come out soon on the other side. Constructive play is the precursor to emerging literacy and other preacademic skills. Play is defined as associative at this stage because children are now talking about their toys to others but not actually playing together. Turn-taking skills begin to form as children talk together to make meaning out of their play episodes.

Pretend Play

Pretending involves creating relationships with others to engage in imaginative play. Developmentally pretend play is considered cooperative because children must engage in problem solving and enlist the support of others to formulate the play activity. For example, you may hear one child instructing the other to be the doctor and themselves the patient so they can recreate a visit to the doctor's office. There is negotiation and strategic planning that occurs during pretend play. Children must be willing to share toys with peers in order to play effectively together. Communication becomes the central mechanic of play during this stage. Piaget (1962) proposed that play stages are sequential cognitive developmental steps children proceed through in order to learn. In a seminal work conducted by Smilanksy (1968), the word *sociodramatic* was used to capture six distinct phases of play covering object make believe, taking on a make-believe role, action make believe, continuing play when presented with barriers, communication in play, and social interaction in play. Play moves from simple to complex as children explore and experiment with their environment.

The studies of teaching pretend play to young children is limited (Barton & Wolery, 2008). The study provided a "pretense taxonomy" of behaviors to promote a method for testing various prompting models that would increase pretend play for young children with disabilities. Six categories of actions in which the child might engage emerged after examining previous descriptions of pretend play: 1) functional play with pretense, 2) substitution of objects or imagining absent objects, 3) sequences, 4) substitution, 5) verbalizations, and 6) scripts. The first set of behaviors involves using objects for their intended action, such as drinking from a cup with no water in it. A child in the second category uses objects for a different purpose than what they are intended for, such as using the cup as a train. The category also refers to when a child pretends to use an object not really there or assigns self or others a role. Sequences involve two different pretense behaviors, such as drinking from an empty cup and serving another cup to a friend. Verbalizations are when specific play roles are determined and described for various participants using voice, such as assigning one child to be the doctor and another to be the nurse. Scripts involve a complete play scenario that is presented to or modeled for the children prior to play, such as a doctor's office where a child is going to receive a shot. Barton and Wolery recommended that future research examine prompting and adult modeling as methods to increase pretend play in children with disabilities. Their findings parallel work by Malone and Langone (1999) who promoted direct intervention approaches to increase play skills in young children with disabilities. Furthermore, Lifter, Sulzer-Azaroff, Anderson, and Cowdery (1993) suggested teaching play skills by assisting the child to change roles by taking the position of agent and then shifting the role of agent to a doll or peer. In this way, more sophisticated play outcomes can be emphasized when the child moves from the central agent to placing control in others such as the doll or toy.

Considering the development of play in stages allows for further refinement of typical opportunities for play at home and in the classroom. For children with disabilities, access to general play situations may not be readily available. Referring to the functional play stages will provide a foundation for both teaching play skills and embedding play events within natural routines. AT supports are possible solutions for expanding the play repertoires of young children with disabilities. The next section will review toys as objects for play and provide suggestions for selection and adaptations.

SELECTING TOYS

Toys are items that children use to explore their environments. Toys are interesting objects related to everyday occurrences and sometimes fantasy or imaginary events that help children develop problem-solving skills. Toys are a means to play and can be characterized by sound, texture, size, and color. Cause-and-effect toys are typically used by children while they are exploring themselves and their senses and determining how an object functions. Young children grasp and shake rattles, stack rings, grip skoosh balls, and hug stuffed animals as a means to cause and effect. Building toys such as blocks, tracks, play dough, snap beads, and cup stackers promote construction of creative designs that may involve working with another child on a project. Multiple opportunities for communication, math, problem solving, socialization, and preliteracy skills often occur while using building toys. Toys that are real-life replicas such as dolls, train sets, shopping baskets with pretend food, and dress-up clothes are appropriate for encouraging make-believe play. Table 6.2 provides more information about types of toys and their characteristics.

Toy characteristics differ in their visual appeal, ease of access, complexity, age appropriateness, and durability. Toys for younger children, for example, avoid small parts that might come off when infants and toddlers are exploring them with their mouths. An infant might be more attracted to a toy with simple patterns and a black and white pattern. Older children may be more interested in multicolored objects that have many gadgets and sound effects to explore. Mistrett (2004) categorized toys by sensory, access, and physical. The first consideration for whether a toy might be appropriate for a child depends on its sensory aspects of sound, visual, and touch. Quiet toys with a soft response sound might be more appealing to infants than toddlers. A child with a sensory stimulation overload issue might be averse to any sound made by the toy. The sound might be acceptable, but the song length might be a problem if it plays more than a few seconds. When considering visual appeal, the amount of variation in light, color, and pattern of the toy may influence its use with a young versus an older child.

Table 6.2.   Types of toys

Type	Play stage	Description	Use
Cause and effect	Solitary/sensory	Toys that have an audible, visual, or tactile response when an action is performed, such as shaking a rattle	Develops the use of senses Increases fine motor control such as grasp and release and crossing midline Introduces early problem-solving skills
Stacking	Parallel/functional	Any item that can be placed vertically in a column or horizontally in a line that completes a predefined pattern, such as a tower of blocks or a stack of rings	Develops the function of objects Helps children with independent play Introduces early math and patterning skills
Building	Associative/constructive	Items such as blocks and playdough are used to construct designs of their surroundings	Helps children create structures that replicate their environment
Real life	Cooperative/pretend	Items are used to imitate actions of daily routines, such as talking on a play telephone and simulating a familiar activity such as reading a book or going to the doctor's office	Allows preschool-age children to enjoy imitating activities to help them understand their meaning, such as cooking in a play cooking area Allows the development of critical thinking skills, problem-solving in social exchanges, and preacademic development

The texture of the toy is also important. Infants typically prefer soft and smooth objects to rough and scratchy ones.

Access to a toy means that a child must be able to touch it, see it, and initiate action. An infant that is watching a musical mobile move around in the crib must be able to see it, hear it, and reach for the dangling objects. If a preschooler selects a puzzle to complete, then the complexity and physical access are key features that need to be considered. If there are too many pieces and no knobs for grasping individual items, then the child may not be successful with its use. Access for children with disabilities is the key factor to consider when examining the appropriateness of toys. Access characteristics allow for determining whether adaptations can be made to the materials in order for the utilization of the toy to be successful.

Physical components of toys include the size, shape, and weight, such as large, ergonomically shaped, lightweight toys for children that may not have fully developed finger dexterity. In addition, the durability of the toy is critical when selecting it for young children who might explore its properties by continually throwing it to the ground or on other objects.

There are several organizations that provide information about toy selection for young children with disabilities. The National Lekotek Center posts 10 tips when buying toys and partners with Toys"R"Us in creating a toy guide for children with disabilities (http://www.lekotek.org; see Table 6.3). The Toys"R"Us guide includes toys categorized by developmental skill, such as fine motor, gross motor, self-esteem, social skills, and tactile; by age; and by brand. The National Lekotek Center provides packets of information on

Table 6.3.   Top 10 tips for selecting toys for children with disabilities

1. Multisensory appeal

   Does the toy respond with lights, sounds, or movement to engage the child? Are there contrasting colors? Does it have a scent? Is there texture?

2. Method of activation

   Will the toy provide a challenge without frustration? What is the force required to activate? What are the number and complexity of steps required to activate?

3. Places the toy will be used

   Will the toy be easy to store? Is there space in the home? Can the toy be used in a variety of positions such as sidelying or on a wheelchair tray?

4. Opportunities for success

   Can play be open ended with no definite right or wrong way? Is it adaptable to the child's individual style, ability, and pace?

5. Current popularity

   Is it a toy that will help the child with disabilities feel like "any other kid?" Does it tie in with other activities such as books and art sets that promote other forms of play?

6. Self-expression

   Does the toy allow for creativity, uniqueness, and making choices? Will it give the child experience with a variety of media?

7. Adjustability

   Does it have adjustable height, sound volume, speed, and level of difficulty?

8. Child's individual abilities

   Does the toy provide activities that reflect both developmental and chronological ages? Does it reflect the child's interests and age?

9. Safety and durability

   Does the toy fit with the child's size and strength? Does it have moisture resistance? Are the toy and its parts sized appropriately? Can it be washed and cleaned?

10. Potential for interaction

    Will the child be an active participant during use? Will the toy encourage social engagement with others?

From the National Lekotek Center. (2008). *Top ten tips for selecting toys for children with disabilities;* The National Lekotek Center, a division of Anixter Center, is a non-profit organization with a national network of affiliates dedicated to making play and learning accessible for children with disabilities and provides supportive services for their families. For additional information on toys, play and technology for children with disabilities, please visit us at www.ableplay.org or www.lekotek.org; reprinted by permission.

toy characteristics and toys for specific disabilities. The Fisher Price web site (http://www.fisher-price.com/us/special_needs/) in collaboration with Susan Mistrett at Let's Play! Projects offers toy ideas based on the level of assistance a child might need reflected in the following categories: seeing, hearing, manipulating toys, thinking and learning, moving, and talking. In addition, the site includes a description of play stages for children with disabilities. The Universal Design for Play Tool developed by Ruffino, Mistrett, Tomita, and Hajare (2006) provides teachers with an assessment for determining which toys might be most appropriate to create more universally designed environments for play. This tool can be accessed at the Let's Play Project web site: http://letsplay.buffalo.edu/UD/FINAL%20final%20Tool%207.pdf

POSITIONING FOR PLAY

Motor development occurs in a progression of movements from beginning internal reflexes to later body coordination and control. When infants reach and grasp for objects, multiple neurological patterns of muscle movement are created, refined, and integrated into total body functioning and control. Typically, motor patterns begin from head to toe, from the trunk to the extremities, and from gross to fine motor movements. When young children's motor development is inhibited by physical disabilities, such as cerebral palsy, muscle strength and control may be compromised. Simple daily actions such as crawling toward a toy, grabbing and shaking a rattle, and reaching and grasping for a ball or block may be unattainable for some children without supports and adaptations. In addition, caregivers and teachers may not be able to discern a child's choice for particular toys, games, and activities if motor control and communication skills are limited. Positioning a child to gain access to a toy, a game, or an activity becomes tantamount to toy selection and participation in play. Positioning for play includes adjusting the environment, individual seating arrangements, toy location, toy's components, and mode of delivery. Each of these positioning concerns will be reviewed further.

Environment

The first assessment occurs in the immediate environment where the toy is located. In the home environment, providing visual, tactile, and auditory labels for toys and environments increases the opportunities for exploring the surroundings. In the classroom, a Picture Exchange Communication System (PECS) and digital photographs of play centers can be placed on shelves and walls at the child's eye level to help discriminate various play areas. Simple choice cards can be created that allow a child to select one toy from another by pointing to a picture. A wide assortment of one-message VOCAs can be placed around the room or included in a toy basket that allows a nonverbal child to press a button to indicate choice. Labeling toys, shelves, cubbies, centers, and rooms increases the likelihood that a child will be able to explore those objects and environments. Using visual, auditory, and tactile labels offers children with disabilities more avenues for recognizing and selecting toys.

In addition, the environment must be free of clutter and organized in such a way that a child can readily identify objects and places in their surroundings. Sections in each room can be created for storing toys and home-based play materials such as plastic containers and pots and pans. A toy exploration area can be marked off in a home with masking tape or a special blanket. Toys can be arranged on low-level shelves for easy access. Placing toys in plastic storage bins and baskets that are color coded and labeled with pictures can aid in keeping toys organized and readily accessible. Creating bins for particular themed toys keeps toy parts and adaptations organized for easier retrieval and clean up.

Child Positioning

The next step to gaining access to a toy is evaluating whether the child is in a position to manipulate it. If a child has difficulty sitting unassisted, then a bolster such as a rolled-up towel on each side of the chair and a simple belt around the chest attached to the chair will help with sitting stability. A variety of commercial bolsters and seating wedges are available for purchase as well. Reaching and grasping improves once a child can sit with support unattended. If the child still has trouble maintaining muscle control of his or her arms and hands, then a head pointer made out of a baseball cap and pencil may be used as an alternative strategy for manipulating the toy or pressing the switch to activate the toy. If sitting is too difficult, then the child may be able to reach and grasp by lying against a large wedge, body pillow, or bolster while reaching to the toy in a horizontal position. Physical and occupational therapists can assist teachers and parents in determining the optimal position for play.

Toy Positioning

Adjustments to the toy may be warranted once the child is in a comfortable position for exploring. A tray table added to a chair arm is another method for offering a contained area for the toy. A slantboard can be commercially purchased or made from a binder with a Velcro-friendly cover to allow toys to stick for easier grasp and reach. Any kind of tray with a lip can be used to confine a toy. Carpet squares and suction cups can also stabilize toys and maintain their location in the child's visual and motor fields. Velcro-friendly materials or soft-sided Velcro can be added to trays and play areas to allow toys to stick to the sectioned off area. Rubber shelf liner added to the tray or table adds a nonskid surface to inhibit slippage and movement.

Toy Adaptations

After the toy is accessible and stabilized, consider adapting the toy parts. A simple solution for steadying toys is to add rough-sided Velcro dots or squares to the underside that allows the toy to stick to a Velcro-friendly surface. Magnets can also be added to toys that will stick to metal trays. If a toy is small or the surface is difficult to hold, then sponge rollers, tape, foam padding, pipe cleaners, and clay can be added to increase the surface amount available for holding. Doorknobs or wooden sticks glued to puzzle pieces provide a larger area for grabbing and maintaining a grasp. Sticky-back foam provides a cushion to rough edges or increases the surface of small pieces. Contact paper added to toy parts increases their durability and visibility. In addition, a variety of materials, such as textured materials glued to toy parts, highlighter tape, colored masking tape, pipe cleaners, and yarn, increase the ways that a child can discriminate between toy pieces, such as the body parts of Mr. Potato Head.

Toy Methods

Last, the mode of delivery for playing with the toy may need to be changed. For example, a ring-stacking toy with lights and colors can be used for basic cause and effect by allowing the child to take one ring off the stacker instead of all five. Later, as the child becomes proficient at taking the ring on and off, additional rings can be provided. A push-toy modified from floor use can then be used on a table. A simple game such as Chutes and Ladders can be adapted with a battery-operated spinner in which the child can use to identify how many spaces each figure will travel on the board.

Table 6.4 provides a list of questions to consider when exploring access issues. By following the guide, users can determine specific information concerning positioning for play in the categories reviewed in the previous section.

SWITCHES

Switches offer access to battery-operated toys or other appliances when the on/off switch or button is small and difficult to maneuver. A switch includes a base that is pressed to activate the toy and a wire that is connected to an adapter either built into an already adapted toy or a plug attached to a battery interrupter that can be connected to any battery-operated toy. Switches come in all shapes and sizes and can also be wireless. Mistrett and Goetz (2000) compiled a resource focused on switch use for children from birth to 2 years old. The document reviewed several characteristics to consider when exploring switches for infants and toddlers. For a younger population, they suggested the team examine the size of the surface, amount of force necessary for activation, amount of play allowed between target and switch activation, type of feedback provided when activated, and durability of the switch components. Because switches come in a variety of shapes and sizes, the recommendations concerning switch characteristics are critical to successful selection.

Switches are created with the individual needs of learner's physical capabilities in mind. To determine the appropriateness of particular switches for young children with disabilities, it is imperative that their physical access style is determined. If a child uses his or her arm to reach for objects, then a larger circumference may be needed. If the child's

Table 6.4.   Positioning for access questions

Environment	Child positioning	Toy positioning	Toy adaptations	Toy methods
Is the environment free from clutter and noise?	Is the child able to hold his or her head up independently? Sit independently? Reach and grasp for objects? Hold objects?	Can the child reach and grasp the toy without adjustments to it?	Is the child able to play with the toy without adaptations?	Can the child play with the toy as intended by the manufacturer?
Are toys organized in individual bins or baskets?	If not, can a towel or pillow be used to stabilize seating position?	Can the child explore the toy with adaptations made to the physical properties?	Can the toy be built with material to increase its surface size for ease of handling?	Can the toy be labeled differently for play?
Is the space too large to allow focus on a particular play event?	Does the child need a physical structure such as a box or laundry basket to maintain balance and control?	Can grasp of the toy be maintained without stabilizers?	Can Velcro be added to increase the sturdiness of the parts?	Can the toy instructions be modified or simplified?
Is there an area designated as a place for storing toys and games?	Can a beanbag chair or adapted chair be provided to improve postural control?	Can the toy be attached to the play surface or other area for the child to have easier access to it?	Can some of the parts be removed to simplify the toy's use?	Can the toy be used for a different purpose than intended?

physical strength is compromised from lack of muscle control, then a touch-sensitive switch might be most appropriate to consider. If a child is visually impaired, then the switch may need to have lighting functions for better viewing or tactile indicators of location. If the switch is activated by the child's head while sitting in a wheelchair, then it will need have attachment components for stabilization. Chapter 9 provides suggestions for including several basic switches for home and classroom experimentation. Table 6.5 lists a variety of switch types, a brief description of their qualities, and how they might be used to activate toys, appliances, and spinners to play in games.

SWITCH TOYS

After selecting toys based on a child's preference, interest, and developmental play level, further adjustments may need to be made before a child can play with the toy. If a toy has an on/off switch powered by a battery, then there are battery interrupters available from several companies such as Enabling Devices and Don Johnston Inc. Adaptivation, Inc. offers directions on how to modify a battery casing to insert a battery interrupter that acts as a switch closure. The interrupter is then plugged into a switch or a plug adapter that allows it to be connected to a switch where the child can easily activate the on/off features of the toy or appliance. Any battery-operated toy can be adjusted to be used by a switch if the battery casing can be reconfigured to fit the copper disc used for the circuit closure. Battery interrupter discs come in various sizes to fit a variety of batteries. Before purchasing the battery interrupter, check the toy to assess the type of batteries it uses and what type of plug is hooked to the end of the switch. There are plug adapters and cords available for connecting to various switches.

Table 6.5.   Types of switches

Type	Description	Purpose	Vendor web site
Homemade switches	A simple switch made out of wire, copper, plug, and tape	Assist a child to activate toys and a computer	http://www.tnt.asu.edu
CD switch	Two CDs with wire, plug, copper, and Velcro that are attached together to create a simple switch	Activate toys and games by pressing down on CD	http://www.rjcooper.com
Textured switches	Provides a large, textured surface with a sensitive touch	Use with children who may not be able to visually locate the switch; provides tactile cues	http://www.flaghouse.com http://www.enablingdevices.com
Finger-size switches	1.1-inch diameter; smaller access switches with a clear plastic cover; audible feedback when touched	For use on wheelchair mounts and activated by a light touch	http://www.saltillo.com http://www.enablingdevices.com
Access switches	Classified under durable medical devices for Medicare coverage; made out of high-impact plastic; 2.5-inch diameter; activated by a light touch; includes multiple colors and a plastic cover for pictures	The size allows for ease of use with children who may have limited fine motor dexterity	http://www.saltillo.com
Animal switches	Touch switches with animal bases and light touch activation	Introduces switch use to young users by providing an interesting base to press	http://www.enablingdevices.com
Jumbo switch	A larger base (5 inches by 5 inches) for activation; available in multiple colors and usually has an audible response	Provides a wider area for activating the switch when coordinated hand and arm control may be compromised	http://www.ablenetinc.com
Pillow switch	Encased in a small pillow (4 inches by 4 inches)	Use with children who may be tactile defensive or have limited strength for activating switch; can also be mounted to a wheelchair	http://www.zygo-usa.com http://www.enablingdevices.com
Plate switch Four-plate switch	Activated when pressing down on a rectangular plate or plates	The slanted rectangular plate base raises the switch on an angle to allow easier access; the four-plate option increases the choices for activation	http://www.zygo-usa.com http://www.enablingdevices.com
Sensory plate switch	Provides a large, textured surface with a sensitive touch and additional sensory cues such as a mirror and dangling beads for activating the switch; may be a stand-alone toy	Use with children who may not be able to visually locate the switch; provides tactile, auditory, and visual cues	http://www.enablingdevices.com

Table 6.5. *(continued)*

Type	Description	Purpose	Vendor web site
Wobble switch	Medicare classifies this switch as an accessory to an SGD; switch is a 3.5-inch spring lever that requires about one fourth-inch movement to activate	Provides a mechanism that requires little movement to activate the switch; for children with limited eye-hand motor movement and control	http://www.saltillo.com
Bright box switch	A touch switch with visual and tactile cues for operation	Used with children with visual/sensory impairments	http://www.adaptivation.com
Latch switch	Any switch that activates a battery-operated toy or appliance and maintains the condition until the switch is hit a second time to deactivate	Use with children possessing limited motor control and movement	http://www.infogrip.com

Purchasing toys that are already adapted is another way for children with disabilities to have access to battery-operated toys. Several companies, such as Enabling Devices, have a wide selection of adapted toys that provide various levels of toy sophistication, such as basic cause-and-effect toys that have lights, sounds, and movement. Mistrett (2005) provided descriptions of toys that can be used with switches to assist in determining toy appropriateness. Stationary toys, such as talking stuffed animals, tape recorders, and music boxes, are the first type to consider because they have responses such as music and vibrations but they remain in a fixed position when activated. Horizontal toys move in one direction, and when the switch is activated, the child can watch the toy move across the table while other visual and auditory cues may also be in effect, such as a barking dog or a mooing cow with light-up features. Mistrett categorized vertical toys as ones that move up and down such as a fire truck with a moving ladder. The child would need some head control in order to track the object traveling in a vertical plane. Circular moving toys, such as roller coasters and mechanical tracks and garages, combine both vertical and horizontal movement and are therefore more difficult to observe if the child's physical motor skills are inhibited. Circular toys typically require some understanding of object permanence, cause and effect, and problem solving. Bump-and-go toys, such as robots and mechanical action figures and cars and trucks that move automatically in various directions, are the last category. Due to the random nature of the movement, the toys in this category require more sophistication to be able to predict potential responses when the switch activates the movement.

PROFILES FOR ASSISTIVE TECHNOLOGY AND PLAY

The next section looks at two children assessed using the FEET: Sean and Abby. The children display characteristics from one of the play stages. The FEET process will be examined for each child, including family concerns and child characteristics, team assessment and planning, observing activity-based intervention, AT action planning, AT observation trials, and AT evaluation. A chart at the end of the section provides a summary of AT action planning to assist in beginning the task of planning for AT and play while keeping in mind the play stages and the developmental needs of each child.

Sean: Sensory

Sean is a 1-year-old child with cerebral palsy. His disability has significantly affected his overall motor development. At age 1, he is able to sit up in a beanbag chair with physical supports for the trunk of his body. His head control is developed and allows him to gaze with his eyes, turn his head toward sound and faces, and actively look at his battery-operated toys and stuffed animals. Scott enjoys having his stuffed animals within visual range. He smiles when the fur touches his face. He can reach out to hit a switch attached to his chair that activates a battery-operated toy. He also likes watching colorful toys that make sounds and music. Sometimes he is placed on his favorite blanket with pillows on the floor where he can watch a mobile suspended from the ceiling. He tries to bat at the moving objects with his right arm. He cannot grasp them but is able to touch them briefly.

Family Concerns and Child Characteristics

Sean has been accepted at an Early Head Start center-based infant/toddler program. Sean's Mom works in an office where she has ongoing training in using computers and the Internet. She wants to have a computer at home with a touchscreen and one at the center so Sean can begin using cause-and-effect software to continue to explore his world. She found out about this type of software while browsing the Internet looking for toys and games for infants/toddlers with disabilities. Sean can use his right arm and hand, so his Mom feels that accessing a computer will offer him opportunities to increase his cognitive skills through using more sophisticated technology. Due to his lack of motor control, his Mom is concerned that he will not develop typical speech patterns. She sees his interest and intent when he gazes at different toys and responds to pictures with his eyes. She wants him to be able to increase his communicative intent through technology support. She also feels that computers are interesting to everyone and other toddlers may want to play with him while activating the touchscreen at the Early Head Start center. FEET Form 1 (Figure 6.1) and FEET Form 2 (Figure 6.2) provide more detailed information about Sean's characteristics and his family's concerns.

Team Assessment Planning

Sean's occupational therapist has already provided some physical supports to allow him more trunk control and reaching. She recommended using a beanbag chair that provides stability for the trunk of his body. Once Sean gains more strength, she is hoping to move him to an adapted chair and stander to gain access to items on a table or tray. For now, the beanbag chair provides Sean with a workable position to grab and reach for objects in his visual and motor field. He has good head control, which allows him to use his eyes and head to indicate his needs. Sean understands how to select a choice between two pictures posted on a communication board. Due to Sean's limited speech output, the infant assessment team was unable to gather much information about his communication and cognitive skills using infant assessment tools. FEET Form 3 (Figure 6.3) describes Sean's team assessment planning.

Observing Activity-Based Participation

The infant assessment team noted on FEET Form 4 (Figure 6.4) that although Sean has no intelligible speech, he is socially aware of the people around him. He has a nice disposition

Family concerns	
Child's name: Sean Age: 1 Parent's name: Sue Address: 123 Pacific Street Telephone: 111-444-2222	Agency name: Early Head Start Referral source: Parent Date of assessment: September 1 Team members: Parent, Early Head Start teacher, and early intervention team Dominant language in home: English

AREAS ADDRESSED	FAMILY COMMENTS
Child strengths/needs 　Vision 　Hearing 　Communication 　Motor	Sean was diagnosed with cerebral palsy at birth. He has limited trunk control but some head control when supported. His vision and hearing is intact, and he can reach with his right arm. He indicates his wants and needs through eye gaze with a communication board with pictures. He has no discernable speech. He can reach for objects but not grab them. He is able to operate a simple Big Red switch to turn various toys on and off. He enjoys this activity with his Mom.
Family daily routines and activities	Mom works during the day while Sean has been attending a family care home where the early intervention team provides services two times a week. Due to the costs of the family care, Mom is enrolling Sean in a center-based Early Head Start program. On weekends, Sean stays at home with a baby sitter while Mom completes the household chores.
Child's preferred activities	Sean likes his battery-operated toys. He has toys he can turn on with a Big Red switch. He needs someone with him, though, when interacting with his toys. He also likes his teddy bear. He smiles when it is placed near his face.
Family priorities for child participation in daily activities	Mom would like Sean assessed for a touchscreen computer that would be available at Early Head Start. He can reach with his right arm and has been exploring his toys with this arm. He may be able to activate the screen for cause-and-effect purposes. Other toddlers might enjoy touching the screen too, which would increase his access to other children.
Family use of technology and priorities	Once Mom begins working full time, she hopes to purchase a computer for the home. She works in an office and is computer competent. The occupational therapist indicated that computer use might offer a way for Sean to communicate and learn.

Figure 6.1. FEET Form 1: Family concerns for Sean.

and smiles when teachers and therapists interact with him. He can indicate which stuffed animal or battery-operated toy he wants by gazing at the picture of the item attached to the communication board. Sean likes to hit the switch to activate the toy dog and the toy butterfly. He seems to display a preference for animals. When offered a stuffed animal or a book, he always smiles at the stuffed animal. Sean likes to have the stuffed animal touching his face. He orients his gaze toward the animal when it is placed within his visual and tactile fields.

Assistive Technology Action Planning

The outcome for Sean in the area of play was to increase his exposure to toys through introducing other battery-operated toys that are switch friendly and creating theme baskets of stuffed animals and books, which is detailed in FEET Form 5 (Figure 6.5). The team decided to continue using the communication board for eye-gaze responses when choosing individual toys and introduce the iTalk2, a type of VOCA, for identifying toy preferences. An additional outcome was to introduce Sean to a touchscreen to teach him cause-and-effect exploration via the computer and assess his responses to a computer-based activity.

Assistive Technology Observation Trials

Sean has not been exposed to a computer or VOCA, but the team would like to try using a single-message VOCA that names his individual toys for him (see FEET Form 6; Figure 6.6). A picture of the toy would be placed on top of the VOCA button using Velcro. Sean could then choose a toy by hitting a switch that says the toy's name. The team decided to use a iTalk2 and a four-item communicator with attachable props to provide voice for the choices he makes around toys. They purchased a farm animal set and attached Velcro strips to the underside of each toy that they then stuck to a slot on the four-item communicator. The

Child characteristics: Communication modalities

Child signal	Elicitation examples	Possible meaning	Adult response	Possible AT strategies
Sean smiles at Mom	Talk with parent, ignore child; parent reports regarding how child asks for hug	Request attention, affection	Picks up Sean to comfort	Photograph of Sean "mad"; adult labels Sean's feeling verbally, then comforts him
Sean reaches toward mobile	Place toy in closed bag or container	Request help	Turns mobile on	Time delay to elicit sign/vocal request from Sean
Sean reaches toward favorite stuffed animal	Show two objects/pictures and wait for response	Request desired object/action	Provides toy that Sean chooses	Hold toy, pair with photograph to transition to symbol request
Sean pushes food away, turns head away, and cries softly	Parent reports regarding how child shows dislike of object/food; expresses "no" to parent; expresses "all done"	Refusal, protest, cessation	Encourages one more bite	Photograph of Sean refusing; adult models no more; encourage Sean to touch photograph
Sean smiles as greeting most mornings when arriving at family care center	Greet child when first arriving	Greetings	Responds with greeting	Provide VOCA that says GOOD MORNING for Sean to activate
Sean looks up at adult expectantly	Make puppet appear; stop and wait for response	Comment: Person/object/action	Gives stuffed animal to Sean to entertain him	Take advantage of teachable moment to elicit request for action with stuffed animal
Sean smiles and reaches out with right arm	Perform "silly" action with puppet and toy animal	Express humor	Performs action again with Sean	Show photograph of Sean "happy," say "funny," repeat action
Sean cries when switch toy does not work	Parent reports regarding what child does to express difficulty with toy/task	Express frustration	Comforts Sean; tries to help	Take advantage of teachable moment to elicit request
Sean cries when mobile is turned off before bed	Parent reports regarding what child does when required to stop favorite activity	Express anger	Takes Sean to bed, turns off mobile	Provide 5-minute warning and picture icon of off before turning off mobile
Sean repeats actions he likes, such as activating toys	Parent reports regarding child is engaged in favorite activity	Express happiness	Repeats favorite actions	Take advantage of turn taking to elicit request for MORE with VOCA or sign language
Sean expresses happiness and frustration	Parent reports regarding child experiences something happy	Express happiness	Acknowledges smile with verbalization of event when possible	Show photograph of Sean "happy," label verbally

Figure 6.2.   FEET Form 2: Communication modalities for Sean.

staff would like to create theme baskets that include a book, a toy, and other activities that match the theme. In addition, the early intervention program administrator contacted a local lending library of AT devices and a regional representative for AT communication systems to experiment with a touchscreen attached to his Mom's home computer and two cause-and-effect software programs prior to purchasing them.

A 6-week trial basis provided daily exposure for the cause-and-effect software. The early intervention teach implemented the computer trials in the family care center during lunchtime in order for Mom to take a break and participate in the sessions. The therapists started with direct instruction techniques such as hand over hand and moved to modeling the action with prompts. The software program they selected was New Frog and Fly because Sean likes animals. Once he gained proficiency with the initial software program, others were added.

Assistive Technology Evaluation

By the end of the 6-week trial, Sean was comfortable using the touchscreen for cause and

Team assessment planning

What we know	Family concerns and child characteristics	Current environments	Current activities/tasks	Current tools
Family concerns form provides family concerns and child characteristics	Limited speech due to cerebral palsy/muscle weakness and control Limited ability to explore toys	**Mornings at home** Dressing/breakfast, car, family care center **Evenings at home** Television time, book time, mealtime, toy time **Weekends** Baby sitter	Sean participates in home, school, and weekend activities with his Mom and family Dressing, eating, riding in car seat, playing with family members, watching television, listening to music/musical toys, having storytime with Mom, bathing at night	Communication is primarily done with no-tech AT: Gestures Smiles Fusses Cries Looks and points to large photographs when linked to favorite activities

What we need to know	What are family's goals and the child's strengths and needs?	How is disability limiting environments? What are possible future environments?	What are desired activities and possible future activities?	What AT tools or strategies will increase participation in activities?
Questions and concerns from family define assessment questions to be answered	Technology to help his communication and play Trunk control for sitting and standing Use of a computer	Environments are focused primarily on home, car travel, and Early Head Start Weekend environments are more flexible Team can seek more community environments for Sean to participate, such as trips to the library and the zoo Communication and motor development are barriers to participation	Weekends have more possible activities with family Mom wants Sean to have more technology support to communicate and play Team can identify choices for preferred activities in community settings	Sean responds to photographs on a communication board Expand use of photograph communication books with choices Use VOCA to take turns in center-based activities Transition photographs to symbols Use computer to build vocabulary and increase cause and effect

Figure 6.3. FEET Form 3: Team assessment planning for Sean.

Observing activity-based participation

Child's name: Sean
Age: 1
Location/setting: Family child care center

Date of observation: September 5
Observer: Teacher, parent, SLP, OT
Begin and end time: 10:00AM to 10:20AM

ACTIVITY/ROUTINE Play musical toys with peer

Child's physical position	Child's actions (what he or she does)	Child's communication behaviors (gestures, sounds, gaze directed toward another person)	Barriers for child's participation	Expectations of typically developing peer in same activity/routine	Discrepancy between child and typically developing peer expectations	Possible AT solutions to increase child's participation
Seated in adapted chair	Orients toward faces Reaches to stuffed toy Attempts to grab stuffed animal with right hand	Shows excitement in body movements Held gaze for several seconds Smiles at Mom Turns toward other adult briefly	Visual attention: Held gaze for several seconds Sean's limited range of motion with right hand impairs reaching and grasping of objects in his visual field Lack of speech and clear communication signals to elicit help from adult	Hugs stuffed animal; feels the texture of the fur	Sean shows limited communicative intent to request assistance with difficult items Chooses from objects provided; limited attention to toy	Provide iTalk2 for selecting one of two toys presented VOCA for communicating simple requests Object board for visual/tactile cues Computer software, touchscreen

Figure 6.4. FEET Form 4: Observing activity-based participation for Sean.

AT action plan

AT access	AT solutions	Environmental adaptations	Resources needed (equipment, funding, training, personnel)	Timelines	Person responsible
Positioning	Beanbag chair with cushions	Limit distractions	Evaluate center furniture to provide appropriate seating and positioning for play, communication, and book time in classroom areas	Immediately	Classroom teacher, OT, PT
Mobility	Supported seating to provide stable base of support	Low table, beanbag chair; eliminate access barriers in classroom, school, and home	Beanbag chair and cushions	6 weeks	OT, PT
Communication	Photograph communication book; Step-by-Step VOCA; object board; computer software to build cause and effect	Place photograph communication book in reach in class and home environments; place object board near musical toys; place computer on accessible table	Digital camera, printer, three-ring binders for photographs; two books—one for home, one for early intervention program; foam core board with lock ties for small musical toys and other favorites for object board; laptop with touchscreen; Simtec and Laureate software	1 week: photograph communication tools; 2 weeks: object board; 3 weeks: VOCA computer with touchscreen and adapted switch	SLP, teacher, parent
Vision	Visual screens annually	N/A	N/A	Annual checkups	Physician
Hearing	Continue to check hearing levels	N/A	N/A	Annual checkups	Physician

Figure 6.5.   FEET Form 5: AT action plan for Sean.

AT observation trials

AT support	Activity 1: Structured play Date/time: Monday/10AM	Activity 2: Free play Date/time: Wednesday/9AM	Activity 3: Outdoor play Date/time: Friday/10AM	AT effectiveness	Modifications needed
AT for communication access Continue using two-choice communication board and introduce talking photograph album, VOCA, and iTalk2	Object board with items representing toys VOCA to indicate wants	Object board with items representing favorite toys Verbal cue to choose which toy to activate	Object board with items representing toys Verbal cue to choose which toy to activate	Sean was able to consistently choose between two toys using the iTalk2	Use time delay with verbal cue to gain attention Wait for gaze, reach, and vocal response from Sean and provide choice quickly
AT for play access Stuffed and Veltex vest; provide battery-operated animal toy; iTalk2	Sean chooses between two stuffed animals using iTalk2; animal is attached to Velcrofriendly material	Sean chooses between two stuffed animals and hears a story about them	Sean chooses between two toys using the iTalk2 and activates the toy	Sean was able to choose between two toys	Increase number of choices to three; add textured objects to select and explore with touch of right hand
AT for literacy access Provide slantboard; adapted books	Slantboard with board book placed in front of him	Mom turns pages and reads the book once Sean glances at the book	Sean glances at the book before Mom begins reading	Sean was able to hold a gaze at each page of the book while Mom read it	Page fluffers and turners; slantboard to prop book up to be within Sean's gaze
AT for computer access Provide computer touchscreen on laptop	Touches screen repeatedly with handover-hand assistance	Touches screen and receives an effect with adjusted hand-over-hand assistance	Provide modeling with extinction and allow Sean to imitate action of touching screen	Sean was able to touch the screen with a prompt by the end of the week	Use hand-over-hand modeling and prompting to teach cause and effect on the touchscreen

Figure 6.6.   FEET Form 6: AT observation trials for Sean.

AT evaluation plan				
AT intervention goal	**AT materials implemented**	**Effectiveness of intervention**	**Need for modifications**	**Person responsible**
Communication Communicative intent; refer to symbol; activate VOCA	Communication photographs enlarged in center and at home; object board with individual VOCA for each item	Sean focused attention on photographs and held gaze for 2 seconds; Sean's attention was brief when introduced to computer on Monday; increased by Friday; Sean hit VOCA to indicate preference between two items	Talking photograph album with bumpers on voice button for expressing needs; provide maximum of two choices on each object board; provide physical cue by holding VOCA toward Sean and wait	Center teacher, SLP, teacher's aide
Play Cause and effect; choice making	Create theme baskets of switch and battery-operated toys, books, and stuffed animals	Sean held his bear while Mom read Brown Bear, Brown Bear; he hit a switch to operate a battery-operated bear	Offer Sean an iTalk2 to select between two theme baskets; attach bear to Sean's shirt with Velcro to maintain hold	Center teacher, teacher's aide
Literacy Attention and engagement with book	Velcro-friendly slantboard with Velcro attached to board books; talking photograph album	Sean gazed at book while Mom turned the pages	Velcro-friendly slantboard and Velcro board books that Mom reads to him	Mom
Computer Cause and effect	Touchscreen and computer with cause-and-effect software	Sean touched the screen with his right hand to activate the software; 1 out of 10 successful trials with hand over hand	Adapted chair; touchscreen	Center teacher, teacher's aide

Figure 6.7.   FEET Form 7: AT evaluation plan for Sean.

effect on four different software programs. The therapists determined that the touchscreen was an appropriate AT support to increase play and communication skills. The addition of a touchscreen and computer in the Early Head Start classroom would also afford Sean opportunities to play with his peers, allowing progression to the next stage of functional play. FEET Form 7 (Figure 6.7) shows details of Sean's AT evaluation plan.

In addition, the theme baskets increased Sean's engagement in toys and offered him a variety of animals to explore. Furthermore, Sean's Mom liked the opportunity to try out different toys to increase his interest in exploring new objects. She also appreciated the basket idea because it helped her keep the toys organized and allowed her to bring some to Early Head Start to demonstrate how to make them with Sean's teachers. Sean improved his play skills and demonstrated emerging functional play abilities along with increasing his picture vocabulary from selecting from two choices to selecting from an animal-themed four-choice communicator. AT devices were provided that helped Sean make the transition from one care center to another.

Abby: Pretend

Abby was born after a long, difficult labor that included a lack of oxygen, which resulted in cerebral palsy. All extremities on her left side have some movement. At 4 years of age, she shows sociability and strong receptive language skills with no clear words. Abby does vocalize in different ways, however, to express her greetings and feelings. She communicates primarily with her eyes, facial expressions, sounds, and gestures. Positioning is difficult for Abby because she has high muscle tone with extension in her arms and legs. She requires support to keep her head up and face forward in her seating system. She reaches and activates toys with her right hand, which requires great effort.

Family Concerns and Child Characteristics

The family is most concerned for Abby's communication skills. Although she smiles and

Team assessment planning

What we know	Family concerns and child characteristics	Current environments	Current activities/tasks	Current tools
Family concerns form provides family concerns and child characteristics	Abby's hearing and vision appear within normal limits Receptive language a strength Communicates with eyes upward to indicate "yes" Family wants to move beyond yes/no indication with eyes Positioning very challenging, high level of extension Family wants more help with positioning Abby	Abby and her family are often in transition. **Mornings at home** Dressing/breakfast, car, school bus, preschool classroom, early childhood therapy clinic **Evenings at home** Television time, book time, mealtime **Weekends** Family gatherings, swimming pool	Abby participates in home, school, therapy, and weekend activities with her family, teachers, and therapists Dressing, eating, riding in car seat, joint book reading, participating in circle time with class, doing art activities, going to therapy sessions, swimming, playing with family, having storytime, bathing at night	Communication is primarily done with no- and low-tech AT: Gestures Vocal sounds Eye gaze to yes/no choices Partner-assisted scanning with two choices Photograph albums of favorite activities to choose
What we need to know	What are family's goals and the child's strengths and needs?	How is disability limiting environments? What are possible future environments?	What are desired activities and possible future activities?	What AT tools or strategies will increase participation in activities?
Questions and concerns from family define assessment questions to be answered	Communication system Optimal positioning support for Abby in sitting Computer access to see digital photographs, software to play games, learn on computer Receptive language and sensory skills are strong	Environments are focused primarily on home, car, travel, school, and therapy Weekend environments are more flexible Team can seek more community environments Physical access is barrier to participation	Weekends have more possible activities with family and swimming Family wants Abby to have more peer interaction Team can identify choices for preferred activities in community settings and provide choices to Abby and her family	Abby responds readily to yes/no questions and choices Low-tech photograph/icon books for choices Activity boards with steps in task Single-message VOCA Multiple-message VOCA Transition to SGD with symbol set to build vocabulary

Figure 6.8.   FEET Form 3: Team assessment planning for Abby.

indicates her wants and needs through eye gaze and physical gestures, her limited speech is unintelligible. She can specify yes and no to communicate her choices of toys and familiar photographs. Abby has some photograph albums that her parents use to help her select her favorite activities. Because of Abby's cerebral palsy, she has a difficult time maintaining a seated position without additional physical supports. She does, however, seem to understand much of what is going on in her home and school environments where she watches activities going on around her. For Abby, physical access is the primary barrier to her successful inclusion and participation.

Team Assessment Planning

The team determined in FEET Form 3 (Figure 6.8) that Abby's play skills were more at a functional level at this time, but they agreed to provide play opportunities to increase symbolic and social play at the emerging level. Abby demonstrated an interest in dolls when she was told to select a toy from four action figures, including a doll. In addition, Abby giggled when she was given a princess crown to wear. Because of her limited verbal expression, the team decided to adapt the play area with voice output to offer Abby more AT tools for indicating preferences and expressing emotion during play with others.

Observing Activity-Based Participation

Initially, Abby was observed during an art activity. She watched the other children reaching for the glue and using it and imitated them with repetitive arm movement toward the supplies. The teacher's assistant provided Abby with a choice of two colors of paper, and she looked toward her preferred color of red. She was able to instruct the teacher's assistant to sprinkle more glue on her paper by pointing to the *yes* sign on her choice board. The assistant asked, "Do you want more glitter?" before each sprinkle. When the assistant became distracted by another student who needed help, Abby was unable to continue to participate in the art activity without extra support.

Later, the teacher told the team that Abby usually prefers watching the children in the pretend play area. The teacher has been moving her closer to the center so she can observe the children playing with the pretend kitchen and clothes. She cannot wear any of the clothes because she has not figured out a way for her to attach them when she is in her wheelchair or stander.

Assistive Technology Action Planning

The sociodramatic play area in the preschool classroom will be the focus of Abby's play (see FEET Form 5; Figure 6.9). The section of the room is already partitioned off with a low bookshelf and a screen with hooks for clothing items hanging there. A kitchen with a pretend stove and a small table with four child-size chairs is on one side of the enclo-

AT action plan					
AT access	**AT solutions**	**Environmental adaptations**	**Resources needed (equipment, funding, training, personnel)**	**Timelines**	**Person responsible**
Positioning	Maintain seating system; supports in car seat/customize form; tumble forms for floor play; adapt materials with Velcro and magnets for doll play	Position materials for access for wheelchair to position at table with other children in class	Review and consult with AT specialist regarding seating system at school; customize form for car seat; tumble forms for play; regional center funding	Within 2 weeks	Regional center (funding), OT, PT, parent
Mobility	Seating system Mobile standing system	Clear obstacles in classroom for ease of access to materials	Consult with OT and PT to evaluate access in classroom and home	Within 3 weeks	OT, PT, parent
Communication	Activity boards with large icons of core and fringe words to choose with eye gaze; single-message VOCAs and sequenced message VOCA; multiple-message VOCA with scanning access	Enlarged icons to represent activities placed throughout classroom on Velcro-friendly background; stabilize toys and switches with rubber mats	Create activity boards with static (core words) and removable icons (fringe words) in AT/AAC resource lab; single-message VOCA ($15); Ablenet Step-by-Step or Adaptivation Sequencer ($150–$175); seven-level communicator with sequencing ($700)	1 each week for 6 weeks; 6 weeks	SLP, teacher, regional center, parent
Vision	Recheck as needed	Position materials in visual field for eye gaze			School nurse, physician
Hearing	Recheck in regular physicals	Ensure attention when communicating with Abby			SLP, teacher, parent

Figure 6.9.   FEET Form 5: AT action plan for Abby.

sure. Another table holds a three-story dollhouse. There is a two-drawer cabinet filled with play dishes, utensils, and pots and pans. Children enter the pretend play area during free choice play.

The team selected two typically developing female peers that would interact with Abby in the play area and assist her with the dress-up portion of the activity. Because of Abby's physical challenges, she had a difficult time keeping the dress-up items on her, even with Velcro closures attached to all of the clothes. One of the team members was able to design a Velcro-friendly apron that Abby could wear during the dress-up time that would allow Velcro-friendly materials and props to be placed on her apron, instead of wearing an actual clothes item. The team also modified the play area by removing the carpet where Abby's wheelchair tended to get stuck.

The team decided to provide themed pretend play containers for each set of clothes represented in the play area. They found plastic beach baskets at the local discount store that were made out of a sturdy woven material with a cloth-lined interior. Each plastic beach basket contained Velcro-adapted items, a four-choice communicator with pictures of emotions, a voice-over labeling the basket with a picture representing the theme and an audible label of it, and a book and videotape with a story about the theme. The baskets were located under the clothes on hooks that represented the particular theme. Digital pictures were taken of the baskets, printed out, built up with sticky-back foam and a contact paper covering, and used as the labels attached to the wall beside the basket. The pictures were placed on a visual scene of the play area, and two items were presented to Abby to select what pretend play activity in which she wanted to participate. A visual scene of each themed basket was also included to provide a way for Abby to talk about what she did during pretend play. The props in each basket were represented in picture form and placed on the visual scene to use later in communicating about what happened.

Assistive Technology Observation Trials

Abby consistently chose the princess-themed basket during pretend play, according to FEET Form 6 (Figure 6.10). The two peers enjoyed pulling everything out of the basket to begin the play activity. Inside the princess basket, steps to becoming a princess were recorded. Abby pressed the Step-by-Step button to indicate each step in the process. The choice board has emotion pictures on it that require Abby to express when she is happy or sad or scared or brave. Abby used her choice board to select the pictures of the items she wanted to have attached to her Velcro-friendly princess apron. In addition, all of the

AT observation trials					
AT support	**Activity 1:** Art & pretend play **Date/time:** Monday/10AM	**Activity 2:** Storytime **Date/time:** Wednesday/2PM	**Activity 3:** Mealtime **Date/time:** Friday/11AM	**AT effectiveness**	**Modifications needed**
AT for play access Switch-activated crayon holder for drawing; thematic play units available in drama area	Switch-activated crayon holder to move crayon around the paper with peer assisting; thematic play activity with peer in drama area	Baggie books of pictures of peers during dress-up time; peer assists Abby to turn pages of book attached to a Velcro-friendly slantboard	Princess-themed cups and plates; all children wear king and queen hats during mealtime	Themed baskets helped the peers to select the already prepared Velcro-friendly equipment and Step-by-Step for the activity; labeling the play center with a voice-over helped to identify play item of choice	Provide emotion words on four-choice templates to use with seven-level communicator or Go Talk 4 to indicate how the doll is feeling; begin with child as agent of play with peer and proceed to doll as agent with props and communication device

Figure 6.10.   FEET Form 6: AT observation trials for play for Abby.

AT evaluation plan				
AT intervention goal	**AT materials implemented**	**Effectiveness of intervention**	**Need for modifications**	**Person responsible**
Play Select at least two play props; use props with peers in pretend play episode	Themed pretend play baskets with visual scenes of the theme and step-by-step directions of the pretend play event	Abby was able to select two out of six props to attach to her Velcro apron	Seating modifications still need to be examined; step-by-step directions with each themed basket would provide a way for Abby to lead the pretend play event	SLP, OT, teacher

Figure 6.11.   FEET Form 7: AT evaluation plan for play for Abby.

props were represented in digital photographs and stored on a visual scene of a princess sitting on a throne. The princess crown was placed on Abby's head. Abby was able press the Step-by-Step when requested by her peer. She was able to select two items from the visual scene to be placed on her princess apron.

Assistive Technology Evaluation

The themed-based pretend play baskets provided a method for Abby's peers to assist in the dramatic play area. The Step-by-Step offered directions to follow for what happens next and offered Abby a way to lead the play event. Abby was able to select two props she wanted to have placed on her Velcro-friendly apron, which gave her a way to participate in the pretend play activity and have the ability to make choices based on her preferences. She still seemed to tire easily while seated in the wheelchair during the activity. The team determined that further evaluation of her positioning by the physical therapist and occupational therapist would provide additional information about seating options. FEET Form 7 (Figure 6.11) gives an overview of Abby's evaluation.

Table 6.6 summarizes the play actions for Sean and Abby. When considering opportunities for play with young children with disabilities, be mindful of the play stage the child appears to be functioning at and consider opportunities for stimulating higher level play skills. Even though children with disabilities may not have systematically moved through the four stages of play in a sequential manner, restructuring the play environment and supporting play through AT devices may increase the likelihood that they will achieve more sophisticated play strategies that will in turn nurture their overall cognitive, communica-

Table 6.6.   Action plan for play

Child	Play stage	Child characteristics	Play outcomes	AT supports
Sean	Sensory-object exploration	Limited physical movement and control; head control adequate; reaches with right arm; sits with trunk support	Orients to physical, tactile, and auditory events	Picture communication board; touchscreen; iTalk2 single-message voice output communication aid
Abby	Pretend	Limited physical movement and control; nonverbal; indicates yes/no on choice board; watches friends during play activities; smiles at children in the play area at school; smiles when given a doll	Engages in cooperative, imaginary play	Theme baskets with props and Velcro-friendly apron; step-by-step directions for sequencing events in play scenario; six picture props on a visual scene provides a low-tech option for communicating about the play event

tion, and social development.

SUMMARY

Play is the vehicle all children use to explore their environments and make predictions about their world. For young children with disabilities, play does not develop in a naturally occurring progression of sensorimotor awareness, object exploration and functionality, and pretend and reciprocal peer interactions. AT coupled with play skill intervention approaches pave the way for children who have difficulty in child-directed activities to be able to have control of their environment. The FEET process offers a methodology for systematically using family input, existing assessment information, observational trials, and action planning to modify environments, toys, and activities to increase the individualization of early childhood play opportunities. The resources listed at the end of the book provide additional tools for supporting the use of AT applications in play.

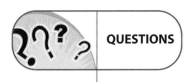

QUESTIONS

1. Describe the difference between learning to play and playing to learn. Provide examples of each.

2. Define the four stages of play related to socialization and the four stages that define functional aspects of play.

3. What kinds of AT devices might you consider for a child that only uses gestures to communicate?

4. What are the five areas to consider when positioning a child to gain access to play environments?

5. What are the types of toys and what play stages would you use them in to encourage play?

TIPS

• Find out about the child's interests and preferences through interviews with parents and teachers.

• Measure the child's physical access for play.

• Evaluate the environment for potential play obstacles.

• Consider Lekotek's toy characteristics before purchasing a new toy.

• Use trials with AT devices in play settings to determine the appropriateness of the toy and methodology.

• Consider ways to move the child from one play event to another.

- Use existing resources to support play environments, such as rearranging furniture or using tape to mark off play areas.

- Talk to specialists about ideas for AT and play.

- Use a team approach when planning for AT and play.

7

Assistive Technology and Emergent Literacy

The emphasis on literacy dominates educational policy and program initiatives for young children. The NCLB is based on the goal that all children will be readers by the time they reach third grade. Research in the development of literacy shows that the varied experiences of children early in life contribute to the ability to read (McGee & Richgels, 2008; National Reading Panel, 2000). To understand how to support all children in developing literacy when reaching the early school years, there needs to be an understanding of the role of broad foundations of early childhood development, including communication, play, socialization, emotions, exploration, cognition, motivation, and language because these areas contribute to literacy, along with the specific skills involved in becoming literate. The connections between all areas of child development and the specific steps to literacy are critical to prepare each child to become a reader and writer. Children begin the process to develop the required knowledge, skills, and tools to become literate by engaging with family, caregivers, and community members. Early childhood professionals now have the tools to enhance literacy development from early in the child's life (Rosenketter & Knapp-Philo, 2006; Snow, Burns, & Griffin, 1998). Research identifies the critical role of basic developmental areas such as hearing, vision, language, motor, and play to support literacy. In addition, there is more explicit understanding of the stages of early literacy that include exposure to words, print awareness, early forms of writing, speech sounds, letter sounds, letter symbols, sound synthesis, phonological awareness, word comprehension, and story comprehension. The child's progress through both the developmental stages and emergent literacy competencies contribute to the ability to learn to read and to write.

For many children, particularly those with significant disabilities, developmental delays in communication, language, cognition, physical mobility, social skills, and play skills present challenges to becoming literate. In 1998, Whitehurst and Lonigan reported that one in three children experienced significant difficulties learning to read. Vandervelden and Siegel (1999, 2001) also reported that children with complex communication needs experience significant risks of delayed and limited literacy development. Furthermore, Koppenhaver (1991) reported that children with complex communication needs have less than a 30% chance of developing reading and writing skills. In addition, Koppenhaver and Yoder (1993) found that specific instruction for literacy development for children using AAC systems was not widely provided. As a result, literacy instruction for students with complex communication needs took a prominent place in AAC research (Clendon, Gillon, & Yoder, 2005; Dahlgren Sandberg & Hjelmquist, 1996; 1997; Erickson & Koppenhaver, 1995; Erickson, Koppenhaver, Yoder, & Nance, 1997; Foley, 1993).

The focus on student assessment increased when academic accountability in schools was emphasized. In early childhood education, an emphasis on academic readiness resulted in developing curriculum standards for children in preschool programs and assessment to measure mastery of preacademic skills through standardized measures. Children with significant disabilities are not consistently included in standardized assessments due to their inability to perform with peers in achievement measures. The resulting reports regarding student mastery of basic preacademic skills reflect only a portion of students—those who are learning without significant learning or developmental challenges. Children with significant disabilities are often not included in standardized academic achievement testing due to the challenges of designing and implementing alternative assessment methods. Early childhood programs, however, are moving toward assessment approaches that include all children. Although the inclusion of students with disabilities in standardized testing is problematic, there are many benefits for including the most challenged students within the accountability measures for all schools. The requirement to include all students in schoolwide assessments creates the opportunity to support all children to learn to read with their peers, even those with the most complex needs. This chapter is provides access to literacy with a range of AT for children with significant physical, cognitive, learning, sensory, and other disabilities that create barriers to becoming literate members of society.

The foundations of literacy begin in infancy and toddlerhood with early communication, play, and exposure to many forms of literacy, including books. This chapter defines key issues that support developing literacy and the particular challenges for children with significant disabilities to acquire these foundations. The chapter focuses on emergent literacy and preliteracy in early childhood that contributes to reading and writing. Next, the chapter discusses variables identified in research that contribute to literacy outcomes in young children, including the role of family literacy experiences, cultural diversity in early literacy, and shared book reading as the foundation of emergent and preliteracy. Children with disabilities face significant challenges to participate and benefit in acquiring preliteracy, emergent literacy, and early literacy competence. AT strategies to support emergent literacy as the stepping stone to early school literacy and later development of reading and writing fluency are provided from several perspectives, including physical access to books, appropriate book selection, book adaptation, supported book reading, and digital books. The importance of vocabulary comprehension and word recognition to build emergent literacy skills is also emphasized and demonstrated with AT approaches that include low- and high-tech methods to support engagement with books and print. Finally, two case studies will be profiled to include assessment and intervention approaches using AT to support emergent literacy and developing literacy skills from infancy through preschool.

PRELITERACY DEVELOPMENT

Prior to becoming literate, children acquire the ability to decode text and to gain meaning from narratives. The complex set of skills that build the foundation for literacy begin in infancy and continue until the early school years.

Definitions in Preliteracy

The terms *emergent literacy* and *preliteracy* are used widely in the literature to describe early stages of skills that are considered to contribute to school literacy, or the ability to read and write (Justice & Pullen, 2003; McCathren & Howard-Allor, 2005). Emergent literacy was adopted from the work of Clay (1993), who recognized that literacy develops from infancy through the preschool years, drawing from informal experiences in the family, home, and community. Preliteracy and emergent literacy are used to describe the same period of development in the infant, toddler, and preschool years. Van Kleeck (2004) recommended, however, that preliteracy include early developmental experiences and emergent literacy include specific literacy skills. As defined by van Kleeck, preliteracy encompasses developmental stages in which children learn about the form, content, and use of language and literacy and more specific skills that contribute to early literacy. Furthermore, van Kleeck suggested that emergent literacy is a narrower term that does not encompass other areas of development such as cognition, language, and social skills that contribute to literacy in children. In addition, early literacy describes beginning reading and extends beyond preliteracy and emergent literacy (van Kleeck, 2004). Dunst and Shue (2005) proposed a model of preliteracy that includes emergent literacy and contributes to the development of early literacy skills with conventional reading and writing.

Figure 7.1 shows the preliteracy model that includes the relationship between developmental areas, emergent literacy, and early literacy presented by Dunst and Shue (2005) and defined by van Kleeck (2004). Erickson and Clendon (2009) emphasized the importance of connections between emergent literacy and literacy skills that enable the child to apply the rules of decoding and encoding text in order to truly read and write. Furthermore, Erickson and Clendon stressed the ability to use the alphabet in a given language as the most critical key to literacy in multiple formats that include reading, spelling, writing, and generating words independently. The challenges for children with complex disabilities and

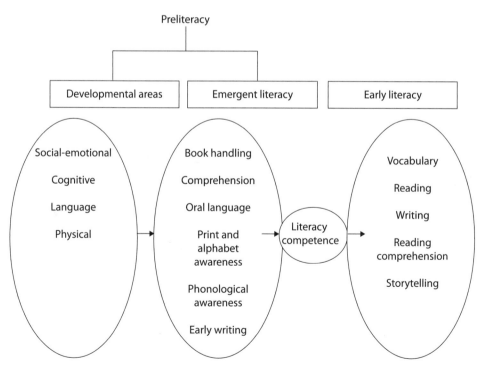

Figure 7.1. Preliteracy development model. (*Sources:* Banerjee & Horn, 2005; Dunst & Shue, 2005; Hemmeter, McCollum, & Hsieh, 2005; van Kleeck, 2004.)

their teachers is to "build core skills and understandings across reading, writing, and communication so that students can move toward conventional uses of literacy to convey meaning to others" (2009, p. 196).

In the following section, developmental domains and specific emergent literacy skills are further defined to extend understanding of the connections between early developmental achievements and emergent and early literacy competencies that lead to reading and writing. Integrating and applying AT principles and practices in preliteracy development is purposefully designed to target challenges for children with complex communication needs and significant disabilities to apply tools of preliteracy to become literate, including oral language, phonological awareness, and knowledge of print.

Developmental Foundations of Preliteracy

Key developmental areas that are considered to be critical in preliteracy include social-emotional development, cognitive development, language development, and physical development (Banerjee & Horn, 2005; Dunst & Shue, 2005). Each of these developmental areas provide the context and opportunity for acquiring emergent literacy skills. The contributions identified in each area of development are described next.

Social-Emotional Development and Play

Through social interaction, children gain social skills of turn taking, understanding rules and routines, having empathy for others, problem solving, and giving and taking (Bannerjee & Horn, 2005). Furthermore, through play that involves social interaction, dramatic play, and sociodramatic play, children develop an awareness of self and establish positive feelings about their own abilities to take part with others. Links between social interaction and play were further identified in a comprehensive review by Roskos and Christie (2001), who found consistent evidence that dramatic play provided opportunities to develop story sequences and act these out in play (sociodramatic play) and master oral language through taking turns and roles in play dialogues.

Cognitive Development

The gradual expansion of the child's world knowledge is thought to grow in a transactional manner. As the child engages in sensory and physical experiences, he or she gains knowledge to approach similar experiences. With the reciprocal influence between knowledge and experience in his or her environment, the child gains increasing complexity in his or her conceptual understanding of events around him or her her. Two major theoretical influences on models of cognitive development include Piaget and Vygotsky. Piagetian stages of cognitive development in the sensorimotor period focus on the increasing sophistication of the child to build cognitive constructs (schema) including cause and effect, means-end, imitation, and object permanence (Singer & Revenson, 1996). Vygotsky's theories and subsequent applications focus both on the child's stage of development and the role of the adult to scaffold or mediate the child's experience and readiness to understand increasing complexity in reasoning skills (Berk & Winsler, 1995). Early cognitive development and experiential learning prepare children to interact with books and to gain new knowledge. The context of each child's daily life influences the type of experiences that are available for learning, such as playing with toys, siblings, or books; going to the park, to church, or shopping; experiencing music; and taking excursions. Connections between early books and experience are considered a means to link more general world knowledge to the child's own experience (Hemmeter et al., 2005).

Children with complex communication needs and significant disabilities are at risk of restricted exposure and experience with a wide variety of daily activities and thus have limited opportunities to develop conceptual knowledge of how things work in the world. Children with disabilities reportedly have fewer opportunities to experience books, which further limits their cognitive connections between direct experiences and more general thematic knowledge found in books. For example, although most children have animal books early in life, they often have connections through their own experiences to visit farms and zoos, a link that may be missing for children with restricted access to community experiences due to developmental delays and disabilities.

Language Development

The role of language development to support literacy development is perhaps the most well-researched and defined role and includes prelinguistic, emerging, and developing language skills. In the prelinguistic stage, infants participate in communicative interactions with caregivers, gaining abilities to maintain attention, take turns, gesture, engage caregivers, and intentionally direct communication. As first words emerge, the child is able to use more conventional forms in symbols or words to express a variety of communicative functions that may include greeting, requesting, refusing, describing, and exclaiming in the process of rapidly increasing vocabulary comprehension and expression. As developing language expands into more complex forms in phrases, sentences, questions, and narratives in the preschool years, the child uses language as a tool to advance development in all areas, particularly literacy. The direct links between communicative interactions, vocabulary, and language development are enhanced and supported by shared book reading (DeBruin-Parecki, 2009). As the child gains understanding of words, both the auditory exposure to the sounds of language and the visual patterns support emergent literacy skills of phonological awareness and print awareness (Justice & Pullen, 2003).

Physical Development

The child's growing physical abilities to maintain eye gaze, develop head control, turn from tummy to back on the floor, sit up with support, reach to toys, grasp and handle toys, move into sitting, crawl, and stand and walk enable him or her to explore activities and objects and interact with people. Children who are limited by physical disabilities may have fewer opportunities for general exploration and specific limitations to gain access to books. Early board books are durable and tolerant of handling. Children with motor disabilities, however, may not be able to hold a book, orient a book, or turn the pages of a book. Dependence on others to handle and present books causes barriers to exposure and experience to books early in life, creating access challenges that must be overcome.

Emergent Literacy

Emergent literacy skills are described generally as a second level of development in young children in the toddler and preschool years, building on early developmental accomplishments in oral language, cognitive, social, and physical development. Specific emergent literacy skills described among typically developing preschool children include vocabulary comprehension, oral language development, story comprehension and retelling, print awareness, alphabetic awareness, phonological awareness, and early writing. Descriptions of each of these domains of emergent literacy follow.

Vocabulary Comprehension

Understanding vocabulary increases with exposure, and the ability to associate words presented orally in pictures and text develops gradually. Children grow in their ability to extract meaning from words they hear in books when they participate in book reading and experience repeated exposure to words and related experiences in their environments (Dunst & Shue, 2005).

Oral Language Development

The ability to use words to communicate enables the developing child to use words as tools to learn more language by gaining a deeper understanding of words and concepts. Furthermore, using words and expanding vocabulary leads the child to understand and use rules for combining words in sentences. In the process of mastering oral language skills, which includes pragmatics (motivation and purpose to communicate); semantics (meaning and vocabulary); phonology (combing sounds to express words); and syntax (combining words to form sentences), the child gains the tools to use language to understand books, words in print, and story elements.

Story Comprehension and Retelling

Understanding stories and the ability to retell and generate new stories are built on emergent literacy skills. These skills and behaviors include 1) increasing knowledge and interest in books; 2) retelling, predicting, and dictating stories; and 3) engaging in activities related to books such as acting out stories or drawing pictures about stories (Head Start, 2000; Justice & Pullen, 2003).

Print Awareness

Through exposure and repeated experiences with books, children gain the ability to recognize that print has meaning and is a direct connection to words that are read out loud. Word recognition increases with exposure, and the child is able to read words that are familiar. Print awareness also includes knowing that books are read from front to back, seeing the appearance and placement of print on the page, and understanding that print has meaning (Dunst & Shue, 2005).

Alphabetic Awareness

Children learn to recognize letters of the alphabet in the context of familiar words and using words in text. The ability to translate letters to the sounds they make first requires the ability to identify letters and to understand that "letters of the alphabet are a special category of visual graphics that can be individually named" (Head Start, 2003, p. 23; see also Dunst & Shue, 2005).

Phonological Awareness

Developing phonological awareness is considered a "watershed" competency that leads directly to literacy and an area that is made up of many skills. Beginning with the ability to listen and discriminate the difference in sounds (phonemes), other key skills of phonological awareness are identifying differences in word patterns that rhyme, identifying words that begin with the same sound (alliteration), identifying the same beginning and ending patterns (rime) in words, and identifying syllable patterns. Increasing ability to listen to sounds and to manipulate beginning, middle and ending sounds in words lead to blending sounds to form words in spoken and printed language (Chard & Dickson, 1999; Dunst & Shue, 2005).

Although there are definitions of the sequence of skills that lead to phonological awareness and the ability to manipulate parts of words, by analyzing the syllables and sounds that make up words and synthesizing parts of words to actually read words, the ages and stages of mastery are not exact. Generally, the literature identifies the following sequence of development in the infant, toddler, and preschool years to indicate the achievement of phonological awareness (Gebers, 2003).

- Being aware of rhymes and alliteration
- Reciting rhymes and making rhyming words
- Segmenting sentences to count the number of words in text
- Segmenting syllables and blending
- Onset-rime, blending, and segmenting
- Blending and segmenting individual phonemes
- Manipulating phonemes by adding, deleting, or substituting phonemes to generate words

Through informal exposure to books and print, children gain awareness of the connection between the speech sounds they hear in their own language and the representation of individual sounds and sound patterns in words in books. More formal instruction at the preschool level with explicit identification of rhyming words, syllables, and sounds in print supports the abilities that are key to recognition and competency to formal literacy skills of reading and writing (Justice & Pullen, 2003).

Early Writing

Written language is based on early writing skills that progress from scribbling and tracing to copying and/or writing letters of familiar words, such as the letters in a child's name (Head Start, 2000).

Each of the areas of emergent literacy described previously are cornerstones to support the development of early literacy. Including more general areas of development for young children provide a foundation for developing emergent literacy and early literacy. The preliteracy period of development encompasses all of early child development, from infancy through the preschool years. Children with developmental delays, significant disabilities, and complex communication needs begin this process at risk of not gaining literacy skills. For this group of children, the challenges to gain access to books, experience shared book reading, and develop vocabulary orally and in print are present from the beginning of life. Experiences with literacy within families, cultural diversity, word knowledge, and storytelling also influence preliteracy development and early literacy outcomes. Each of these areas are discussed in the following sections, and AT strategies to enhance preliteracy development with children with disabilities are provided.

FAMILY LITERACY AND ASSISTIVE TECHNOLOGY

Experiences that support early literacy development occur in typical daily activities within the context of family life. Routine activities, such as grocery shopping with a young child while the adult points to the logo or label on favorite cereals, help promote recognition of symbols and print awareness. Throughout daily environments, young children frequently experience exposure to print as they observe adults and family members making lists and reading menus, newspapers, magazines, and books.

Often, children with significant disabilities reportedly experience less opportunity to develop preliteracy skills. Researchers identified differences among families with children with significant disabilities. The experience of having a child with a significant disability influenced family priorities regarding preliteracy activities. Light and Kelford Smith (1993) found that families of preschool children indicated that functional skill development was more important to them than supporting literacy. Families ranked literacy and social development lower in priority with children with significant disabilities. Conversely, families of children who were typically developing rated literacy, social skills, and communicative skills as high priorities and functional skills lower in priority. Differences in priorities among families appear to influence the type of preliteracy experiences and opportunities provided to their young children, with children with disabilities having far less opportunity to benefit from repeated exposure to books, resulting in risk of literacy failure.

Naturally occurring activities with young children become linked to literacy development through adult intervention to highlight and focus the child's attention to such literacy elements as spoken words, speech sounds, rhyming sounds, printed words, and letter names. Family literacy practices include both informal and intentional literacy activities (Wasik & Hendrickson, 2004). Dunst and Shue (2005) identified a number of daily activities that adults routinely conduct together with their children, such as reading store and street signs, picking out movies and books, playing with computer keyboard letters, looking at family photograph albums, making a scrapbook, play rhyming games, repeating jingles from commercials, making grocery lists, having pretend telephone conversations, sending and receiving mail, and nature walks. Notari-Syverson and Challoner (2005) also provided examples of early literacy-rich activities in home settings. Based on the work of these authors, further adaptations with AT strategies are applied to extend naturally occurring family literacy activities to all children, in particular those with the most significant disabilities. Simple adaptations to daily activities can enable children to participate, take turns, make choices, and build language skills to support emergent literacy skills. Table 7.1 demonstrates selected routines and activities that may typically occur in home settings for many families and create a literacy-rich experience. AT strategies are provided that further adapt typically occurring family activities with young children.

Cultural Diversity in Family Literacy

Thus far, descriptions of literacy-rich experiences for young children in home and family settings assume that print and text-based literacy formats are commonly available in the home. Literacy across cultures takes different forms, in addition to print-based approaches. In families of diverse language and cultural backgrounds, an emphasis on storytelling exists through oral modalities, with less emphasis on text. With changes in society and immigration patterns in cities worldwide, the diversity of languages and cultures represented in families with young children contributes to increased interest and research regarding the influence of culture on home literacy experiences (Wasik & Hendrickson, 2004). Research indicates that family approaches to literacy vary by culture and language, in addition to socioeconomic and educational differences in families (Tabors & Snow, 2001). Research influences practice, and, as a result, programs for young children increasingly address the needs of children whose primary language is not

Table 7.1.   AT strategies to support literacy in home environments

Routines	Activities	AT strategy	Preliteracy skills
Family photograph albums	Family photographs Family events Family stories	Obtain a talking photograph album (http://www.attainmentcompany.com). Print names of people in photographs. Add key word to identify event. Record comment about each picture to play, taking turns.	Print awareness Comprehension of family names Recognition of own name
Looking at picture books	Shared reading Turn pages Identify favorite pictures	Select book with repeated lines, such as *Are You My Mother?* by P.D. Eastman. Record repeated line on single-message voice output communication aid (VOCA) (http://www.attainmentcompany.com). Place photograph of main character on VOCA. Encourage and then fade cueing for child to activate VOCA for repeated line throughout the story.	Book handling Turning pages Taking turns in dialogic reading with parent "Read" part of story with repeated line
Sound and word games	Repeat sounds in books, such as alphabet books Play with sounds and imitate Say words that begin with same sound	Adapt an alphabet board book, such as *Dr. Seuss's ABCs.* Using small magnetic letters, place a piece of magnetic tape on page and attach corresponding magnetic alphabet letter. Read book with child and assist him or her to remove magnet letter to place on cookie sheet. Return to pages and assist child to choose letters to return to book, matching letters and sounds.	Sound–symbol awareness Alphabet awareness Book handling Symbol matching to page
Music and songs	Listen to children's songs Sing favorite songs Play music	Provide photograph of CD label and two choices for child to choose favorite music. Collect props to represent favorite fingerplays/songs; for example, a small star for "Twinkle, Twinkle, Little Star" or a toy spider for "Itsy-Bitsy Spider."	Phonological awareness of beginning sounds Phonological awareness of rhyming words Listening to patterns and rhythm
Car/bus ride	Talk about going for a ride in a car or on a bus Point out places en route	Adapt story to keep in car (http://www.vanderbilt.edu/csefel/resources/strategies.html).	Oral language Book handling Predicting events

the dominant language in a given society. The importance of the primary language, the language spoken at home with the child and family, is more often recognized in early literacy programs than in the past. Research supports the critical role of language development in the child's primary language to support subsequent success in literacy and learning (Snow & Tabors, 2001).

With a growing awareness and practice to address the needs of children who are acquiring the dominant language (e.g., English in the United States) as a second language comes greater understanding of differences among families and cultures to integrate language and literacy in daily life. Studies that compare cultures regarding storytelling and book reading within families show both differences and similarities across cultures. For example, Yaroz and Barrett (2001) found that storybook reading was similar among families of various cultural and language backgrounds and that income, family size, and education contributed to more differences across cultural groups than ethnicity alone. African American families reported that storytelling was prevalent and adults encouraged children to also create oral narratives (Heath, 1983). The different variations of Spanish spoken in the United States create the need to consider differences across families regarding literacy practices. Families who have recently immigrated often want their children to speak English in order to succeed in school and thus may limit their use of Spanish in reading and storytelling at home. Other families encourage bilingual development and provide literacy experiences in Spanish at home while encouraging speaking English at school and in the community (Strucker, Snow, & Pan, 2004). Although differences and variations in the type and amount of preliteracy experiences clearly exist both across and within cultures, the expectations for children entering preschool settings focus on conventional forms of literacy that lead to reading and writing.

Children from diverse cultures and languages who are learning English as a second language are often identified as at risk of reading failure (Strucker et al., 2004). This finding may be more related to differences in school and family expectations than in literacy development. Pellegrini observed that "the degree of similarity between home and school literacy events predicts success in school-based literacy" (2001, p. 55; as cited in Wasik & Hendrickson, 2004). The mismatch between the expectations of the preschool, the family, and home literacy activities may result from diverse approaches to literacy across cultures. The preliteracy experiences of young children range from informal exposure to storytelling, oral narratives, and printed materials to more formal adult scaffolding in shared book-reading activities.

In addition to different expectations in families of diverse cultural and language backgrounds, individual child characteristics influence outcomes in emergent literacy skills. Children with significant disabilities often do not experience the same level of exposure to books, print, storytelling, and language development opportunities as typically developing children (Wasik & Hendrickson, 2004). In addition, if the child with a disability also lives in a family who does not speak the dominant language of the society, then different expectations may limit the child's opportunity to experience all forms of literacy and print forms. For children with disabilities from diverse language and cultural backgrounds, the complexity increases when planning for AT to support literacy development. Considerations of cultural, linguistic, and family literacy traditions need to be included in AT strategies. A number of preliteracy, emergent literacy, and early literacy materials are available in multiple languages for young children, and many of these resources are listed at the end of this book. AT approaches such as physical adaptations to books, book selection guidelines, digital book formats for computer use, literacy kits, and thematic approaches will be described in upcoming sections of this chapter, with particular attention to families and children with diverse language backgrounds.

ASSISTIVE TECHOLOGY AND PRELITERACY PRACTICES

AT provides opportunities and access to develop preliteracy skills for young children with significant disabilities. Recommended practices to enable children with disabilities to benefit from exposure and experiences with books beginning early in life build the foundations for literacy competencies in several stages that include handling books, awareness of text in words and sentences, and gradual mastery of the multiple skills leading to phonological awareness and early literacy. Practices that apply AT with young children include initial access to books, considerations for selecting appropriate books, shared and supported book-reading strategies, narrative development, and explicit focus on phonological awareness. In this section, research-based approaches for AT and preliteracy are provided. Following this section, AT supports for emergent literacy within preschool curriculum are provided.

Access to Books

The natural pleasure of sharing a book can be severely compromised for young children with disabilities, particularly those with physical, cognitive, sensory, and communication challenges, placing the child at risk of not establishing a foundation to experience books. Erickson and Clendon (2009) stated that reading materials need to be physically, linguistically, and cognitively accessible in order to support students with significant disabilities to benefit from learning with books. In addition, children with vision or hearing difficulties may need sensory alternatives to gain access to books, such as tactile input, enhanced auditory feedback, and visual representations of sign language. Each of these areas of access to books are considered next.

Physical Access

Although the child's physical position is the first consideration to gain access to any type of activity, including books, toys, and computers, a number of positions may be explored for gaining access to books. For a young child, sitting on a parent's lap may be natural and comfortable. For a child with a physical disability that involves muscle stiffness or involuntary movement related to many motor disabilities, however, finding optimal positioning requires a seating system adapted to the needs of the individual child. Developing a seating system for optimal positioning for book sharing is beyond the scope of this book and can be best developed in the context of the child's family and professional team. Following the development of optimal support for positioning, access to books and other activities can be developed. For further information on seating and positioning, the reader is referred to the Wisconsin Assistive Technology Initiative (WATI; 2010).

Physical access to books includes positioning the book for optimal viewing or reaching, keeping the book in place, and a finding a way to manipulate and turn the pages of the book. Several means of improving physical access to books are available, including commercial products and teacher-made materials. Initially, positioning books can be accomplished with slantboards to provide an angled surface for viewing. In addition, Velcro can be used on the back of a book that is placed on a textured fabric on the slantboard, such as tempo loop display fabric, also known by the brand name Veltex®. For young children, optimal physical positioning may be sitting or sidelying on the floor with an appropriate bolster or other supports based on input from the physical and occupational therapist. The location and position of the book, with or without positioning on a slantboard, is related to the most comfortable and available position for the child.

After developing a stable position for looking at a book, the child needs a method to turn pages. Several adaptations, which are referred to as "page turners," include fitting materials to the edges of the pages to make page turning easier, such as foam pieces attached by an individual paper clip on each page or plastic clothes pins to more easily grasp the edge of the page and turn. In addition to page turners that are attached to the book, adapted AT tools may include a cap with a pointer fixed to the bill of the cap or magnetic wand to attract magnetic tape placed on the edge each page. Table 7.2 provides additional examples of page turners.

In addition to page turners, "page fluffers" are recommended to place within the pages of books to create easier access to young children with limited fine motor abilities to separate each page. Detachable photographs or icons to match pictures in the book can be affixed with Velcro and also serve to "fluff" pages. Other materials that may be used for this purpose include small, adhesive "picture bumpers;" small, adhesive furniture floor pads; and foam pieces. Table 7.2 provides additional examples of page fluffers.

Table 7.2. Summary of AT for access to books for young children

Physical access	Linguistic access	Cognitive access	Sensory access
Page turners	*Simplify vocabulary*	*Relevant themes*	*Tactile adaptation*
Chip clips	Stick-on labels to cover	Pets	Object choice boards
Hair tie loops	text	Farm animals	to represent songs
Hefty tabs	Wordless picture books	Zoo animals	and books
Index tabs	Highlighter tape on key	Ocean life	Story boxes with
Magnet	words	Bugs	children's book and
Paper clips with foam	Books with repeated	Family	related objects
piece	lines	Grandparents	Beginning braille books
Popsicle sticks		Vehicles	(as determined by
Shower curtain ring		Foods	team)
Small plastic clothes			Tactile books with
pins			shape of object and
Sponge pieces			textures
Page fluffers	*Simplify text*	*Props for books*	*Auditory adaptation*
Foam curler	Stick-on labels to cover	Stuffed toy	Push-button sound
Hot glue drop	extra text	Battery-operated toy	books for children
Large buttons	Highlighter tape on key	Scanned images	(e.g., *Bright Baby,*
Magnet	phrases	Photographs	*Noisy Car* and *Bright*
Packing styrofoam	Predictable patterns in	Boardmaker icons	*Baby, Noisy Barn* by
Picture bumpers	text with one or	Picture props mounted	Roger Priddy)
Plastic washers	more repeated lines	on sticky-back foam	Children's books
Pom poms		Picture props mounted	adapted with single-
Puffy paint dots		on Ethafoam	message voice
Sponge pieces			output communi-
Velcro dots			cation aid with
			repeated line
			Computer books with
			voice output
Slantboards		*Graphic representation*	*Visual adaptation*
Three-inch binder		Boardmaker images to	Sign language icons to
covered with		match key phrases	match key words
microfiber		Text and picture	Computer books with
Commercial slantboard		programs such as	visual animation
covered with Veltex		Writing with	Computer books with
Hands free		Symbols and	sign language
Baseball cap/visor with		Symbolate in	animation
pointer attached		Boardmaker Plus	

From Grant, D., Justice, P., & Maltby, K. (2001). *Beyond the book: Infusing literacy and assistive technology into the classroom.* Presentation at the 2001 CSUN International Conference on Technology and Persons with Disabilities, Los Angeles; adapted by permission.

In addition to creating greater access through adapting hard copies of books, digital books are increasingly available at little or no cost. A number of software programs are available commercially to provide book-reading experiences for young children on the computer. Online libraries are widely available with children's books in digital format and require a computer with Internet access. For children with limited physical access to books, digital formats offer the opportunity to experience favorite stories more easily. More extensive computer applications for literacy are addressed in Chapter 8.

Linguistic Access

Simplifying books is a critical element to meet the developmental needs and language level of each individual child. Books for young children include those without words, those with minimal text, and those with more extensive stories. In order to simplify language to make it accessible to each child, adults need to stress key words, shorten sentences, and abbreviate the text within books to maintain the child's attention and engagement while reading the book together. Several strategies using low-tech AT with books in print include covering up excessive text so that only key words are visible. In addition, transparent highlighter tape that is available in office supply stores can be used to emphasize key words in the text that relate to pictures or story elements in the book. While reading with the child, adults can editorialize the text to shorten phrases, simplify concepts, and use vocabulary that is within the understanding level of the individual child (Erickson & Clendon, 2009).

Cognitive Access

Cognitive development influences the child's early experiences with books. According to cognitive development theories, the child's knowledge and understanding of the relationships between the objects, people, and events in his or her daily environments enables further learning. For example, the infant who begins to understand that his or her own cries and vocalizations result in further attention from caregivers gains the tools to communicate in increasingly complex social interactions. The child's familiar circle of daily activities becomes more meaningful, allowing connections with more abstract representations found within books. In order to support cognitive access to books, adults need to assist children to connect their experiences with the contents of the books. Book themes for young children are often related to animals, feelings, families, actions, and other familiar activities that assist to make book contents relevant and meaningful for the child.

Additional adaptations using low-tech AT include using props in the form of objects, photographs, icons, and other materials that extend the concepts and vocabulary in the book to the child's cognitive understanding. Examples of props include pictures mounted on thin sticky-back foam and laminated with Velcro attachments to the pages of the book. Stuffed animals, puppets, or toys may also be used as props when related to the concepts in a particular book, such as a teddy bear for *Brown Bear, Brown Bear* by Bill Martin, Jr., or a battery-operated frog with *Jump, Frog, Jump* by Robert Kalan. Research demonstrated that children increased attention and interaction when props were used to support key concepts and vocabulary in selected books (Culatta, Aslett, Fife, & Setzer, 2004). The connections between actual objects, pictures, and vocabulary content in books assist young children to make the cognitive "leap" and gain meaning from participation in book reading.

Additional alternative formats to assist in creating meaning for young children in early book exposure include graphic symbols to support text. Erickson and Clendon (2009) suggested providing pictured symbols to represent text in order to build awareness of the print and to make stories more understandable to children in beginning stages of literacy.

Sensory Access

Vision and hearing access can be bridged using alternative formats. Children with limitations in vision, hearing, or both areas require special consideration in applying AT with early literacy experiences. Focus on tactile experiences with books may be the most critical modality to introduce books with children who experience vision and hearing loss. Furthermore, consulting with specialists in these areas, such as a vision specialist or audiologist, is needed to design specific interventions to meet individual needs of children with sensory disabilities. Visual access includes attention to the size, clarity, and contrast of pictures in books. Although this is important for all young children, particular consideration is needed for children with visual impairments. As visual development and disability occur in a range of needs, developing AT strategies to support visual access to books and print also occurs in a range of modified visual input to reliance on auditory and tactile input, based on the strengths and learning modalities available to each child. In a similar manner, children with hearing impairments may benefit from augmented visual support to participate with books, such as highlighted text using highlighter tape or other means, clarity of pictures, and simplified language concepts. In addition, children who are provided with amplification early in life through either hearing aids or cochlear implants continue to benefit from visual support in addition to auditory input. Those children who rely on sign language as a primary means of learning language and communication interaction skills may benefit from visual symbols representing the sign language symbols that accompany the vocabulary in a given book.

Book Selection

Selecting appropriate books for young children, particularly those who require support to gain access to and learn preliteracy skills through experiences with print, words, pictures in books, work patterns, sentence patterns, and story elements, requires consideration of several variables. Selecting books to promote physical, linguistic, cognitive, and sensory access is the first level of decision making. Books that can be adapted to create more accessible formats must be durable with clear pictures and simple text. In addition to the physical format of books, attention must be paid to the design and purpose of books for children. Hemmeter et al. (2005) outlined expected emergent literacy skills that are typically observed in preschool settings to support the development of conventional literacy in the early school years, including comprehension and expression of printed forms of vocabulary, sentence patterns, grammatical rules, story sequences, phonological awareness, and the alphabetic principle. Geber (2003) developed an extensive guide to selecting and using books with young children to target specific emergent literacy skills that are particularly critical for children with complex disabilities. Table 7.3 includes considerations for selection of books and books identified by Geber to target specific literacy developments.

Shared and Supported Book Reading

The practice of shared book reading with young children develops many language and literacy skills, including listening, taking turns, print awareness, phonological awareness, vocabulary development, story comprehension, and storytelling. The benefits for young children to participate in shared book reading extend beyond literacy skills to social-emotional development and nurturing relationships with family members and caregivers. The frequency of shared book reading with young children is linked positively to reading readiness in the preschool and early school years. Several studies showed specific effects of shared book reading with increased oral vocabulary among toddlers and preschool children and potentially positive effects to support the development of print awareness, reading, and writing skills at school entry (Justice, Kaderavek, Bowles, & Grimm, 2005; Lonigan, Anthony, Bloomfield, Dyer, & Samwel, 1999; Lonigan & Whitehurst, 1998; Whitehurst et al., 1994; Whitehurst & Lonigan, 1998; Zevenbergen, Whitehurst, & Zevenbergen, 2003).

Shared book-reading practices vary widely across families and settings due primarily to cultural and linguistic diversity, socioeconomic conditions, and parents' education level. Among highly educated families, shared book reading begins quite early in the child's life because reading is highly valued among these families (van Kleeck, 2004). Specific practices of shared book reading include both interactional strategies and talking about the books with children. Language interaction strategies used by parents are key to shared book reading because there is an exchange of social closeness with the

Table 7.3. Guidelines for books to target selected preliteracy skills

Preliteracy skill	Considerations in selection	Examples
Vocabulary comprehension: familiar themes	Choose books that connect words to child's familiar experiences Find books that include names of things, actions, locations, and describing words Get books that describe concepts of size, shape, color, and number that relate to child's world Select books with minimal text, such as wordless picture books Look for books with broad quantity and quality of words to expand vocabulary base	*The Grouchy Ladybug* by Eric Carle *The Baby Beebee Bird* by Dian Redfield Massie *Big Red Barn* by Margaret Wise *Mr. Gumpy's Outing* by John Burningham
Two- and three-word phrases	Select books with short phrases and minimal text on page	*It's the Bear!* by Jez Alborough *Jamberry* by Bruce Degan
Print awareness	Highlight text of key words in book or story Look for repeated phrase patterns and repeated lines in book Look for books with clear and simple pictures that are associated with text	*Farmer Duck* by Martin Waddell *Dinosaurs, Dinosaurs* by Byron Barton *Geraldine's Blanket* by Holly Keller
Grammatical awareness: questions	Look for books that pose questions repeatedly in the story Allow pauses when reading for child to answer questions Look for "what," "who," "where," "why," "how," and "when" questions	*Who Sank the Boat?* by Pamela Allen *Jesse Bear, What Will You Wear?* by Nancy White Carlstrom *Is Your Mama a Llama?* by Deborah Guarino *Freight Train* by Donald Crews
Grammatical awareness: verb tense	Look for books with events and actions Seek a variety of action words Select books with clear pictures and limited text to highlight actions Select stories with a series of events that can be reviewed in the past	*The Adventures of Taxi Dog* by Debra Barracca and Sal Barracca *Fortunately* by Remy Charlip *I Went Walking* by Sue Williams *Corduroy* by Don Freeman *Fortunately* by Remy Charlip
Grammatical awareness: plural forms	Seek books with multiple examples of singular and plural items Seek books with increasing numbers and quantities, such as counting books Select books with clear pictures of single and multiple items	*The Very Hungry Caterpillar* by Eric Carle *School Bus* by Donald Crews *Mr. Gumpy's Outing* by John Burningham *Peter's Chair* by Ezra Jack Keats *Sheep on a Ship* by Nancy Shaw
Story sequence awareness	Look for books with sequenced events in logical, temporal order Choose books that reflect child's own experience Include books with basic story grammar structure with main character, setting, events, outcomes, and feelings of characters Seek books with key words including *first, and then,* and *next* to sequence story elements	*Good Dog, Carl!* by Alexandra Day *That's Good! That's Bad!* by Margery Culyer *Planting a Rainbow* by Lois Ehlert *If You Give a Mouse a Cookie* by Laura Numeroff *The Carrot Seed* by Ruth Krauss *Daddy Makes the Best Spaghetti* by Anna Grossnickle Hines
Phonological awareness	Look for books with repetition, rhyme, and verse	*Hairy Scary, Ordinary* by Brian P. Cleary
Rhyming	Select books with repeated sounds at beginning for words for alliteration	*Zin! Zin! A Violin* by Lloyd Moss *Noisy Poems* by Jill Bennett *Lilly's Purple Plastic Purse* by Kevin Henkes *Click, Clack, Moo, Cows that Type* by Doreen Cronin *Sing, Sophie* by Dayle Ann Dodds
Alphabetic principle	Seek books organized by alphabet letters Look for rhyme and repetition in the phrasing to establish patterns for learning alphabet Seek books with multiple examples of words paired with each letter Select books with simple, clear pictures and text labels	*Alligators All Around: An Alphabet* by Maurice Sendak *Chicka Chicka Boom Boom* by Bill Martin, Jr., & John Archumbault

Source: Gebers (2003).

Table 7.4.   Shared book-reading practices

Talking about books: language content			Talking about books: interaction strategies		
Use increasingly abstract language	Focus on word meaning first, then print	Increasingly frame book as unique context	Tune into child's interests and experiences	Be semantically contingent with child's contribution	Prompt child's verbal participation
Use concrete language Use more decontextualized, abstract language	Talk about pictures/story Talk about letters and print	Use book-related vocabulary Talk about authors	Relate book to child's life	Use initiations and expansions Use semantic extensions Use clarification requests Respond to child's questions	Ask questions Vertically scaffold Hold child accountable Provide praise and encouragement

From van Kleeck, A. (2004). Fostering preliteracy development via storybook-sharing interactions: The cultural context of mainstream family practices. In C.A. Stone, E.R. Silliman, B.J. Ehren, & K. Apel (Eds.), *Handbook of language and literacy: Development and disorders* (pp. 175–208). New York: Guilford Press; reprinted by permission.

child as well as an exchange of knowledge from adult to child. Table 7.4 summarizes the language and interactional exchanges that occur within the context of sharing a book with a child.

The process that parents use changes as the child develops from infancy through the preschool years and his or her language becomes more abstract and complex. In turn, parents increase the cognitive demands on the child to talk about books using more "decontextualized" language that is not directly related to the book. More demands appear related to rhyming words and identifying letters, sounds, and familiar text in shared books as children progress in development and mastery of emergent literacy skills. The practice of shared book reading is identified as "culturally relative" for families with high priorities to prepare children for school entry and readiness to read.

For children with significant disabilities, the opportunities to engage in shared book reading are limited by reduced opportunities to handle books, participate in sustained interactions, barriers to verbal communication, and difficulties in attention and motivation. Liboiron and Soto (2006) identified the importance of increased adult scaffolding with children who use AAC in order to participate in shared book reading. Soto, Dukohvny, and Vestly (2006) refer to the practice as "supported book reading" and provided intervention strategies to increase support for children to respond to questions and to interact with storybooks. In addition to the strategies to support children to interact with books, the development of an extensive command of words is key to advancing literacy development. The next section focuses on vocabulary development, both receptive and expressive.

Vocabulary Knowledge

Understanding and expressing words in oral language in the early toddler years are strong predictors of subsequent language development skills at more complex levels in typically developing children. Children who are identified to be at risk of language delays also require a core vocabulary in order to progress to using phrases and sentences in language development (Light & Draeger, 2007). In a parallel process, Justice and Pullen (2003) summarized early literacy research and identified the critical role of vocabulary knowledge in the preschool years to support further competency in becoming literate in the early school years. The importance of building word knowledge is thus underscored with young children with disabilities, particularly those with limited verbal speech-language development.

Word knowledge in printed form involves several basic skills in the young child, beginning with comprehension and connection between words presented in text with their own experiences. Hearing a word and linking the word pattern to a referent that may include a previous experience, concrete object, or person within the child's environment provides a foundation for comprehension and building further meaning associated with each word learned. Wilkinson and Albert (2001) described the process of vocabulary development in typically developing children as "fast mapping," which involves rapidly learning words and meaning by attaching a label to an object, action, or person. Children apparently apply the fast mapping process with only limited exposure to a word, linking the word to an immediate object or experience, often with incomplete or even incorrect meaning. Over time, children gradually construct more complete meaning with words by expanding knowledge and experience. Children with limited verbal development may rely much more on receptive understanding of words rather than expression (Cress, 1998). The challenge to build vocabulary knowledge in the context of books includes developing a reliable method for the child to communicate recognition and knowledge of familiar words. AT strategies to provide vocabulary development opportunities that match the child's experiences and also assist to expand word knowledge and use include many approaches already referred to earlier in the chapter. More specifically, emphasizing relevant words with repetition and links to meaning are needed. Word recognition provides the foundation for reading comprehension.

In order to meet the challenge and needs for young children with disabilities to have opportunities to have repeated vocabulary exposure, experience, and learning, early intervention and preschool professionals need to plan for the child to gain access to core and fringe vocabulary easily. Identifying high-frequency words that are found in the vocabularies of children from preschool through adult years provides a guideline for practitioners to focus on words that can be used in many activities. For example, the following words are among the 25 most frequently used words in the conversation of English-speaking preschool and kindergarten children: *the, and, a, you, he, is, with, they, I,* and *have* (Marvin, Beukelman, & Bilyeu, 1994). More extensive core vocabulary lists are available through the University of Nebraska, Barkley Center, at http://aac.unl.edu. Although core vocabulary research is based on oral language use, there is a high correspondence to Dolch lists developed as high-frequency reading words for young children. Dolch lists are based on research conducted by Edward Dolch (1948), who reviewed children's books for high-frequency words and developed a list of 220 words that are recommended for mastery in the early school years.

In addition to the concept of core vocabulary, fringe vocabulary are the content words found in children's language learning experiences and in children's books. General nouns, verbs, adjectives, prepositions, and specific names of characters in books are some of the frequent fringe vocabulary words unique to each book. Some words such as colors, sizes, number concepts, shapes, and other descriptors often generalize from book to book and may be considered as core vocabulary rather than fringe vocabulary, which is specific to individual books or activities. Both core and fringe vocabulary need to be included for young children with disabilities when using AT support for literacy development. Erickson and Clendon (2009) provided the example of developing communication boards to assist in building vocabulary comprehension to use with *Brown Bear, Brown Bear* (Martin, 1983) that extends beyond the specific vocabulary within the book. Rather than restricting the child to a communication board that is book specific, Erickson and Clendon advised designing a low-tech communication board or programming a high-tech device for the child with core and fringe vocabulary words. Core words that can be used in reading activities, such as *I, you, the, and, he,* and *she,* can be included along with color, number, and size words. Combining core and fringe vocabulary within AT tools to support early vocabulary knowledge allows the child to use words more independently by indicating appropriate color and animal names to answer questions and to participate in the shared book-reading activity.

Because the high-frequency words in English (Dolch words) are not easily decoded phonetically, they typically are learned as sight words, which are important for gaining meaning from verbal and written language yet do not assist children to master the phonological properties of words. Print awareness and word knowledge are cornerstones of emergent literacy, and phonological awareness is the other critical piece to move beyond sight words and learn new words through conventional reading. Attention to phonological awareness is also key in emergent literacy and early literacy when implementing AT tools to support vocabulary development. Strategies to develop phonological awareness using AT strategies are more targeted and specific to sounds, rhymes, word onset patterns, and decoding and encoding sounds in words, and these are addressed in following sections.

Story Comprehension and Prediction

The ability to identify elements in a story and retain relevant information from the sequence of events within a book leads to reading comprehension in the process of developing conventional literacy skills. Young children benefit from repeated reading of familiar stories because memory of the key events becomes a pattern to understand the structure and organization of stories. Young children then gain a structural organization that helps to develop the skill of predicting what might come next, based on the information presented. Books such as *If You Give a Mouse a Cookie* (Numeroff, 1995) and *Jump, Frog, Jump* (Kalan, 1991) provide a pattern of events and repeated lines that allow the child to anticipate and guess what comes next in the story. AT strategies to support prediction and comprehension of story sequences are directly related to the book selected. Table 7.3 lists examples of books that are noted for providing a repeated pattern with predictable outcomes. In addition to selecting books with elements of predictable and often amusing outcomes, the additional use of AT tools such as a communication board with icons representing the sequence of "What happened first?" "What happened second?" and "Then what happened?" will provide support for the child to comprehend and retain the story elements. In addition, using a VOCA with a sequence of recorded messages enables the adult to record the story sequence ahead of time and the child to replay and retell what happened several times.

Narrative Development

Developing the ability to tell stories begins with the child relaying information to caregivers and family members about events that are personally relevant and important. Westby (1985) described the development of storytelling in young children as a process that begins with "heaps" of words and sentences that may not be in order or have incomplete information about something that just happened. Often, adults must fill in missing information when young children convey their excitement and feelings about an event that either caused them to be delighted or angry. Soto, Yu, and Henneberry (2007) highlighted the importance of strong feelings to assist the memory of events and stories that children tell about their experiences because the affect that is attached to a given event can provide a link to remembering details of the event. Stories become more organized and complete as the child gains more vocabulary and language facility. Children form cohesive narratives that have a beginning, middle, and end as they get ready to enter the primary grades.

Children with complex communication needs and related learning difficulties often have trouble with language processing that requires sequential memory and retention of information. Soto and Hartmann (2006) analyzed the narrative development skills of children who used AAC and found that each of the four children observed demonstrated significant difficulties in several types of narrative tasks—retelling a story in a picture book, completing a story with a "story starter," and constructing a novel personal narrative. Soto et al. (2007) followed this analysis with an intervention study that implemented a co-constructed narrative approach to provide scaffolding for an 8-year old girl to tell stories using visual and communication support. From the results of the narrative intervention and the adult co-construction strategies used in the narrative intervention, Soto, Hartmann, and Wilkins (2006) identified communication techniques used by the child in the study that contributed to her ability to construct her own narratives. Furthermore, Soto et al. (2007) proposed a series of facilitative steps to assist in co-construction of narrative development. Because research by Soto and her colleagues in narrative development with children who use AAC and AT is limited in sample size, conclusions can only suggest the challenges and potential intervention directions to assist children with complex needs to achieve independence in generating narratives.

EMERGENT LITERACY IN PRESCHOOL ENVIRONMENTS

As young children reach preschool age, more formal expectations and curriculum are put into play. In particular, preacademic experiences take the central role within the context of experiential learning, and teachers provide direction and facilitation of learning toward locally and nationally determined standards. Preschool curriculum models differ across the nation and the world, with differing degrees of structure and expectations for child performance within the preschool setting. The affect of curriculum standards exists both in general early childhood education and early childhood special education programs, in particular, with a focus on emergent literacy. Research informs practitioners that literacy-rich environments in preschools are beneficial for all children. Johnston, McDonnell, and Hawken (2008) reported that children in literacy-rich environments in preschools showed 3–10 times more engagement in early writing and reading behaviors than children in traditional settings. Literacy-rich preschool environments are those that emphasize making transitions to using printed forms of language throughout the preschool day. Justice and Pullen (2003) and Morrow (2007) described literacy-rich preschool classrooms that include many of the following exemplars.

- Visual display of target vocabulary in a "word wall" format
- Books selected to focus on particular emergent literacy skills
- Literacy-enriched play centers with graphic and text labels for items in each center
- Multiple opportunities for adult–child shared book reading
- Explicit focus on phonological awareness to include rhyming, alliteration, initial sounds, alphabet awareness, and sound–letter correspondence
- Oral language development to focus on correspondence of objects, photographs, pictures, and print
- Oral language development to focus on words in print to form sentences according to language syntax rules in basic sentence types

These practices are also echoed in the work of Goosens' et al. (1992), who developed and demonstrated engineered classrooms with extensive visual communication tools with children with disabilities. The engineered classroom environment provided a system of enlarged graphic symbols, pictures, and props with print to accompany each activity in the classroom including morning greeting, songs, books, meals, individual play, computer time, outdoor play, and making transitions between activities. The parallels between the current recommended practice of literacy-rich classrooms and the previous model of engineered environments are striking. In another version of the engineered classroom, KingdeBaun (2007a) included more focus on print in the making language visible approach. Recommendations by Goosens' et al. and King de Baun include extensively using visual supports, adapted books, and vocabulary icons with text in both low- and high-tech formats throughout the classroom. The similarity of approaches in general and special education curriculum for young children shows an integration and blending of approaches that can be complementary and support inclusion of children with disabilities. Furthermore, the principles of universal design for learning and response to intervention (RTI) approaches that are recommended practices in educational settings for all children are in concert with methods to make language and literacy visible and explicit to all children. Specific practices to support implementing AT for literacy in preschool settings include literacy-rich environments and phonological awareness strategies, which are discussed next.

Assistive Technology for Literacy-Rich Preschool Settings

Literacy-rich preschool environments provide an easily adaptable context for implementing AT support to meet the needs of children with disabilities. Within the preschool classroom, learning centers provide the context to develop and expand low- and high-tech tools that support participation and learning for all children. Regarding literacy development, Justice and Pullen (2003) identified evidence-based practices to facilitate emergent literacy skills including shared book reading, literacy-enriched play centers, and explicit focus on phonological awareness. Adult–child shared book reading was discussed previously and strategies to support phonological awareness will be discussed in the following section. Literacy-enriched play centers are the focus of this section because the natural extension of AT tools with current preschool learning centers provides an initial entry point to expand access to literacy for all children. Table 7.5 describes using AT tools with low-tech picture communication tools using text and picture icons in preschool learning and activity centers.

In addition to designing and preparing AT materials to enhance literacy opportunities in play and learning centers, AT literacy tools can be embedded in the regular early childhood curriculum. Embedding adaptations for children with disabilities in regular preschool classrooms is described as a blended curriculum (Grisham-Brown, Pretti-Frontczak,

Table 7.5. AT tools to support emergent literacy skills in preschool play and learning centers

Centers	AT access to literacy
Pizza parlor	Pizza menu with picture icons and printed words for pizza toppings Velcro-backed icons with picture/word to place on Velcro-friendly clipboard to place orders
Baking	Pictures with text labels of recipe in page protector on clipboard Magnetic-backed icons/text of ingredients to place on cookie sheet or metal bowl
Dress up	Dress-up theme pictures/text (e.g., princess, ballerina, pirate, cowboys) Program voice output communication aid (VOCA) with steps in script to "tell the story" (e.g., character, feelings)
Pet store	Animal photographs with text labels with Velcro backing Program VOCA with script for buying animal/pet (e.g., pet, cost, feeding)

Table 7.6.   AT extensions within preschool thematic units for literacy

Theme	Suggested book	AT tools for literacy themes
Seasons	*The Fall of Freddie the Leaf* by Leo F. Buscaglia	Communication board with core and fringe words in each book
Bugs	*Under One Rock, Bugs, Slugs and Other Ughs* by Anthony D. Fredericks	Adapted book for access
		Laminated photographs of actual items in each book
Dinosaurs	*The Most Amazing Dinosaur* by James Stevenson	Props in basket to represent book contents
Family	*Abuela* by Arthur Dorros	Voice output communication aid programmed with sequence of events in book
Feelings	*Everybody Has Feelings* by Charles E. Avery	

Sources: Meinbach, Fredericks, and Rothlein (2000), Morrow (2007), and Preschool Rainbow (2009).

Hawkins, & Winchell, 2009). In addition, the RTI approach encompasses adaptations for children along a continuum of learning needs. Applying AT strategies provides a means to extend each of these approaches in preschool settings that include children with significant disabilities with consideration of the additional access methods that are needed. Thematic units provide an additional context for extending literacy to all students. For example, thematic units designed to focus on particular concepts such as foods, zoo animals, pets, and family often use a book as the central focus with extension activities to reinforce vocabulary and build on child knowledge. AT tools provide an additional means to extend and create access for those students with significant challenges in communication, mobility, learning, and other areas of development. Table 7.6 demonstrates specific examples of AT solutions to extend and provide access to literacy development within literacy-based thematic units in preschool curriculum.

Assistive Technology for Phonological Awareness

Each of the emergent literacy skills and AT strategies to support literacy development discussed thus far lead to the link between preliteracy development and conventional literacy. Phonological awareness is the link that enables the child to gain conventional reading and writing abilities. Although high-frequency words, print awareness, and story knowledge complete some of the puzzle to build literacy, phonological awareness provides the piece of the literacy puzzle that allows the child to manipulate sounds and letters in order to read and write in his or her own words.

Phonological awareness results from the development of several skills that were listed and discussed earlier. Justice and Pullen (2003) further identified skills that are considered to be critical to support making the transition between emergent and conventional literacy, including written language awareness and phonological awareness. Written language awareness skill areas identified by Justice and Pullen showed considerable overlap with those skills defined thus far as emergent literacy skills and include alphabet awareness, alphabet names, book handling, print awareness, recognition of print forms, and early writing. Phonological awareness skill areas identified by Justice and Pullen coincided closely with other researchers in early childhood literacy development and include alliteration awareness, sound blending, phoneme identity, rhyme awareness, segmenting, syllable awareness, and word awareness. Justice and Pullen advocated for an explicit focus on the areas listed, particularly for children at risk of reading failure. Erickson and Clendon (2009) further emphasized the pivotal role of alphabet knowledge and phonological awareness for children who use AAC and AT systems to communicate. In particular, they recommended focusing on first letter cueing to support the learning of letter names and sounds. Additional strategies to build phonological awareness include the use of alphabet books, association of letters with sounds, and low- and high-tech AT tools for children to indicate their choices when asked to identify correct target sounds.

Furthermore, Erickson and Clendon (2009) recommended explicit focus on spelling-based instruction, referred to as Making Words, developed by Cunningham and Cunningham (1992). The Making Words approach begins with a limited letter set with a single vowel. In a series of prompted steps, children are guided to form 1-, 2-, 3- and 4-letter words with immediate feedback and application in generating new words. The steps in the Making Words approach follow a phonics-based approach that is commonly used for all children with additional AT tools to support visual attention and alternate modalities of communication to demonstrate word encoding skills. Although Erickson and Clendon recommended a direct instruction approach to learning phonics as a means to strengthen phonological awareness and support early literacy development, they also recommend implementation within the context of shared book reading. For example, children could indicate recognition of a target sound, such as /s/ when the teacher reads selected passages from *Silly Sally* (Wood, 1994), through a number of AT strategies including: 1) holding up a large sign with s, 2) activating a single-message VOCA to say I HEAR S!, 3) indicating the letter s on a communication board, or 4) activating their high-tech SGD to respond THAT'S IT! Providing a method to visually represent the letter, hear the sound, and respond allows every child the means to participate in the context of shared book reading and gain letter and sound knowledge in the process.

Goals for Emergent Literacy

Each of the approaches described to support literacy development are supported in research. Recommended approaches include a combination of strategies complemented by AT tools that increase access and overcome barriers for each child to progress and learn the components of becoming a literate individual. Hemmeter et al. (2005) outlined emergent literacy outcomes for young children as follows.

- Excitement and love of language and print materials
- Comprehension and meaning from print materials
- Phonological awareness (the ability to hear, identify, and manipulate the sound structure of oral language)
- Alphabetic principle

When considering these outcomes as a guide for designing AT supports to engage children with disabilities in literacy learning, practitioners can ground their work in research-based practice and develop meaningful educational goals.

ASSISTIVE TECHNOLOGY AND LITERACY: FEET PROFILES

Examples of implementation with AT to support emergent literacy are provided with the following profiles of two children, Scott, age 3 years, and Abby, age 4 years. Each of these children have differing needs and abilities, and AT supports for literacy are designed to demonstrate individualized assessment and planning. The steps in the FEET process serve as a guide for teams to design effective AT strategies for literacy with young children. Examples of selected sections of the FEET forms are included in the following section. More extensively completed FEET forms and case material are included on the CD-ROM.

Scott: Preliteracy

Scott, age 3 years, was discussed in Chapter 5 where his FEET profile is presented more fully. As a young child with emergent communication skills, he is beginning to show interest in photos and access to books. His FEET profile is discussed here in the context of planning AT to support his development of preliteracy skills.

Family Concerns

Scott's parents reported their concerns regarding their son's limited verbal communication, something that he was beginning to do at 18 months and then discontinued. His parents and team have not arrived at a clear diagnosis or explanation for his apparent regression in development, although characteristics of autism spectrum disorders were discussed. Because Scott's parents are both well versed in computer technology, due to their professional backgrounds as computer programmers, they are eager to expand technology to support their son's development. In particular, they have begun to develop photograph albums on the computer of Scott's daily routines and software programs with simple stories and music. After consulting with the team, Scott's parents obtained additional programs tailored to meet his current needs and extend his attention through cause-and-effect programs and turn taking. Using the software features tool provided in Chapter 8, the team assisted Scott's parents in planning for his early literacy and language development. A complete summary of Scott's family concerns is included in Figure 5.2.

Child Characteristics

Through assessment conducted by each team member, including the early childhood teacher, occupational therapist, SLP, behavior specialist, and Scott's parents, the team identified Scott's current strengths and needs in all areas of development, including preliteracy skills. He demonstrated brief interest in picture books and computer-based books, touching pictures and vocalizing for short periods of time. A complete summary of Scott's communication modalities is shown in Figure 5.3.

Team Planning

After collecting each team member's assessment findings, a plan for further observation and intervention using AT strategies for literacy was developed. After considering his daily routines and enjoyable activities, the team further identified potential environments to focus on increased communication, social participation, and building his understanding of the words and sequences in familiar routines.

Within the context of his day, potential AT tools and strategies were identified. Regarding literacy, the team focused on Scott's emerging interest in books and his need to have experiences in handling books, manipulating props attached to pages of the book, turning pages, and being exposed to familiar vocabulary in pictures and print. Computer-based literacy experiences were also targeted when considering Scott's need to increase his sustained attention, realistic pictures, vocabulary repetition, musical themes, turn-taking opportunities, and ease of physical access using a touchscreen. A complete summary of team planning for Scott is included in Figure 5.4.

Observing Activity-Based Participation

Observations were conducted during storytime to gain further information about Scott's participation within the activity. FEET Form 4 (Figure 7.2) demonstrates Scott's brief

Observing activity-based participation						
Child's name: Scott Age: 3 Location/setting: Preschool				Date of observation: September 5 Observer: Parent, OT, SLP, early childhood education teacher Begin and end time: 11:00AM to 11:30AM		

ACTIVITY/ROUTINE Storytime with adult and one other child						
Child's physical position	**Child's actions (what he or she does)**	**Child's communication behaviors (gestures, sounds, gaze directed toward another person)**	**Barriers for child's participation**	**Expectations of typically developing peer in same activity/routine**	**Discrepancy between child and typically developing peer expectations**	**Possible AT solutions to increase child's participation**
Seated on floor with adult Old MacDonald or similar book with large pictures of animals in visual range Animals to represent pictures in basket nearby VOCA programmed with "Old MacDonald" song	Looks toward adult briefly when asked to name animals Looks at book, reaches toward pages of book Looks at other child briefly, moves away to another part of room Returns to story, shows curiosity with book and stuffed animals Randomly hits VOCA with lines in Old MacDonald	Shows interest in book, adult, and peer with brief eye gaze Reaches toward book, adult, and stuffed animal as if to request interaction or more of activity Vocalizes occasionally when hearing VOCA with recorded lines in "Old MacDonald" song	Attention to story, book, pictures, props, and peer are very fleeting Turning pages of book not accessible to child Method to communicate requests for more of the book, song, and activity are not available Adult responds more often to peer who is verbal	Peer of same age responds verbally, naming animals when teacher asks questions about pictures Sings "Old MacDonald" with teacher when looking at pages in book Chooses animal from basket when pause in song, "On his farm, he had a..." and names animal Offers stuffed animal to peer independently	Scott listens and looks briefly at book, does not name animals or verbalize Scott reaches toward book when teacher reads/sings song Scott vocalizes in response to song when others sing and on VOCA—imitation only Scott requires support to choose animal from basket Scott does not offer toys to peer	Tempo loop display board with laminated photographs of animals, one at a time to gain attention Link stuffed animal to photograph with Scott Provide animal prop to keep Scott engaged Support Scott to activate VOCA, taking turns signing OLD MACDONALD Photograph of next activity to support transition Develop visual schedule

Figure 7.2. FEET Form 4: Observing activity-based participation for Scott.

interest in books and VOCA tools programmed with repeated lines. He occasionally vocalized and responded when hearing voice output and being provided with opportunities to handle props associated with the book. Several barriers were found, which included Scott's limited attention to the activity and his difficulty turning pages of the book. Although he made infrequent attempts to communicate, adults often responded more to verbal peers in the shared book-reading activity. Additional AT solutions resulted from summarizing this observation, and the team moved toward developing AT tools to increase Scott's participation and learning in the following ways.

- Providing laminated photographs to highlight key words, animals, and events in the book to be placed one at a time on a black background (Velcro-friendly material).

- Assisting Scott to associate props such as stuffed animals and photographs during storytime.

- Cuing Scott to take turns with the VOCA, using repeated lines in stories.

- Providing a photograph cue for next activity to assist in making transitions and developing a visual schedule.

- Planning for stories to be linked to computer-based activities such as reading *Old MacDonald* in the storytime circle and using *Old MacDonald* software by SoftTouch at the computer station.

Action Planning

Following observation, the team completed their action plan to address his needs and implement appropriate AT tools. The team planned a literacy-rich environment to match Scott's needs and developed several AT approaches in response to his emerging interest in photographs, books, props, and computer-based stories. Specific AT tools to target literacy development with Scott include using a touchscreen on a laptop computer, computer software including My Own Bookshelf by SoftTouch, VOCA application with repeated lines from books, adapted books for ease of physical access, laminated photographs to attach to pages of books, and a collection of stuffed animals and objects to relate to the books selected for Scott. Scott's action plan is included in Figure 5.5.

Observation Trials

Implementing planned strategies using adapted books and computer-based literacy activities requires repeated observation. Through observation, the team determined the needs for further modifications and fine tuning in applying AT for literacy development with Scott. As Scott showed limited attention and was easily distracted, methods to limit choices and to increase cueing were implemented. AT strategies developed by Scott's team are illustrated in FEET Form 6 (Figure 7.3).

Evaluation Plan

Through repeated observation, the team determined appropriate levels of cueing and prompting to engage Scott with books, both in hard copy and computer formats. As his attention increased with AT tools, more complex story elements and vocabulary concepts were introduced, such as sequences of events, action words, location, and describing words. Expanding his vocabulary with pictures, photographs, and icons were consistently paired with print. Ongoing evaluation was conducted by the team, including Scott's parents, in order to determine the next level of literacy development and advancement in AT tools for Scott. Figure 7.4 shows a portion of completed FEET Form 7 for Scott, with a focus on literacy.

Abby: Emergent Literacy

Abby, age 4 years, was profiled in Chapter 6. As a young girl with developing language skills, she demonstrates emergent literacy skills as evidenced in her awareness of words and eagerness to engage with books. Her FEET profile is discussed with a focus on developing AT tools to support her literacy development.

AT observation trials				
AT support	**Activity 1:** Book corner **Date/time:** Monday/10AM	**Activity 2:** Outdoor play **Date/time:** Wednesday/9AM	**Activity 3:** Mealtime **Date/time:** Friday/11AM	**AT effectiveness**	**Modifications needed**
AT for literacy access Provide adapted books; detachable props to engage attention; photographs of actual objects to increase comprehension; computer-based photograph books	Adapted books with large photographs of animals and vehicles	Photographs of outdoor place; make baggie book with photos of Scott on swing and slide	Adapted book with photographs of favorite foods to take home	Scott attempted to turn the pages of the adapted book of zoo animals during a literacy center/free choice activity; he was able to point to one outdoor picture in the baggie book when teacher's aide made a verbal request	Add carpet squares to literacy corner; parents adapt computer to use PowerPoint photograph album at home; parents explore Mayer-Johnson Mobile Activity Player for book reading

Figure 7.3. FEET Form 6: AT observation trials focusing on literacy for Scott.

AT evaluation plan				
AT intervention goal	**AT materials implemented**	**Effectiveness of intervention**	**Need for modifications**	**Person responsible**
Literacy Book handling; attention and engagement with books; increase vocabulary comprehension and development; increase print awareness	Adapted books; baggie books; stabilize book with Velcro on back of book on rug surface; PowerPoint photograph albums of animals and switch interface	Scott was able to pick out a favorite book when given two choices and turn the first two pages; Scott was able to attend to the first page of the baggie book with familiar pictures but lost interest after that; Scott was able to choose between two animal pictures when given a choice of the lion and the giraffe	Carpet squares for stabilizing floor position in literacy center; slantboard with Velcro on back to stabilize placement; props to match photos in book for vocabulary development; flap books with surprise elements to maintain engagement; highlighter tape or eye lighter to emphasize key vocabulary words in books in which he shows interest	Parent, teacher, SLP, teacher's aide

Figure 7.4.   FEET Form 7: AT evaluation plan focusing on literacy for Scott.

Family Concerns

Since Abby was a toddler, her family has focused much of their time and resources on obtaining comprehensive services for her health and development. Now that she is approaching kindergarten, her family is concerned that she might not be able to participate with other children who are learning the alphabet and other early reading skills. Not only is Abby's communication a major priority for her family, but also her ability to read. FEET Form 1 (Figure 7.5) summarizes her family concerns.

Child Characteristics

The results of an assessment conducted by the team in Abby's special education preschool setting highlight a range of Abby's strengths and needs. Her physical access to use AT tools for communication, play, literacy, and computer use remain challenging due to her changing positioning needs. In the past year, Abby gained increased mobility by using a mobile walker, which contributed to increased initiation toward her peers and teachers in daily activities (Escobar, Leslie, & Wright-Ott, n.d.). Her extensive receptive vocabulary and reliable response to picture icons on her eye-gaze board further document her progress in language development. Abby has participated in the early childhood center, adjacent to her special education classroom, and often shows interest in printed words presented by the teacher. Up until this point in her education, Abby has experienced books on the computer and adapted books that are placed on a slantboard on her wheelchair tray. Her responses to specific sight words and letter sounds are inconsistent; thus, a focus on her emergent literacy skills became a central priority to her family and team.

Team Planning

In a meeting with Abby's parents, her preschool intervention team reviewed assessment findings and developed a plan to target literacy in the coming school year. Based on her interests, several books were selected from the preschool curriculum and related to themes that appear highly motivating for Abby. Topics such as animals, family members, dress up, and princess characters were identified as the basis for several thematic units for Abby. Each thematic unit was organized around a book, communication symbols on her eye-gaze board, a multiple-message VOCA, and computer program. A plan for further observation and intervention using AT strategies for literacy was developed. The completed team plan is demonstrated in FEET Form 3 on the CD-ROM.

Family concerns	
Child's name: Abby Age: 4 Parent's name: Naomi Address: 123 B Street Telephone: 888-666-4444	Agency name: Our Town Early Intervention Center Referral source: Hospital social worker Date of assessment: March 1 Team members: Early intervention team (social worker, nurse, PT, OT, SLP, early intervention specialist) Dominant language in home: English

AREAS ADDRESSED	FAMILY COMMENTS

Child strengths/needs
  Vision
  Hearing
  Communication
  Motor
	Abby smiles when familiar people enter into her field of vision, which appears quite strong. She uses her eyes to communicate often, and we have established a yes/no system with her to look up for yes and down for no. Her hearing seems normal because she responds to even faint noises inside and outside of our home. Due to her type of cerebral palsy, Abby does not move independently except to roll on the floor. Her arms, legs, and torso are quite stiff, yet often in a reflex pattern with constant movement. This makes it hard to hold her comfortably because she is always extending her legs and arms, which causes stiffening through her body. She does seem to understand much of what we say, smiling and looking at the people, toys, photographs, and even small drawings that we name with her.

Family daily routines and activities	Our days are so busy with getting the new infant up and getting Abby ready for the school bus to come. We often miss the bus and have to drive her to school and pick her up to get to extra therapy appointments. Her assessments are completed through the developmental services center in our county and are up to date. So most of our days are spent in the car, going to and from appointments. At home, we have some book/television time, meals, bathing, and bed. Sometimes, just relaxing on the sofa and floor with the whole family together is our only down time.
Child's preferred activities	Abby is playful and loves when her grandpa tickles her and plays with her. She is most comfortable playing on the floor, where she can reach for the ball or dolls to play with her older cousin.
Family priorities for child participation in daily activities	We need to have more toys and ways for her to play with her cousins and kids her age. I know there is more we can do to develop her communication beyond eye contact and facial expression. She fights her car seat and cries often when put into her wheelchair. I want to know what is going on in her head and how to help her be more comfortable physically.
Family use of technology and priorities	We bought a laptop computer for Abby to use on her third birthday. Our family is learning to use it, and several of the early intervention team members have put on different programs for her to use. She enjoys photographs of our family and books on the computer. She has a hard time reaching the switch to "click" on pictures and words.

Figure 7.5. FEET Form 1: Family concerns for Abby.

Observing Activity-Based Participation

Activities within Abby's school day were targeted for observation, specifically story-time, computer use, and peer play. After forming the team plan, observations were conducted during storytime to gain further information about Abby's participation within each activity. She demonstrated extended attention and interest in each book, when directly engaged with an adult. Her attention to books was limited when peers were enlisted to read with her, and this was attributed to her reliance on adults to provide choices regarding turning pages and emphasize specific components of the story.

Following initial observations, several AT strategies were developed to support Abby's attention and engagement with the books she chose with her eye-gaze communication system. Furthermore, specific skill areas were targeted, such as sound identification in targeted vocabulary words, sight word recognition, and association of printed words with picture icons. Several AT tools were identified for Abby, including enlarged print with pictures on the back of cards, storyboards with pictures and print to "act" out familiar songs and stories with peers, computer-based books to correspond with printed books, and computer programs such as Intellitools Classroom Suite to develop individualized phonological awareness activities for Abby. The completed FEET Form 4 is shown in Figure 7.6.

Observing activity-based participation						

Child's name: Abby
Age: 4
Location/setting: Preschool classroom

Date of observation: March 5
Observer: Parent, SLP, OT, PT
Begin and end time: 9:00AM to 9:20AM

ACTIVITY/ROUTINE Art activity with peer

Child's physical position	Child's actions (what he or she does)	Child's communication behaviors (gestures, sounds, gaze directed toward another person)	Barriers for child's participation	Expectations of typically developing peer in same activity/routine	Discrepancy between child and typically developing peer expectations	Possible AT solutions to increase child's participation
Seated in supported seating system with wheelchair, trunk, and head supports	Looks at art supplies on table	Looks at art supplies on table	Physical barriers to manipulate art materials	Peer reaches toward art supplies	Abby's initiation of communication is limited; waits for teacher to offer choices	Provide visual access to communication board with art activity items, actions, and place in visual proximity to use eye gaze
Table surface easily accessible to chair and Abby pushed up to table	Reaches toward art items	Looks toward teacher repeatedly, to request	Reaching toward art items, but was not able to grasp	Peer verbally requests colors, paper, glue, and glitter when needed	Vocal and verbal use of vocabulary to talk about art project lacking	VOCA device that allows Abby to choose art supplies and comment on peer's work
	Watches peer complete pasting shapes on paper and shaking glitter	Smiles at teacher in response to question about art activity	Reliance on adult to provide choices of art supplies rather than independently gaining access	Peer offers items to Abby to choose	Gestural and vocal communication only in response to teacher and peer questions	Set up scanning on multimessage device with switch location for Abby to activate START and STOP with scanning to select colors
	Remains focused on activity for entire observation	Looks toward her preferred color of paper, markers, and paint when offered choice of two items including glue stick, glitter shaker, paintbrush, and sponges to stamp shapes	Independent communication tools not available for Abby to indicate choices	Peer comments on location of shapes and what she is creating on paper	Turn taking with peer limited to peer initiations toward Abby	
			Adult responded to peer who was verbal, thus limiting turns for Abby to communicate	Peer answers questions about her glue, shape, and glitter project when asked by teacher		
				Peer shows her creation to Abby voluntarily		

Figure 7.6. FEET Form 4: Observing activity-based participation for Abby.

Action Planning

After observing and identifying further AT solutions to support Abby in her emergent literacy skills, specific steps were planned for implementation. A comprehensive approach to developing literacy was planned across several activities in her school day, adding printed sight words throughout her environment. For example, each area of the preschool such as the dress-up corner, book corner, kitchen area, and pizza parlor were labeled with printed words and picture icons to assist Abby and other students to associate print with their favorite activities and routines. A "star sound of the week" was featured and highlighted through the environment with scavenger hunts and other activities to find the star sound. Abby was provided with multiple means to communicate her awareness and identification of target sound using eye gaze, computer programs, a preprogrammed VOCA, and various noisemakers that were attached to her wheelchair tray. Increased opportunities for phoneme identification and print recognition in her activities and in the context of books, both in print and on the computer, contributed to her growing skills to gain phonological awareness. FEET Form 5 provides an example of the completed step in the FEET process and is found on the CD-ROM.

Observation Trials

Repeated observation of Abby's participation using the AT strategies across her day at school allowed the team to conduct ongoing assessment. Initially, Abby required frequent support and repeated cues to look at target words and sounds. Her communication system

AT observation trials					
AT support	**Activity 1:** Art & pretend play **Date/time:** Monday/10AM	**Activity 2:** Storytime **Date/time:** Wednesday/2PM	**Activity 3:** Mealtime **Date/time:** Friday/11AM	**AT effectiveness**	**Modifications needed**
AT for literacy access Provide adapted books with high-interest themes; reduce clutter in text and pictures; provide stable surface for books; select books with phonological targets for rhyming, alliteration, and sound awareness skills; provide eye-gaze method to select letter	Adapted books with princess themes; page turner that is soft and can be grasped easily (sponge roller, makeup sponge); repeated patterns in words with rhyming words, repeated lines, and fill-in words at end of phrases	Adapted books that teacher selects per curriculum theme with props; prop for Abby to handle and select to respond to specific word or line in book; VOCA activation to participate in repeated line in book/story; eye-gaze method to select letter to correspond with the sound the teacher names	Placemat for food items and choices during mealtime at home	Abby showed sustained attention and motivation to participate with adapted books, especially the princess theme; difficulty turning pages due to grasp and release problems; positioning difficult to maintain due to changing muscle tone; eye gaze to correct letter with sound required two to three prompts; accuracy improved quickly	Stabilize books on slantboard with Velcro backing on book; white-out tape on excess text; reduce clutter on page; highlighter tape on key text; large sponge rollers on edge of pages to grasp and turn; eye-gaze board with target words and letters for sound-awareness

Figure 7.7. FEET Form 6: AT observation trials focusing on literacy for Abby.

to date had emphasized picture systems with gradual transition from photographs to picture icons. Although text was always paired with pictures, her attention to print was not a major intervention focus. With the shift in priorities in her daily education, she appeared confused and became nonresponsive at times. Portions of completed FEET Form 6 (Figure 7.7) demonstrate AT strategies for literacy.

Evaluation Plan

Following repeated problem solving, Abby's teacher found that a combination of strategies worked to engage Abby in literacy activities. First, by emphasizing pictures in books and then making the link to print by showing printed words with each picture, Abby sustained her attention to the activity. Next, the teacher found that computer practice helped to reinforce the words and sounds that were targeted in the daily storytime. Abby demonstrated increased participation and success through a combined effort to introduce printed words gradually and connect daily literacy activities thematically. Abby's evaluation plan can be seen in Figure 7.8.

SUMMARY

Young children with complex disabilities face enormous challenges in gaining access to learning environments with their peers. Recognizing the importance of literacy as a key to continued learning drives much of today's education policy and programs. With highly sophisticated learning technology, opportunities exist for children formerly left out of learning to read and to write to overcome barriers.

AT evaluation plan				
AT intervention goal	**AT materials implemented**	**Effectiveness of intervention**	**Need for modifications**	**Person responsible**
Literacy Increase book handling with adapted access; increase language development regarding phrase complexity and length; increase print awareness; increase phonological awareness	Adapted books with page turners/fluffers using sponge materials; slantboard with 3-inch binder and microfiber to hold Velcro-adapted book; highlighter tape to focus on phrases in text; all reading curriculum to focus on initial phonological awareness and sound blending skills; computer-adapted books with MOB on favorite themes	Abby mastered eye gaze to appropriate letter targets to correspond to sounds with minimal prompting; physical access to turning pages is difficult	Alternative computer activation for book access with eye gaze or air-puff technology is recommended	SLP, teacher, parent

Figure 7.8. FEET Form 7: AT evaluation plan focusing on literacy for Abby.

This chapter took a developmental approach to becoming a literate individual, beginning with the contributions of domains of socialization, language acquisition, play, cognition, and physical and sensory abilities that establish the foundation for emergent literacy skills that lead to early literacy as the child begins school. Many aspects of preliteracy, including developmental foundations and emergent literacy competencies, were examined from the perspectives of researchers in the field of early childhood, including those who study typical child development and those who focus on children with disabilities. Key areas that contribute to becoming a reader and writer include early experiences with books, vocabulary knowledge, print awareness, phonological awareness, and mastery of the alphabetic principle.

AT tools and strategies that include adapted books, supported book reading, VOCA devices to provide speech output, and SGDs to generate speech were integrated into the context of sharing books with children with disabilities. The importance of deliberate, explicit teaching in the milieu of book reading was highlighted as a means to overcome barriers to literacy for children challenged by physical, cognitive, language, behavioral, and sensory disabilities. Links to curriculum standards for young children were made with additional infusion of AT within daily learning environments. In many ways, the state of the art in AT to ensure that all children have opportunities and appropriate interventions to become literate is just emerging. Finally, one approach or one type of technology cannot be expected to foster language and literacy, and literacy must be approached as a comprehensive system beginning early in life for all children.

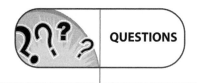

QUESTIONS

1. Describe the three major components of literacy development in young children. What are the relationships between each component?

2. Describe the contributions of early development in infancy to the emergent literacy experiences of young children. Identify particular challenges for children with physical, cognitive, language, and sensory disabilities.

3. Review the specific skills that contribute to phonological awareness in typical child development. What are particular challenges for children with complex communication needs and how might low-tech AT strategies reduce barriers?

4. Place yourself in the position of an early childhood teacher with both typically developing children and children with complex disabilities in your classroom. How will you design a learning center to promote emergent literacy for all children? Identify the theme of your center and a range of low- and high-tech AT tools and strategies you will use.

5. You are planning a shared book-reading session and thematic unit around spring, gardening, and nature in the backyard. What book will you choose and how will you implement at least three AT tools and strategies in your unit?

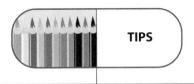

TIPS

❍ Identify the strengths and abilities of each child in your program regarding his or her exposure to books and emergent literacy development by consulting with the assessment team.

❍ Select appropriate books with a range of topics and vocabulary that are relevant to the experiences of the children in your program.

❍ Develop literacy kits around themes with a book, props, VOCA, and pictures of core and fringe vocabulary to have ready in the program.

❍ Take time to review Internet resources available with ready-made communication boards and adaptations for most children's books.

❍ Consult families regarding their children's favorite books and incorporate parents in shared reading activities.

❍ Identify traditions of literacy among the families of children you serve and incorporate their favorite stories, songs, and oral histories into the classroom.

❍ Conduct a thematic unit around families and develop individual narratives with family input, photographs, and stories.

❍ Create homemade books with English and the primary languages of families you serve.

❍ Plan to provide explicit instruction for phonological awareness within the classroom in small groups with selected books as a focus.

❍ Create visual tools to develop a literacy-rich classroom setting through photographs and text, a word wall, and literacy tools in all learning centers.

8

Assistive Technology and Computer Access

Technology applications have revolutionized how we learn about the world. In the 1990s, personal computers entered the mainstream of education and increased the ease and efficiency of writing composition. Only since the 2000s has the advent of online resources and software development offered new and innovative approaches to entertainment, recreation, social networking, and learning. Children have access to incredible amounts of information via the Internet. Families and young children alike are bombarded with new and innovative computer applications to enhance early childhood development. Software programs are now available that teach infants and toddlers cause and effect and preschoolers their alphabet skills. Typical households have at least one computer available for playing computer games and searching the Internet. Modes of communication have been altered due to technology innovations. E-mail, texting, social networking via the Internet, and video teleconferencing are all commonplace in homes, schools, and communities. Communication has been expanded to include multimodal avenues for connecting with others by using computers and computer applications.

Exposing young children to the benefits of computers has been a slower developing process due to developmental considerations concerning readiness for acquiring computer skill and understanding software content. As discussed by Vernadakis, Avgerinos, Tsitskari, and Zachopoulou (2005), preschoolers need not be left out of the information technology explosion because of their apparent lack of cognitive, social, behavioral, communication, and motor capacity for learning. Although there has been a lack of rigorous studies on the benefits of CAI over traditional methodologies for young children with disabilities, some efforts hold promise for offering technology strategies as another approach to supporting access to curriculum for children who may not learn as fast and efficiently with more typical teaching instruction and learning tools (Hitchcock & Noonan, 2000; Hutinger, 1996; Kinsley & Langone, 1995; Lau, Higgins, Gelfer, Hong, & Miller, 2005; Mioduser, Tur-Kaspa & Leitner, 2000; Vernadakis et al., 2005). This chapter reviews the literature that supports computer use with young children and highlights the benefits of the technology option for gaining access to inclusive settings and embedded learning opportunities. Furthermore, the chapter describes computer readiness skills and the various skill domains in computer use. A section is devoted to adaptations available for child positioning and computer access. Another section is devoted to software considerations, how to select appropriate software for young children with disabilities, and resources available for various software applications. The chapter culminates with examples of computer and software adaptations using information from the FEET assessment model from previous case studies introduced in the book.

RATIONALE FOR COMPUTERS AND YOUNG CHILDREN

Although computer use as a teaching tool is prevalent in K–12 education, there is a lack of consensus in the early childhood literature (Watson, Nida, & Shade, 1986) as to the benefits of computer access for young children. Other studies have advanced the notion that computers can be as effective as other methodologies in teaching preacademic subjects and increasing opportunities for peer interactions in play (Hitchcock & Noonan, 2000; Mioduser, Tur-Kaspa & Leitner, 2000; Vernadakis et al., 2005). Computers make learning more accessible for all children and, in particular, those who learn better with pictures and sounds. In 1996, the NAEYC published a set of guiding policies concerning technology use with young children. The position supported technology's role in supporting the education of young children by encouraging teachers to investigate the benefits of technology use and better prepare themselves to incorporate technology into their teaching strategies. When developmentally appropriate software is selected, developmental trajectories for play and learning are enhanced. The policies emphasized that software programs do not replace sound early childhood practices such as multisensory exploration through play and creativity. Furthermore, the document promoted integrating technology into children's daily learning environments. The statement challenged educators to assure equitable access to computers by all, not just the students who are most successful with other modes of learning that receive computer use as a reward for success. Using computers in the classroom is influenced by teacher attitudes as well as teacher knowledge and skills (Judge, 2000). The document included a separate section on children with special needs, with an emphasis on computers as a bridge to inclusive classroom opportunities and a vehicle promoting independence. The policy promoted the feature matching concept as critical in not only infusing technology throughout curricular supports and teaching practices overall, but also linking specific characteristics of software features to the needs of the user. Although the technology policy was developed in the mid-1990s, it still provides a baseline for early childhood educators to consider when promoting computer use with young children.

In a seminal work on recommended practices for young children with disabilities and their families, a chapter is devoted to recognizing the importance of professionals accessing technology to support learning in the early years (Stremel, 2005). The practices are defined across three technology domains including assistive, instructional, and informational. Recommended practice reinforces the literature that emphasizes technology use in intervention programs as a way to increase development and as a vehicle to family guidance and support. One of the main issues concerning computer applications for young children, however, is the lack of teacher awareness of what is available on the market and the exponential nature of software development that is occurring in all facets of technology-based curriculum and teaching materials (Mistrett, 2005; Parette, Boeckmann, & Hourcade, 2008). As mentioned by Parette et al., educators miss opportunities to implement successful software programs that enhance literacy and other early academic skill developmental areas due to the overabundance of new software programs. In addition, the lack of research along with readily available information on the highlights of specific software programs fuels the continued underutilization of computer-based learning tools in the preschool classroom. Furthermore, teachers lack adequate training in computer use themselves along with integrating it into their teaching strategies. When surveying teachers concerning their perceptions of computer use with young children, Judge (2000) found that even if teachers are comfortable with computer use, they may not have the tools to weave software programs into various curricular areas such as play, literacy, art, and other daily events.

Vernadakis et al. (2005) emphasized that computers and technology have become an integral part of daily living and there is no reason for young children to be left out of the digital world. In their review of several international studies on the effectiveness of computer use for young children, they concluded that computers provide an avenue for learning a wide range of preacademic skills at the preschool level. They emphasized the interactive nature of teaching with computers, a known benefit to learning. Children learn best through multimethod and multimodal learning techniques. The computer offers an interactive platform for teaching skills, above and beyond some traditional educational approaches, which Vernadakis et al. agreed is probably the most important finding of their review. Another positive outcome to computer use in teaching young children is the self-paced process of various software programs that allows children who may be functioning at different developmental levels to move along at their prescribed acquisition speed. In addition, attention span has been shown to increase through the use of computer programs (Vernadakis et al., 2005). Finally, computers are interesting, spark curiosity, and are part of the everyday fabric of the 21st century. Hitchcock and Noonan (2000), in their comparative study of computer-assisted instruction (CAI) and teacher-assisted instruction (TAI), summarized that computers motivate children to explore problem-solving activities through activating items on the touchscreen or keyboard. The child-centered approach, which computers offer, capitalizes on increasing child independence, satisfaction with learning, and self-reliance, all prerequisite skills for participating in inclusive learning environments. Although the literature is evolving in examining the positive effects of computer use with young children, there is a small body of research that has demonstrated gains in preacademic skill development (Hitchcock & Noonan, 2000; Mioduser et al., 2000; Parette, Hourcade et al., 2000) and justifies thoughtful consideration for supporting young children with disabilities in inclusive educational settings.

COMPUTERS AS A TOOL TO SUPPORT DEVELOPMENT IN ALL AREAS

Young children with disabilities are sometimes left out of the information highway due to difficulties with easily accessing computer hardware and learning how to navigate software programs through trial and error and casual observation. NAEYC (1996) provided the foundation for teachers to consider computer use as an effective method for increasing young children's cognition, social development, and independence, and Campbell et al. (2006) provides a review of six evidence-based research studies on the effectiveness of computer use for infants and young children. Although some benefit was indicated, researchers found that beliefs and knowledge regarding computer use with very young children influenced their lack of consideration of CAI. Similarly, Vernadakis et al. (2005) offered multiple international studies that have demonstrated the potential for increasing preacademic and social skills through the adoption of CAI. Findings included increased attention span for children using the computer, learning gains from the use of a vocabulary computer program, and higher math test scores achieved by preschoolers exposed to CAI activities.

As Parette, Hourcade, and Heiple (2000) suggested, keyboarding and computer skills may need to be taught to children with disabilities through more structured training on how to use the computer. They furthered the concept of computer use for young children with disabilities by emphasizing the link between computers and software that supports a more constructivist notion of learning in classrooms where child-directed approaches are embraced. Computer use then becomes a gateway to learning by offering additional pathways of curriculum and curricular supports found in many software applications for young children, such as phonological awareness and letter recognition skills. Mioduser et al. (2000) indicated that CAI provides an avenue for young children at risk to increase their reading competency comparable with same-age peers using written materials alone. In their study of CAI, they compared traditional teaching modes of learning with CAI and found not only that children's reading skills had benefitted but also their motivation toward learning improved. Similarly, Hitchcock and Noonan (2000) supported the use of CAI with preschoolers with disabilities when involved in teaching shapes, colors, and numbers. Software programs that have been rigorously researched may enhance overall learning success in many preacademic areas as well as increase social-emotional capacity for success and self-confidence. The next sections provide an overview of the studies linking computer use with young children with disabilities' development and academic performance.

Literacy (Reading and Writing: Early Exposure to a Keyboard)

Computer programs and peripherals provide tools for young children with disabilities to engage in literacy-rich learning activities typically out of their reach due to limitations of access. A child that may have sensory impairments such as hearing and vision problems or lack attention for sustained participation may benefit from exploring learning concepts in a computer-based format in which an individualized approach can be geared toward the needs of the learner.

Parette et al. (2008) provided an overview on the effectiveness of using software to promote literacy development in young children, including making a transition to symbol recognition in learning to read. Children at risk of reading difficulties often experience the most difficulty in learning to read due to the challenge of connecting the symbol of printed text in words and letters to represent auditory comprehension and representation of spoken words. Parette et al. identified strategies to use picture icons with text to support awareness of symbols as representation of words and to assist in developing print awareness. The authors reviewed specific software available on the market that promotes literacy skills, such as Writing with Symbols (WWS), Boardmaker with Speaking Dynamically Pro, and Clicker V Software. The article provided examples of applications using WWS to enable children to "read" text with visual support of picture symbols paired with words. In addition to generating stories about daily activities and supporting comprehension of familiar books, WWS can be used for children to generate their own stories about their experiences, thus creating personal narratives. One of the main recommendations emphasized is for early childhood educators to become familiar with the availability of software with some research-based support to increase literacy skills in young children.

Hutinger, Bell, Daytner, and Johanson (2005), in a technical report reviewing findings from a nationally funded study of an early technology curriculum for young children with disabilities, described a technology curriculum used to increase literacy skills in preschool children with disabilities. Results showed that the availability of an integrated technology curriculum increased access to literacy-rich learning activities and benefitted children with disabilities. Children demonstrated gains in literacy and technology skills greater than the comparison group. Other behaviors were noted as well, including developing computer-related vocabulary, engaging in conversations about the activity, problem solving, making judgments, improving listening skills, and increasing social interactions among peers regarding the software program. Children demonstrated turn taking and providing assistance to each other during wait times. The literacy technology curriculum revealed benefits beyond literacy instruction. Research has provided information on the effectiveness of CAI for preliteracy skill acquisition in young children and its value for creating avenues for exploring literacy environments typically not readily available to young children with disabilities. Computers may be the most important tool of the 21st century for bridging the literacy gap for young children with disabilities. This, in turn, moves pedagogies away from a focus on developmental skill building to exposure to higher level cognitive activities such as literacy. Literacy at any level is a gateway to the world of learning, and computers are the vehicle to transport children with disabilities down the path toward full inclusion.

Language

In addition to software programs emphasizing the development of preacademic prerequisites and attention to the task, there are a few companies that offer language acquisition software including Laureate Learning Systems and SoftTouch. Moore and Calvert (2000) found that preschoolers with autism demonstrated greater vocabulary gains with a software program compared with individualized teacher-directed instruction. Researchers have shown that language intervention software offers a methodology for increasing language skills similar to training provided in a clinical setting (Sweig Wilson, Fox, & Pascoe, 2008). Grant and Singer (2004) observed software use with infants and toddlers over a 3-year period and found that the staff reported increased vocal output during computer activities as compared with other infant development activities at the center, and the researchers were able to quantify the observation during several single case study designs. The researchers found that the touchscreen provided the most uninhibited access for young children. Having multiple formats to develop language increases the likelihood that children who are nonverbal or possess limited verbal abilities such as those with autism or developmental delays will be exposed to language development in various ways and in a multitude of educational settings.

Play

Not only are young children with disabilities often left out of preacademic activities, but their exploration with peers during play is also inhibited. Much of the focus of the research on computer use with young children with disabilities has focused on CAI for increasing computer skills and preacademic development. Lau et al. (2005) investigated how involving teachers in the computer activity increases social interactions in young children with disabilities. Lau et al. indicated that teacher-facilitated computer use increased socialization and cooperative play among typically developing children and those with disabilities. Previous research demonstrated that children with and without disabilities exhibited more cooperative play when using computers over toys (McCormick, 1987). Lau et al. used a peer-reviewed software program called Elmo's Workshop that allowed the children the freedom to create various artistic designs. They had the opportunity to select colors, characters, and other animated objects to build various pictures. The open-ended structure of the software allowed children opportunities to engage in conversations and take turns using the mouse. Because children with disabilities tend to have limited social interactions as compared with same age peers, Lau et al. recommended using a computer activity to encourage more appropriate peer exchanges through the modality of the software program. Considering the computer as a means to building more sophisticated interactions between peers with and without disabilities provides another social skill intervention approach to increasing social behavioral reper-toires in young children with disabilities.

Hitchcock and Noonan (2000) found that CAI with teacher-facilitated instruction on computer use was effective not only in promoting early academic performance but also in motivating children to enjoy the event. Hitchcock and Noonan noted laughter from participants when effectively pressing the keyboard or touchscreen to activate a response. Thus, computer technology offers an approach to increasing preacademic, social, and play skills in young children with disabilities.

Another study conducted by Calvert, Strong, and Gallagher (2005) examined the aspect of control over computer use and the resulting gains in attention and involvement in the task. User control was found to be an important engagement feature for children's attention and motivation during computer activities. Control is a behavior necessary to develop self-regulation skills in young children. When a child has a disability that inhibits his or her opportunities for choice making, learned helplessness results. Furthermore, the study revealed that attention was higher when the activity was child directed.

In summary, research focused on computer use in young children is still in the form-ative stages of testing and development. Studies since the 2000s have revealed potential for adopting computer technology to enhance young learner's exposure to preacademic skill building through programs that emphasize an interactive, problem-solving approach coupled with drill and practice opportunities. Some studies have demonstrated benefits to teaching preacademic skills using computers over and above more traditional methodolo-gies using written materials. Possibilities abound for integrating technology into teaching methods aimed at introducing preacademic concepts to young children. More research is needed to confirm computer technologies as a recommended practice for young children. As mentioned by Vernadakis et al. (2005), teachers need to recognize that technologies may offer an interactive and motivating multimodal learning milieu in which children advance their performance at higher rates than with just a single teaching method alone. With this recognition comes a willingness to consider alternative forms of teaching and practicing learning concepts through various computer mediums. As with other types of teaching methodologies, computer technology requires some training and time devoted to becoming computer savvy prior to interweaving technology approaches into typical teaching strategies. In addition, learning the mechanics of the computer is only a first step in mastering the use of the technology. Teachers need to be well versed in software eval-uation to assure the appropriateness of computer applications and various web resources for enhancing CAI. Mioduser et al. (2000) remarked that technology is not a stand-alone product for successful teaching practices and needs to be thoughtfully reflected on as a means to expanding evidence-based pedagogies recognized as recommended practice for young children. Technology is a means for young children to learn preacademic skills and social-emotional strategies for successfully participating in multiple learning arenas.

For a young child with a disability, computers may provide the necessary tools for cap-italizing on the critical early learning periods often missed due to limitations in language, motor, and cognitive challenges. As young children gain readiness for learning about their world, children with disabilities need supports to alleviate the disconnect between their gaps in development and their access to learning situations usually reserved for those who are ready developmentally. This chapter emphasizes that children with disabilities may not always be ready for engaging in preacademic tasks and initiating peer interactions. By set-ting the stage for learning through accessing computer technologies, however, a window into the exciting world of early childhood education may be opened for them. As empha-sized by Hutinger et al. (2005), computer applications act as a way to even the playing ground for young children with disabilities by providing the tools necessary for them to gain access to daily routines and learning experiences. In their review of the literature on computer use with young children with disabilities, Hutinger et al. emphasized that research and practice reveal that children with disabilities are more successful when able to access various technologies than those children not exposed to computers. The next segment of the chapter focuses on the first step to linking a young child with disabilities to technologies—physical access.

CHILD CONSIDERATIONS FOR COMPUTER USE

Through team-based assessment, including a review of child characteristics and gathering input from families, considering using a computer begins with information about the child's physical positioning for the task. As emphasized by Drescher (2009), positioning at the workstation is the first step in determining access to a computer. Depending on the type of disability, the child may or may not have adequate trunk control and stability to maintain a seated position, a typical requirement for computer access. Both occupational and physical therapists provide information about a child's positioning and physical capabilities and help determine the best supports for computer access. Other developmental disabilities such as autism may have positioning issues related to sensory disruptions such as the type of chair the child is seated in or the visual, external environment surrounding the computer space. A child may have adequate structural support and head and trunk control, but the amount of time the child can maintain the position may be limited due to muscle weakness or condition. A child with Down syndrome may have the ability to sit in a chair but not maintain the position required for a long term period. The FEET profile provides information on the child's physical strengths and needs along with other developmental skills that inform the team's consideration for positioning. While observing the activity, the team explores the present seating options for the child and considers other potential supports that may provide the most advantageous milieu for computer use.

Seating and Positioning

In Step 5 of the FEET process, action planning begins with positioning. For computer access, a child will need to be able to reach a mouse, keyboard, or touchscreen. A child will need a seating option with maximal trunk and head support. Focusing on learning versus continually adjusting the seating arrangement is the key to effective positioning. An occupational therapist can evaluate the need for physical supports such as an adapted chair to enable the child to reach the computer screen, mouse, switch, and/or keyboard. There may be several ways for maintaining the child's balance in the chair. Often, a typical chair can be adapted with a nonskid surface attached to the chair legs such as shelf liner or furniture bumpers and several rolled towels placed under the child's arms and around the trunk and head to create an adapted version of a chair already available in the environment. Gel-filled wrist supports are also available that can be used for supporting arms and other body parts of young children with disabilities. Beginning with what everyone else uses and considering the least intrusive adaptations is the easiest and most sensible place to begin. In the home environment where laptops may be more frequently available, a lap tray on a couch may be more feasible than setting up a simulated workstation in the room where the child might then require additional equipment, furniture, and materials to be seated correctly. Once the child is comfortably seated in a chair with supports, such as Velcro straps across his or her chest to keep him or her maintained in the chair, the team can identify the type of mechanism for computer control that best suits the individual's learning, cognitive, and physical needs.

Another aspect of the seating arrangement is the child's proximity to other children who may be involved in the activity or interested in participating in the event. Computer use can be an individual learning opportunity that might include cause-and-effect software or basic preacademic drill and practice. The computer station can also be a location for peer interaction and social skill development such as turn taking and reciprocal communication of the fun experienced with the computer program. The team needs to examine the location of the computer in proximity to other daily events such as using the actual computer station that all children have access to or setting up a new computer center to include accommodations for the child with the disability and others in the program. Again, by starting with what is typical for all children, incorporating a universal design principle to computer stations will inevitably assure participation from all children.

Vision and Hearing Concerns

When the child is positioned comfortably in a seating arrangement that supports access to the computer hardware, some adjustments may need to be made so the screen is located for optimal viewing. The child needs to be situated about a foot away from the computer with an eye level corresponding to the top mid-portion of the screen for effective viewing opportunities. Mistrett and Goetz (2009) suggested that when a child is playing with a computer while sitting on a parent's lap, a viewing level of 10–15 inches away from the screen is appropriate. When the appropriate viewing distance is determined, the child is ready for piloting the various software programs targeted for young children's developmental levels and interests.

In addition to the physical positioning in the chair or lap, the team has gathered data on the sensory needs of the child, including vision and hearing status. The position of the child in the seat needs to be angled in such a way that capitalizes on his or her visual strengths. If a child sees well from a peripheral view, then the chair can be tilted to adjust for the viewing field. If a child has difficulty seeing from a distance, then the chair can be arranged to be as close to the computer screen as possible by using an adjustable height table, a slantboard, or a tray that brings the computer closer to the child's face. The actual screen can be adapted to use large fonts or visual highlighting to discriminate between the items displayed. There are also magnifying systems that can be incorporated into the visual screen portion of the computer.

For a child with either a unilateral or bilateral hearing loss, the team would need to adjust the angle of the chair toward the speaker system and may need other adaptations depending on the level of hearing loss. The volume control may be adjusted to accommodate for minor hearing difficulties. An SLP may have additional suggestions for positioning the child for gaining access to sound.

Fine Motor Control Options

Once the child is comfortably seated for computer access, the team needs to evaluate his or her fine motor control and identify the most appropriate type of computer mouse, keyboard, or alternative to maneuvering the computer activity. Adaptations and alternatives are available for the mouse, keyboard, and screen. If the child is unable to use a standard mouse, then the next alternative might be to build a simple mouse house to provide one-hand touch to clicking the mouse. There are also a variety of switch interfaces that allow basic switches to be plugged into the computer via an external port. The team may want to invest in a sampling of mouse alternatives such as a trackball, touchpad, or touchscreen. A whiteboard on which the child can write and the message appears on the screen is a more expensive alternative but is becoming more available at schools.

Speech-recognition software offers children with limited fine motor access but adequate speech development another alternative to a mouse. An eye-gaze system or laser-activated coin forehead disk are other options for children with limited to no fine motor abilities. The systems require some head control to maintain gaze on a particular item on the screen. The touchscreen may be the easiest adaptation to start with for young children that are just learning computer skills. If a child is familiar with switch use, however, and has already been assessed for a particular switch device, then starting with what he or she is already familiar with and using in daily learning activities is recommended. As the user advances to more complex software programs, additional hardware may be more appropriate, such as keyboard adaptations. The type of hardware needs to support the skill level of the child. A touchscreen used for cause and effect and choice making may not be as appropriate for a child ready to explore higher level problem-solving software programs. Table 8.1 reviews the various types of computer peripherals and interfaces that may be beneficial for a young child unable to access the computer. The list of example devices covers some of the products either free or available for purchase from various companies. The list is not exhaustive but offers a place to start.

Questions to Guide Arranging the Physical Environment for Computer Access

Seating and Positioning

1. Where is the computer located in the room?
2. What other areas might be better suited for locating the computer for optimal access by all?
3. Does the child require special seating to be positioned with body at midline? If so, what types of seating are available?
4. Are there basic adjustments to the seat that would allow access?
5. What types of materials are already available that might support the child's seating position?
6. Will the computer be available to all children even after the seating and positioning adjustments have been completed?

Visual and Hearing Concerns

1. Does the visual or auditory status of the child potentially inhibit access to the computer programs?
2. What visual supports are needed to adequately view the computer screen and observe other participants in the activity?
3. What are the auditory supports that need to be provided to experience the sound portion of the computer program?

Fine Motor Control

1. Describe the child's fine motor capabilities for reaching, grasping, and maintaining hold on an object.
2. Can the child move and manipulate a computer mouse without adjustments?
3. If adjustments are necessary, has the team explored an adapted mouse or other peripherals such as a switch interface device or a touchscreen?

Table 8.1. Computer adaptations and mouse alternatives

Type	Description	Uses	Example devices
Mouse house	Handmade container for the mouse	Creates a larger platform for mouse click	http://www.lindaburkhart.com
Pointers	Alternative to finger pointing	Provides a low-technology tool for mouse or touchscreen pointing	Head pointers http://www.scoe.net/seeds/AT Pointers, mouth sticks http://www.sammonpreston.com
Trackball	Large ball that is moved with the hand or fingers	Allows for larger fine motor movement to activate mouse click	Wave switch http://www.ablenetinc.com Big Track http://www.infogrip.com Enabling Devices http://www.enablingdevices.com Sam Trackball http://www.rjcooper.com Indemouse http://www.acctinc.ca
Touchpad	Touch-sensitive pad usually found on laptops but available as external devices	User brushes his or her hand/fingers across the pad to move the mouse	Touchpad http://www.infogrip.com
Touchscreen	Screen attaches to computer screen	Touch-sensitive screen allows direct touch to the computer program	TouchWindow http://www.riverdeep.net/edmark Magic Touch http://www.rjcooper.com 3M Micro Touch http://www.solutions.3m.com
Built-in touchscreen	Touch-sensitive screen built in to a computer	Laptop with touch-sensitive, rotating screen	Microsoft Company http://www.microsoft.com Mobile Activity Player http://www.mayer-johnson.com
Foot mouse	Mouse controlled by the foot	Offers a child with foot control a way to navigate the computer	No Hands Mouse http://www.infogrip.com Foottime Foot Mouse http://www.visualtechnology.info/technology/the-foot-mouse/
Head mouse	Mouse controlled by head movements using a reflective dot	The dot can be worn on glasses, the forehead, or the bill of a hat to move the cursor or online keyboard coupled with a switch	Tracker Pro HeadMouse Extreme http://www.orin.com Head Master System http://www.prentrom.com
Eye-gaze mouse	Uses eyes to move cursor on the screen	Provides users with functional eye movement to control the cursor	My Tobii http://www.tobii.com ERICA http://www.dynavoxtech.com

Device	Description	Company/Website
Mouth and other body parts mouse	Joystick game controller adapted with switch jacks that can be used with body parts, including the mouth — An alternative to a switch device for controlling computer programs	Jouse2 Joystick http://www.jouse.com; Quadjoy for mouth or chin http://www.quadjoy.com; Lipsync http://www.acctinc.ca
Switch-adapted mouse	Mouse that has ⅛-inch plugs for two switches — Provides access to a regular mouse by plugging in a switch directly to the mouse for switch access	Infogrip Inc. http://www.infogrip.com; R. J. Cooper http://www.rjcooper.com
USB switch interface	Multiple outlets for switch plug-ins — Interface allows for using switches to activate the cursor	Crick Company http://www.cricksoft.com; Switch Interface Pro http://www.donjohnston.com; Switch Interface Plus http://www.quizworks.com; Switch Hopper http://www.rjcooper.com
Switch click	Switch mouse with a USB port plug — Plugs directly into the computer USB port	TASH Inc./Ablenet Company http://www.tashinc.com
Speech-recognition software	Transcribes the spoken word into text — Children with age-appropriate speech articulation and language skills can use it instead of a keyboard	Dragon Speaking Naturally http://www.nuance.com
Keyboard adaptations	Overlays to change the texture, size, or symbols on the keyboard keys; plastic covers protect from moisture and dirt — Modifies keyboards to provide alternatives to standard letter keyboarding	Enlarged and programmable keyboard http://www.intelliKeys.com; Big Keys http://www.rjcooper.com; Online Keyboards; Onscreen http://www.comfort-software.com; WiViK on-screen keyboard http://www.wivik.com; REACH Interface Author http://www.ahf-net.com/reach.htm
Plastic covers	Plastic skins can be purchased through most computer companies	
Other hardware possibilities	Tablets; Other new technologies — Tablet laptop computers without a keyboard and mouse	Microsoft and Apple Companies http://www.microsoft.com http://www.apple.com; AbleData http://www.abledata.com

4. What are the results of the trials for using one or more of the computer mouse and/or alternatives?

5. Has the team considered what tool might be used after the existing mouse alternative needs to be changed due to the needs and skill levels of the child in order to ensure that they move to the next level of computer sophistication?

SKILL DOMAINS FOR COMPUTER USE

Just as children develop skills for play, communication, and learning, there are specific competencies to consider for computer use. The computer environment can be experimented with and can provide novel opportunities to explore sensory input through seeing, touching, hearing, and moving. Once the child's sensory skills have developed, language and learning follows. When a child has limitations with sensory inputs and outputs, such as low vision or hearing deficits, cognitive delays, communication difficulties, and physical challenges, the computer may provide the means to growing and learning in a simulated environment. Computers offer opportunities for participation in play and learning not otherwise accessible to children with disabilities. There are specific developmental skills needed for accessing a computer. The lack of competencies does not forego a child's exposure to computer use, however. Computers are a way to access multiple learning settings. An awareness of the basic skill sets for moving from basic cause-and-effect software to advanced problem-solving software allows for the child to experience age- and developmentally appropriate computer software programs geared toward their individual learning needs.

The following section presents the various developmental areas addressed when exploring computer use. Although the categories follow a developmentally appropriate age progression of acquisition, teachers and parents need to expose children with more significant disabilities to a variety of computer hardware and software programs. When computers may be the only vehicle to connecting with the world around them, it is critical not to limit exposure to early sensory tasks alone. The caveat is offered as a way to approach computer use in a multifaceted process by beginning with identifying both age-appropriate and developmentally targeted technology while keeping in mind the individual child characteristics that may inhibit accomplishing simple computer tasks such as cause and effect in a linear fashion. In this way, young children with more complex disabilities will have opportunities to explore computers similar to other children without being confronted by access issues. Mistrett and Goetz (2009) reminded readers that children do not need to know how to use a mouse or keyboard to experience cause and effect. The easiest approach to engaging a young child with a disability to participate in a computer activity is helping them discover that touching any key will elicit a response. Once a child is able to determine simple causality, he or she is able to generalize to other software programs and move through other computer skill sets as described here.

Attention (Perception and Sensory Exploration)

At the initial stage of computer use, the child needs to have a brief attention to what is happening on the screen. Software programs that have one or two pictures incorporating simple actions are preferred over programs with a multitude of colors and effects. If abstract caricatures are too advanced to initiate a brief look or focus on the screen activity, then young children enjoy real objects and pictures of family members and friends. Software programs that allow the user to import familiar pictures may spark attention to the task. Attention grows as the child becomes accustomed to the screen.

Cause and Effect (Early Cognition)

Simple cause and effect is the next developmental progression for computer use. Software programs available for young children, including children with disabilities, emphasize cause-and-effect competence. The child may touch the screen or hit the keyboard and notice a change in the screen graphics. The first attempts at cause and effect on the computer are usually random. Beginning software programs typically include options for an immediate response on screen when a child hits any key or touchscreen. Cause and effect is the basic computer skill needed to build later problem-solving strategies. Providing a variety of software programs that include cause-and-effect functions ensures that the child will enjoy the experimentation and not lose interest in the routine. Eventually the child learns that something happens when a key is pressed or the screen is touched.

Turn Taking (Social Skills)

Turn taking with the parent encourages social interactivity with young children. The child learns that an action occurs when the parent or caregiver touches the keyboard, mouse, or touchscreen. The child notes the action and understands that by waiting, he or she will have an opportunity to attempt the action. Turn taking with parents and caregivers builds confidence early on that can be transferred to situations involving other children. For children with disabilities, turn taking in naturally occurring social situations is not always easily accessible to them due to their communication, cognitive, or other developmental delays. Learning turn taking on the computer provides a vehicle for early socialization not otherwise available to them in free-play activities.

Social Interaction Between Adult and Child (Social)

Building relationships with familiar adults provides the foundation for learning and developing other social skills, such as interacting with peers. The California Learning Foundations for Infants and Toddlers (California Department of Education [CDE], 2009) emphasized fostering relationships between adult and child as the basis for all other development. Learning to rely on a caregiver for assistance early on paves the way for seeking out support from an adult in a classroom setting and understanding nuances in social situations with peers in play. A young child will need the encouragement and guidance from a familiar adult and possibly additional physical support in order to participate in a computer game or activity. Grant and Singer (2004), in their multiple case studies of infants and toddlers computer use, found that when changing a teacher's affect during a computer game, did not change the children's engagement with the computer activity, but altered their social exchange with the teacher. The children tried to enlist the teacher in the activity when the teacher's manner was more subdued versus animated and engaging. They found that CAI within planned adult–child social interactions offered positive benefits to young children with disabilities through planned and engaging exchanges during computer use. The relationship between adult and child may begin with the adult as sole initiator of the social activity. As the adult and child work together to solve the cause-and-effect software, the relationship becomes more reciprocal. Once the child feels comfortable interacting with the adult, the behaviors gleaned from the one-to-one situation may be applied to interactions with other peers. The computer event allows for modeling of appropriate behavioral responses to frustration with the activity potentially not available to young children with disabilities in typical play routines, which are usually less structured and more difficult to script sequentially.

Choice Making and Sequences of More than Two (Cognitive)

After grasping basic causality with a computer, the child learns how to choose between two objects on the screen with an increase in difficulty as he or she becomes proficient in sets of two. Once a child can click and cause a frog to eat a fly, he or she can try programs that require more than one option, such as a cat meowing or a cow mooing. Item matching on the screen is another type of activity that provides exposure to choice making on the computer. Moving from single choice to multiple choices promotes the development of problem-solving skills. Similarly, once a child can select between more than one item, computer scanning can be introduced. Software programs are available that include a scanning component. The child touches a switch or screen to indicate a choice when the cursors lands on the item of choice. Choice making is a critical feature required for using more sophisticated software programs.

Vocabulary Building with Sounds, Words, and Pictures (Communication)

Young children can be introduced to basic vocabulary through computer programs. A child with limited verbal skills has the opportunity to build vocabulary using this medium. Through repeated exposure to a range of words presented auditorially and visually, the child learns to discriminate and choose. The software program provides repetition of basic vocabulary not always available in other daily routines. Different pictures are displayed with a voice output labeling the action or object presented. Beginning software programs include basic vocabulary found in young children's language. Although other children may be speaking in full sentences by the time they are 2 years old, this may not be the case for a child with a cognitive, communication, or physical disability. Real pictures of items in the environment can be added to software programs, such as My Own Bookshelf, that allow users to create programs that meet the individual needs of children. Vocabulary exposure in a contrived environment such as a computer provides drill and practice opportunities in a fun and engaging way. The computer allows for individual pacing of vocabulary development that is more geared toward the learning needs of the child with a disability. Although acquiring vocabulary within typical routines is the primary mode of communication skill development, children with disabilities can increase their receptive and expressive vocabulary through computer options targeting word learning that may not as easily occur in natural settings.

Language Skills (Communication)

Understanding the nuances of language follows vocabulary development. Syntax and grammar programs exist to teach language concepts. Laureate software programs emphasize developing language skills and offer software emphasizing various language components such as prepositional phrases. Children watch items on a screen move to different positions and are asked to choose when the object is located on top or under a box or table. The programs follow a developmental sequence for acquiring language concepts. A child with a limited vocabulary and language skills can benefit from programs that sequentially move through various language rules. The one-to-one nature of the computer allows the child to review language concepts at his or her own pace and level of expertise. In addition, software programs provide visual cueing often necessary for some children, such as those diagnosed with autism, to make a connection between the spoken word and its meaning. Pictures provide the means to accomplish language concepts that may otherwise go unlearned due to the limited multisensory experiences available in a typical conversation or preschool classroom learning event. As evidenced by Light (2005), children with disabilities increase vocabulary and language use through exposure to computer-based visual scenes. Computers provide additional opportunities for communication skill development that allow for individualization of specific vocabulary and language needs.

Early Literacy Skills (Preliteracy)

Early exposure to oral reading is a precursor to later literacy acquisition. For children with disabilities, listening to storytelling may be difficult due to sensory deficits and attention difficulties that inhibit sustained focus on the activity. Children who are unable to experience storytelling can develop listening skills and sustained attention to a story through computer programs. There are software programs that provide onscreen versions of favorite children's books. Children who are unable to focus specifically on a storybook reading from beginning to end can revisit the story on a computer and share the experience with one or two friends. The computer version offers hands-on versions in which children have to touch the screen or click the mouse to turn a page. Exposing children to books on the computer enhances their initial experience during circle time. Books on computer provide a method for multiple opportunities to support individualizing skill development and pacing according to the child's attention and understanding. Furthermore, the visual and auditory cues offered with books on a computer increase the likelihood that the child will attend to and follow the story sequence as compared with a story with only auditory input, such as circle storytime.

Sequential Story and Song Development (Preliteracy)

Preliteracy skills move from listening and focusing on a story to following the story sequence and engaging in songs. If a child is nonverbal and cannot follow along during storytime, then their access to story sequencing is curtailed. Computers provide a means of pacing the story at various speeds to account for individual differences. A child who is unable to pronounce all of the words in a song being sung by a small group of children during a sing along is able to sing along with the computer by self-activating the next line of the song. The child is able to control the story in order to experience the complete sequence and learn through repetition—the primary line of the story. Online books and software programs with books and related games and activities provide an avenue of storytelling that capitalizes on a child's control of his or her environment. The books on computer offer an enhancement to curricular activities focused on storytelling and oral book reading. Children with disabilities are then offered multiple options for gaining experience with learning songs and following a story sequence in addition to the traditional presentation during circle time. Other children may enjoy exposure to books on the computer as well.

Basic Concepts (Preacademic)

Drill and practice software includes activities that punctuate basic preacademic skills in reading, math, and writing. Many children in the 21st century are being exposed to preschool learning software that emphasizes basic concept development. For children with disabilities, basic concepts presented in preschool may need to be remediated in the primary grades due to lack of acquisition in preschool. Basic concept software promotes a review of preacademic tasks in a fun and interesting format that allows for self-pacing and reinforcement of concepts taught during small- and large-group classroom activities. There is a variety of software available in this category, and attention to difficulty level is important. Some programs are simple to use, whereas others require more advanced computer skills and maneuvering through complex visual scenes not appropriate for a child with complex physical and communication challenges. Children that do not readily grasp basic skills such as colors, shapes, numbers, and the alphabet are exposed to the concepts repeatedly in a game-like format that sparks curiosity and interest in often mundane matching or labeling tasks that quickly loses their attention. Matching objects, alphabet letters, and numbers during a puzzle activity may be out of reach for a child with a physical disability. The computer software program of basic concepts provides simulated matching activities that engage the learner and eliminate the physical access requirement of a puzzle or other matching activity.

Problem Solving (Later Cognition)

Children begin exploring their environments early in their development (see Chapter 6). Infants begin to perceive differences and similarities in objects, which initiates the brain's function of classification. They initiate various actions to experiment with what works and what does not work. Simple cause and effect grows to multiple solutions for why something happened. Toddlers observe others solving basic dilemmas, such as reaching for an object that is under a table by moving their position or trying different-size lids on a jar until one fits. Three-year-olds have solidified their problem-solving techniques to determine what might work, such as picking out the small lid for the small jar automatically without having to go through a trial and error process as they did as an infant. They also know that others can help them figure out challenges and they seek out that help. Problem-solving skills are a predictor of later academic success (CDE, 2008). Because problem solving is tantamount to later school performance, children with disabilities need increased exposure to activities that pose predicaments. Problem solving on the computer involves the simple cause-and-effect programs that lead the way to more sophisticated scenarios. Preschool software is available that teaches specific problem-solving skills in which children are required to respond to a series of choices about an event. Blue's Clues software is a case in point in which Steve assists the learners to help Blue choose which items she needs to maneuver through the house to get to the hidden treasure. Problem-solving software is typically geared toward preschool learners corresponding to the developmental progression of cognition and learning. Using cause-and-effect software programs with young children with disabilities may expose them to learning opportunities early that provide a foundation for later exploration of problem-solving software. Although problem solving in actual activities is preferred over simulated versions available on the computer, problem-solving software can be an alternative to consider when a child's disability inhibits his or her involvement in daily routines in which problem solving occurs naturally and frequently. Problem-solving software affords an opportunity for children with disabilities to initiate solutions in a more controlled learning environment that may otherwise not be available. Experiencing problem solving in a contrived environment helps them garner the skills necessary to build self-confidence for trying things out in a more natural setting. The next section reviews the various software options available and provides a method for selecting software appropriate for young children with disabilities.

SOFTWARE CONSIDERATIONS

Just as toys need to be fun, popular, and appealing for young children, software programs need to have similar characteristics. Children enjoy software that is engaging, with bright colors and lights, familiar animation, and motivating content. The purposes of the material now available for computers are as varied as toys, books, and games for young children. Some software suites include curricular supplements focused on drill and practice of preacademic skills such as alphabet and number knowledge, phonemic awareness, vocabulary development, and matching. There is a wide range of difficulty levels for preschool tutorial software that may not always be the best fit for a child with a disability. There are specific companies that specialize in switch-accessible software programs and those more focused on cause and effect and switch scanning. Software considerations are many and can be readily evaluated by trial and error. There are also web sites dedicated to children's software review such as Children's Technology Review (2009) and Super Kids Educational Software Review

(Knowledge Share, 2009). Consulting both online sources as well as other parents, teachers, and staff about what has been used with other children is recommended in order to ensure the software program selected will be appropriately matched to the child's learning needs. Furthermore, becoming familiar with the research supporting various software programs and their purpose increases the likelihood that the software purchased will have been field tested and comply with recommended practice that supports using evidence-based learning materials for young children. With the advent of other online networking sources such as Facebook and Twitter, gathering information about the potential of various software programs becomes much more attainable.

Determining the child's strengths and needs through the FEET evaluation process is the first step in discerning whether a software program is going to be appropriate for a young child with a disability. Once the child's characteristics have been documented and the computer hardware and positioning requirements specified, parents and teachers select software programs based on a set of software features. There are several educational software evaluation checklists available for downloading that address several aspects of software features appropriate for younger children including Linking Software Evaluation to the IEP Part 3 (Forgan & Weber, 2001); Instructional Software Evaluation Checklist (Rittner, 2002); Software Evaluation Form (Schrock, 2007); and Evaluating Software for Young Learners (Haugen, 2001). Buckleitner (1999) emphasized that the multidimensional nature of computer software as compared with two-dimensional books poses challenges in evaluating its appropriateness and is more similar to measuring an interaction between a teacher and child. He suggested several questions be answered in order to determine whether a software program will meet the needs of a particular child including such queries regarding the program's purpose, pedagogy (constructivist versus behavioral), developmental level for the intended audience, and whether the program is the most sophisticated in terms of current technology design. Hofmann (1985), in an examination of a process for assessing the utility of educational software, recommended that teachers focus on the type of learning expected, such as teacher facilitated, memorization, or cognitive development, and combine that with the amount of user control allowed to determine the effectiveness of the software for its intended purpose. He recommended that teachers emphasize the utility of the software for the target audience and deemphasize evaluating the general software characteristics. In order to capture the important components of software potential for young children with disabilities, all of the previous considerations need to be addressed when choosing software programs. The software features chart in Figure 8.1 provides a method for formally reviewing and recording the appropriateness of software programs specifically for infants, toddlers, and preschoolers with disabilities.

TYPES OF SOFTWARE PROGRAMS

There are different types of software programs that might be considered depending on the child's characteristics and the expected outcomes. The following categories provide a brief description of each software type. Table 8.2 contains the vendor, types, and titles of available software. Although not an exhaustive list, the information offers a starting point for selecting software appropriate for young children with disabilities. Each program will still require an evaluation of its appropriateness for use with particular children.

Cause and Effect

There are several companies that offer cause-and-effect software programs for young learners, such as Marblesoft/Simtech and SoftTouch. Usually, programs are switch, keyboard, and/or touchscreen adapted, allowing the user to simply touch the peripheral for an action to occur

Software Features Checklist

Evaluator: _____   Date: _____

Title: _____

Vendor: _____   Cost: _____

Switch accessible: ____ touchscreen ____ single switch ____ switch scanning

Type: ____ cause and effect ____ problem solving ____ drill and practice ____ art ____ basic concepts
_____ vocabulary/language development ____teacher designed ____text to speech

Technology compatibility: ____Mac ____PC ____Both ____Wii ____Xbox 360 ____online access ____other

Age level: ____ infant ____ toddler ____ preschool

Feature	Description	Evaluation			
		Disagree	Neutral	Agree	N/A
Age appropriateness	CAI matches developmental skill levels of age indicated	1	2	3	0
Design	Simple, interesting, and easy to use	1	2	3	0
Background	Uncluttered or visually distracting display	1	2	3	0
Color	Bright, appealing, and high contrast	1	2	3	0
Volume	On/off switch and volume control available	1	2	3	0
Sound effects	Age appropriate, element of surprise, and attention getting	1	2	3	0
Pictures and animations	Age appropriate, engaging characters that are popular with young children	1	2	3	0
Activation	Easy to turn on and off; activate pictures with simple touch of screen or movement of mouse	1	2	3	0
Control	Pacing program to meet child's needs	1	2	3	0
Difficulty level	Motivating and developmentally corresponding to skill level of child	1	2	3	0
Response time	Immediate versus delayed	1	2	3	0
Feedback mechanism	Positive auditory and visual feedback when correct	1	2	3	0
Text-to-speech capability	Can convert speech to text or text to speech	1	2	3	0
Teacher data collection	Data on child successes can be monitored through a data collection system	1	2	3	0
Cost	Low cost	1	2	3	0
Compatibility	Works with all computer systems	1	2	3	0
Cultural independent content	Uses universal design and avoids culture-specific language, colloquial phrases, color, design, pictures, and themes specific to one cultural group	1	2	3	0
Technical adequacy	Reliability and validity of program available for review; other online sources of evaluation provided; clear directions provided	1	2	3	0
Rating total: Add number of circles in each column to determine highest amount		____	____	____	____
Comments:					

Figure 8.1.   Software features checklist.

Table 8.2. Software list

Vendor	Software type	Software titles
Adaptivation http://www.adaptivation.com	Cause and effect; color recognition	Splatter-Splatter ($55) (Windows only) Kaleidoscope 2 ($55)
Broderbund http://www.broderbund.com	Preliteracy; preacademics; art	Disney Fun and Skills Toddler, Preschool Dr. Seuss® ABC Adventure Workshop Kids Pix 4 ($19.99 each) Reader Rabbit Preschool Favorites ($9.99)
Creative Communicating http://www.creativecommunicating.com	Preliteracy	Storytime Collection Farm Fun ($20) Storytime Kit, ten books ($250)
Don Johnston http://www.donjohnston.com	Single-switch story scenes to develop computer input skills; cause and effect; preliteracy	Press to Play Series: Speedy, Zoo, Animals, and Sports ($59) UKanDu Switches, Too! Eensy and Friends, Humpty Dumpty and Friends ($55)
Edmark Early Learning Series, available through River Deep http://web.riverdeep.net/portal/page?_pageid=818, 18_dad=portal&_schema=PORTAL	Teaches preacademic skills; includes a progress reporting option	Bayley's Book House Millie's Math House Sammie's Science House ($79)
Inclusive Technologies http://www.inclusive.co.uk	Cause and effect; preacademic; switch or touchscreen accessible	Alphabet Paint 1-2-3 Paint Abracadabra Happy Duck Big Bang Switch It Original ($60–$75)
Intellitools http://www.intellitools.com		Click It! for customized scanning ($99)
Judy Lynn Software http://www.judylynn.com	Cause and effect; activated by a single switch, mouse, or touch window	Amusement Park Look and Listen Intro to Cause and Effect Scan and Paint Match It ($39)

(continued)

Table 8.2. (continued)

Vendor	Software type	Software titles
Knowledge Adventure http://www.knowledgeadventure.com/	Toddler and preschool preacademic games	A variety of games available for toddlers and preschoolers, such as Tub Time and ABC Game.
Laureate Learning Systems http://www.laureatelearning.com	Vocabulary and language development	Creature series First Words First Verbs ($85–$235)
Learning Magic http://www.learningmagicinc.com	Cause and effect; puzzling using Clicker 5 software	Cause and Effect Puzzle Collection for Clicker 5 ($69.95)
Linda J. Burkhart http://www.lburkhart.com	Cause and effect; vocabulary and stories; software and games/handouts; works on Intellipics Studio	Two Switches to Success! Early Songs and Play The Gingerbread Man ($40–$50)
Marblesoft/Simtech http://www.marblesoft.com	Single switch/cause and effect; step scanning; linear scanning	Cause and Effect Sights and Sounds New Frog and Fly Switch Kids ($30) The Picasso Series Scan and Match 1–3 ($50)
Marblesoft/Simtech http://www.marblesoft.com	Cause and effect; preacademic; IntelliKeys; single- or dual-switch scanning	Early Learning Series Cause and Effect Potato Face ($59)
SoftTouch http://www.softtouch.com	Books and games that work with a switch or touchscreen and promote language development; My Own Bookshelf is an authoring software to make your own talking books	Switch Basics Teach Me to Talk Monkeys Jumping on the Bed My Own Bookshelf Old MacDonald's Farm Songs I Sing at Preschool Wheels on the Bus ($99–$139)
Access and Productivity Tools, Synapse Adaptive (made by Inclusive Technologies) http://www.synapseadaptive.com	Developmental sequence of skills including cause and effect, turn taking, basic concepts, and problem solving to motivate students to use a switch	Switchlt! Software Suite: Pictures, Scenes, Patterns, Opposites ($200)

on the screen. What happens on the screen varies from whole-screen changes to items moving from one location to another. For instance, Simtech's cause-and-effect software has different objects that move around on the screen combined with music. The objects are brightly colored with high-contrasting elements. Marblesoft's Switch Kids uses children's faces to display changes, such as blowing up a bubble and then popping it. SoftTouch Company has a series of software for young children that promotes cause and effect using various familiar animations, such as penguins, and provides three levels of difficulty for building scenes.

Choice Making

Choice-making software allows the learner to select between two or more choices. For instance, Inclusive Technology offers a series of products providing opportunities for choice making, such as Choose and Tell Fairy Tales and Choose and Tell Nursery Rhymes. Teach Me to Talk allows choice making using changeable screen formats that offer teachers options for choosing from two to nine items at a time on the screen. Picture placement can be varied in different locations on the screen. Some squares can be left blank to determine if a child is actually using scanning to select choices. The changeable format provides options for setting up forced choice situations, such as placing a favorite choice or picture in the upper part of the screen. The child who may hesitate to cross midline from left to right is then offered a favorite picture prompt that encourages a new or uncomfortable physical movement.

Other software applications include fantasy and fun to engage the learner and spark curiosity to experiment with the programs. Reader Rabbit Toddler includes a game in which the user navigates the Dream Ship around the screen to uncover hidden animations and sound. Look for programs that embed choice making into the activity, such as vocabulary selection and preacademic tasks. Starting with beginning choice-making programs provides skill development for more complex selection based on a theme, color, letter, or number in a sequential pattern, such as needing to first choose the color red among other color choices before moving on to the next screen. If a child is unable to effectively move the cursor to make informed selections, then scanning systems in which the child moves through a sequence of items and clicks on the preferred option are viable alternatives. Adapting keys on the keyboard is another mode of selection. IntelliKeys creates keyboard grids that correspond to various software packages available for purchase. Keys can also be removed and adapted with material, symbols, pictures, or other choices by using low-technology modifications such as Velcro and glue to change the symbol on the key to match the symbols in the program.

Switch Accessible

Switch-accessible software alleviates the need to make further adaptations for switch use. Several companies specializing in software for children with disabilities produce software programs that are already switch accessible for cause and effect and choice making. With switch-accessible software, the program is designed to respond when a switch is activated by touch or once released as opposed to requiring multiple movements of the cursor. Most of the cause-and-effect and choice-making software presented in Table 8.2 includes the switch-accessible component. Modifying the size and style of the cursor icon is another way to make software more accessible for young children with disabilities. R. J. Cooper offers a program called Biggy Cursor, and other basic computer programs such as Microsoft Word often provide a built-in adjustment for the cursor.

Vocabulary

Several software companies specializing in programs for young children with disabilities include options for vocabulary development in structured and unstructured formats.

Laureate Learning Systems provides a more structured approach to word acquisition. The company produces a variety of software programs that are geared toward increasing vocabulary skills, such as First Words and First Verbs. The company recommends the programs for children from pre-K through sixth grade with disabilities involving communication skills such as autism, developmental disabilities, language disorders, learning disabilities, physical disabilities, low vision, hearing impairments, and English language learners. The programs focus on 100 nouns and 50 verbs to reinforce basic vocabulary skill development. A less formal introduction of beginning vocabulary can be found in software programs that present nursery rhymes and other children's stories, such as Monkeys Jumping on the Bed by SoftTouch, Spider Song by Linda Burkhart, and Dr. Seuss' ABCs by Broderbund.

Language, Grammar, and Syntax

In addition to basic vocabulary development software, Laureate Learning Systems provides software programs that reinforce basic syntax and expressive language skills and offers a myriad of programs that teach simple sentence structure, prepositions, and pronouns. Teachers are able to track student's responses, which allows ongoing measurement of progress to determine goals to be modified and programs to be adjusted according to the specific growth of the child. Eensy and Friends by Don Johnston is another example of language development software. A click will change an object to its exact opposite on the screen. In addition, the software serves multiple purposes in that it teaches basic concepts including identifying colors and counting.

Text to Speech

Text-to-speech software converts text into synthesized speech. There are widely used computer programs such as Microsoft Word and PowerPoint that have the text-to-speech function. Freeware such as Natural Reader can be downloaded and used to adapt computer programs to accommodate text to speech on any program in your computer. Clicker 4 and Clicker 5 software provides simple word processing that incorporates writing of words and phrases and the addition of pictures that are supported by speech. Similarly, Writing with Symbols 2000 creates symbols that are matched to text to speech. In a software review concerning text-to-speech options for struggling readers, Balajthy (2005) noted three existing text-to-speech word processing programs marketed for children with disabilities, including KidPix 3 by the Learning Company, IntelliTalk 3 by IntelliTools, and Write:OutLoud 6 by Don Johnston. Dragon Naturally Speaking 9 from Scan Soft Inc. is a more expensive speech-recognition software program that converts text to speech. Other text-to-speech software programs are BuildAbility and IntelliPics Studio 4, which include talking books that consist of pictures, text, and auditory output.

Preacademic

Several companies offer preacademic skill development using a game-like format. Edmark software products include an early learning series that focuses on literacy, math, science, and social studies. The activities use animal characters and colorful visual screen displays to present basic concepts. Jump Start by Knowledge Adventure offers preacademic skill-building software targeting various age levels, including toddlers and preschoolers. The programs are inexpensive and use animated characters to guide children through preliteracy and math activities incorporating beginning mouse skills. Parallel to the Jump Start

Series is Reader Rabbit Learning System available through Broderbund. The screen offers boxes with different games, and clicking on a box begins the game. New versions include popular themes such as Disney characters and Dr. Seuss. Songs and music accompany the games focused on preacademic skills.

In addition to preacademic packages, there are several software programs that include favorite storybooks and rhymes that are animated and set to music. Storybook packages such as Old MacDonald's Farm and Five Little Ducks focus on preliteracy and include audible stories and games. Don Johnston markets several series focused on familiar nursery rhymes such as "Humpty Dumpty" and other popular stories. The stories selected emphasize repetitive lines, which encourage the development of emerging literacy development. Creative Communicating publishes software called Storytime Kit that presents early literature coupled with recognizable songs. Table 8.2 lists available software programs for building and enhancing preacademic skill development.

Art and Drawing

Art software programs are the next level of cause and effect and allow users to create their own pictures and designs using the mouse, keyboard, and/or touchscreen. Several companies offer software geared toward computer art and vary in the amount of user control and difficulty levels provided as well as switch option availability. Kid Pix, a graphics software program by Broderbund, provides a variety of mediums adapted for the computer to create pictures. Animations and special effects can be incorporated into the design, which can also be printed out for display. The One Switch Picasso Series by Marblesoft-Simtech Company has a paint palette that allows the user to color in pictures. Alphabet Paint and 1-2-3 Paint are other programs that combine basic concepts and art. Tux Paint, a free software download appropriate for preschool through sixth grade is a drawing program with a variety of tools available for creating computer canvases. Although compatible with many computer operating systems, the program would need modification to use with a switch. Art programs usually allow flexibility in user control and foster creativity and problem solving.

Problem Solving

Preacademic skill-building software tends to employ basic skill and practice techniques for increasing content area knowledge as compared with problem-solving software that emphasizes critical thinking skills. Software that enhances memory and cognition tends to be developmentally more appropriate for children at the late preschool age range. Humungous Entertainment Company has several problem-solving series, including Putt Putt Joins the Race, in which users navigate through areas to find hidden clues, and Freddi the Fish adventures. Cause-and-effect software with difficulty levels may be a better starting point to enhance problem-solving skills in young children with disabilities.

Teacher Authored

Authoring software provides a platform for creating programs that capitalize on the interests and characteristics of young children with disabilities. The flexibility of using a more personalized approach to CAI benefits children with complex communication, cognitive, and physical needs that may not always respond to commercially designed products. SoftTouch Company's My Own Bookshelf software program allows authoring of books and choice-making activities. Choose It! Maker 2 by Inclusive Technologies, in which authors can arrange decision-making screens, and Picture It by Slater Software, which links pictures and stories, are additional examples of authoring software. There are several vendors that specialize in software for children with special needs that are listed in Table 8.2. Online reviews of software for young children, such as the SuperKids Software Review site, are another avenue for exploring possibilities. The best approach for selecting software is to try it out. Sometimes libraries carry a variety of educational software programs for young children that can be checked out for a short period. Companies offer free trial downloads of products as well. Another source to consider is searching online companies specializing in used software, such as eBay and Amazon.com. Obsolete software programs can sometimes be located for a low cost on one of the online sites. Parents with older children may be willing to donate software that no longer is age and developmentally appropriate.

PROFILES FOR ASSISTIVE TECHNOLOGY AND COMPUTER ACCESS

Each of the children assessed using the FEET model included identifying the computer as a potential learning tool. The earlier chapters reviewed the FEET outline for each child, including family concerns and child characteristics, team assessment and planning, observing activity-based intervention, AT action planning, AT observation trials, and AT evaluation. In Chapter 6, Sean, a 1-year-old with cerebral palsy, participated in several trials using a touchscreen and cause-and-effect software to increase skills in communication and play. The following section will review the FEET model for Jorge and Abby, with a focus on computer access.

Jorge: Cause and Effect

Family Concerns and Child Characteristics

Jorge has a developmental delay with vision impairments. He has limited communication skills. His Mom wants to explore computer use as an avenue for learning. He has access to a computer at his school. Jorge is mobile and is able to sit unsupported in child chairs.

Team Assessment Planning

Jorge likes music and likes to watch the games that other children play on the computer. He reaches toward his Mom when frustrated and looks to her for help when he is unable to reach a toy or object.

Observing Activity-Based Participation

Jorge reaches for a toy and tries to activate it. Because Jorge has experienced some success in using basic switches, the team decides that a single switch would be the most appropriate peripheral device to help Jorge access the computer. Because he is at the basic cause-and-effect stage and his visual skills are limited, the team wants to look at software that capitalizes on his current developmental level.

Assistive Technology Action Planning

The team has evaluated and purchased several cause-and-effect software programs. They decide to use Marblesoft/Simtech's Sights and Sounds due to the high-contrast

AT action plan					
AT access	**AT solutions**	**Environmental adaptations**	**Resources needed (equipment, funding, training, personnel)**	**Timelines**	**Person responsible**
Positioning	Seating at small table to assist in attention focus	Limit distractions; provide high visual contrast; large photographs; gradually reduce size	Evaluate classroom furniture to provide appropriate seating and positioning for play, communication, and book time in classroom areas	Immediately	Classroom teacher, OT, PT
Mobility	Supported seating to provide stable base of support; walker with basket to carry toys	Low table, child-size chair; eliminate access barriers in classroom, school, and home	Obtain child-size walker and fit with front basket to carry toys	6 weeks	OT, PT, social worker
Communication	Photograph communication book; Step-by-Step VOCA; object board; computer software to build vocabulary concepts	Place photograph communication book in reach in class and home environments; object board placed near musical toys; computer on accessible table	Digital camera, printer; three-ring binders for photographs; two books, one for home, one for early intervention program; foam core board with lock ties for small musical toys and other favorites for object board; laptop with touchscreen; Simtec, Laureate software	1 week: photograph communication book; 2 weeks: object board; 3 weeks: VOCA; computer with touchscreen and adapted switch	SLP, teacher, parent
Vision	Continue to monitor vision to ensure that glasses are appropriate	Large and high-contrast materials in classroom displays	Black construction paper on bulletin board for high contrast; large visual displays	Ongoing; 3–6 months observation	Vision specialist, teacher, OT, parent
Hearing	Continue to check hearing levels	Assure auditory attention with music and sound cues	N/A	6-month checkups	SLP, teacher, parent

Figure 8.2.   FEET Form 5: AT action plan for Jorge.

colors, music, and switch capability. They attached a large, textured switch using a switch interface to the computer to add tactile cues for Jorge. FEET Form 5 (Figure 8.2) shows Jorge's complete action plan.

Assistive Technology Observation Trials

A peer models the software program while Jorge watches. He shows interest in the screen events and begins to whine because he is not getting a turn. Because Jorge is mobile, he is able to gain access to the existing computer chair easily and begins touching the switch to activate screen designs. Every time he hits the switch, the screen creates new designs. FEET Form 6 (Figure 8.3) describes Jorge's observation trial.

Assistive Technology Evaluation

Jorge's first trial with the cause-and-effect software is successful. He focused on the task for 10 minutes and enjoyed laughter with two other children watching him change the screen pictures with the touch of the switch. A teacher assistant observed the task but did not need to provide any additional physical support for the activity. The team decided to experiment with other cause-and-effect software that required just one click of the switch

AT observation trials

AT support	Activity 1: Music Date/time: Monday/10AM	Activity 2: Playtime Date/time: Wednesday/11AM	Activity 3: Outdoor play Date/time: Friday/9AM	AT effectiveness	Modifications needed
AT for computer access Provide cause-and-effect software to increase generalization of cause and effect	Cause-and-effect software, Sights and Sounds by Simtech	Jorge watches his peers activate the program and whines when he cannot get a turn	Jorge initiates sitting in the computer chair and starts hitting the switch to change the screen designs	Jorge attended to the computer task for 10-minute intervals and interacted with laughter with peers present	Peer models to show Jorge how to activate switch; allow Jorge to position himself and direct the activity once he understands the task

Figure 8.3.   FEET Form 6: AT observation trials for Jorge.

for activation until Jorge's computer skills improved. See FEET Form 7 (Figure 8.4) for Jorge's evaluation plan.

Abby: Preacademic and Problem Solving

Four-year-old Abby has cerebral palsy and uses her eyes and gestures to communicate. She needs support in maintaining head and trunk control. She uses her right hand to activate toys.

Family Concerns and Child Characteristics

The family is hoping that Abby's communication skills will increase when she is introduced to the computer. They recommend computer software programs to provide Abby with opportunities to look at photographs, play games, and learn preschool curriculum. Although Abby's physical challenges inhibit participation in many typical preschool activities, she is alert and cognizant of activities going on around her.

Team Assessment Planning

Abby showed interest in doll play during previous observations. Positioning Abby at the computer was the primary hurdle for the team to overcome. The team used the checklist for proper positioning developed by Lau et al. (2005) to address the steps to consider in successfully maintaining a comfortable position for Abby.

Observing Activity-Based Participation

The team tried a switch-adapted mouse because Abby was able to reach with her right arm. A toggle switch was used to take advantage of her large movements. The team decided to try My Face by Marblesoft, a cause-and-effect software program that creates faces.

AT evaluation plan

AT intervention goal	AT materials implemented	Effectiveness of intervention	Need for modifications	Person responsible
Computer Learn cause and effect; turn-taking skills	Cause-and-effect software with colorful pictures and designs	Jorge hit the switch to activate the screen designs multiple times; Jorge laughed with peers on each screen change	Choose software with bright and colorful screen images that are high contrast; make sure Jorge is positioned within close proximity to the screen for optimal viewing	Teacher, SLP, vision specialist, teacher's aide

Figure 8.4.   FEET Form 7: AT evaluation plan for Jorge.

AT observation trials					
AT support	**Activity 1:** Art & pretend play **Date/time:** Monday/10AM	**Activity 2:** Storytime **Date/time:** Wednesday/2PM	**Activity 3:** Mealtime **Date/time:** Friday/11AM	**AT effectiveness**	**Modifications needed**
AT for computer access Cause-and-effect computer software programs; switch and switch interface for activating software	My Face software by Marblesoft with a toggle switch and switch interface for activation			Two peers modeled software demonstration on the first day; Abby activated toggle switch after two attempts on software on the second day	Begin with two peers as models of action; Abby observes on first trial and participates on second, continuing in a turn-taking fashion

Figure 8.5. FEET Form 6: AT observation trials for computers for Abby.

Assistive Technology Action Planning

The team asked the two female peers who enjoy playing with Abby to participate in the computer trials. Each child modeled how to use the toggle switch to activate the software program. Abby was positioned in her wheelchair with additional bumpers under her arms and trunk. A foam cushion was placed under her right arm attached by Velcro to the wheelchair in order to provide adequate support for the arm she would use to hit the switch. The trials were scheduled for 5-minute sequences in which each of the girls took turns activating the My Face software.

Assistive Technology Observation Trials

Abby and her friends were situated at the computer station, and the teacher helped the first child begin the program. Because all of the children were unfamiliar with the My Face program, they all learned together how to begin the activity. Abby watched during the first session while the other two students mastered the program. They all expressed surprise as the face was created. Abby's turn came on the second day. She was able to hit the toggle switch after two attempts and watched as the face appeared. The other girls clapped, and Abby hit the toggle switch a second time. By the fifth day, all students were competent switch and software users. FEET Form 6 (Figure 8.5) describes Abby's observation trial.

Assistive Technology Evaluation Plan

The computer activity allowed Abby to be a full participant in an interactive cause-and-effect software game. She has mastered the basic one-switch activation and is now ready for listening to storybooks on the computer and attempting basic concept software. Abby enjoyed playing the game with others, which supported social-emotional skill development along with cognition and basic skills. See FEET Form 7 (Figure 8.6) for Abby's evaluation plan.

AT evaluation plan				
AT intervention goal	**AT materials implemented**	**Effectiveness of intervention**	**Need for modifications**	**Person responsible**
Computer Demonstrate understanding of cause and effect on a computer; move from single actions to two or more; provide two switches for choice making	My Face cause-and-effect software program with toggle switch and switch interface	Abby has mastered the basic one-switch activation and is now ready for listening to storybooks on the computer and attempting basic concept software	Provide peer models to orient Abby to task prior to introducing functions; increase difficulty level as Abby achieves single action; move to choice making, storybook reading, and basic concept software as successive trials indicate progress	SLP, teacher, parent

Figure 8.6. FEET Form 7: AT evaluation plan for computers for Abby.

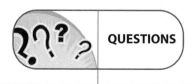

QUESTIONS

1. What specific research supports computer use with young children?

2. Describe the types of prerequisite computer skills necessary for a young child with a disability to access software programs.

3. How can computer software be used to increase literacy development in young children?

4. Describe the different ways computers can be adapted to allow access by all children. List some of the peripheral devices available for this purpose.

5. Describe the types of software available for use with young children that promote preacademic skills. Include a list of software characteristics to consider when purchasing a software program for use in an early childhood educational setting.

TIPS

○ Use the FEET to assess the learning needs of the child and whether CAI might be beneficial.

○ Incorporate software trials and maintain ongoing data on the child's progress when using particular software systems/programs.

○ Use the software features chart when considering the purchase of software programs.

○ Reference the current NAEYC and DEC recommended practices along with recent literature as a rationale for purchasing software and hardware.

○ Visit web sites focused on early childhood special education frequently to keep abreast of new information on computers and software.

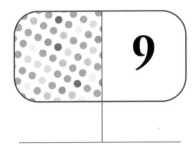

9

Bridging the Divide with Assistive Technology Toolkits

Throughout this book, each chapter unveils a wealth of resources to bring AT within the reach of children with disabilities, their family members, and early childhood teams. As demonstrated in previous chapters, the keys to developing AT services are readily available. Literature and web-based information and materials on AT for children with disabilities are extensive. Providers and families require tangible examples in order to develop a system of AT services and devices that is accessible for all children who may benefit from technology support in early development and learning. The literature makes it clear that AT needs to be available in the form of adapted books, toys, communication modalities, and computers. Furthermore, AT tools can assist early childhood teams to conduct AT assessment and intervention planning.

Often, AT services are perceived as synonymous with high financial costs. Although early childhood service systems across the nation and the world increasingly recognize the need to establish AT services, limited resources do not allow expensive AT equipment to be purchased. In remote and rural areas, the needs for resources are heightened by distance and extremely limited numbers of specialized professionals with background in AT. On the positive side, developing AT services is not entirely dependent on large budgets. Initially, providing low-tech AT support is possible with low-cost materials that can be made with everyday supplies such as Velcro, microfiber, plastic page protectors, and clear plastic picture frames. High-tech equipment such as speech-generating software, digital book publishing software, adapted switches, electronic toys, and other computer peripherals are also needed and require more funding. As technology advances, however, costs will decrease, and the availability of computer-based products will increase. The availability of equipment loans in most states is an additional resource for AT equipment and is supported by legislation through the ATA of 2004 (Wissick, 2006; see Chapter 2). When it is determined that purchasing high-tech and high-cost equipment is appropriate, funding sources exist through legislated policy and programs. In order to bridge the divide between research and practice in AT with young children with disabilities, we must begin with the theoretical foundation for AT services in the early childhood years. Although it is understood that AT is beneficial to support young children to develop and learn, a valid and reliable approach to providing AT services is grounded on early development and learning theory (Lane & Mistrett, 2002; Langone et al., 1999; Long et al., 2003).

Starting with the theoretical bases of child development allows practitioners to match AT solutions to the individual developmental stages and functional activities of each child. From a theory-based approach that is fortified by research, a range of AT tools can be organized so that providers have the means to discover each child's access needs for AT support. A comprehensive framework and consideration of AT materials and equipment for each individual child led to the development of AT toolkits. AT toolkits are a collection of equipment and supplies that enable early childhood providers to readily adapt activities for children with complex needs to participate in daily activities and learning environments with their peers.

This chapter brings together the resources described throughout the book into an organized guide for early childhood teams to integrate AT within their systems of services for young children. Each of the areas discussed in the book, thus far, show processes and adaptations to include low- and high-tech AT devices within environments and daily activities for the purpose of enabling young children with disabilities to participate with peers, according to individual developmental stages and functional needs. Initially in this chapter, theory and research provide the rationale for developing and implementing AT toolkits with young children across daily routines. From a research perspective, guidelines for organizing and applying AT toolkits follow. Within the organization of AT toolkits, different toolkits are described with four different categories, including communication, play, emergent literacy, and computer use. Each of the four AT toolkits include key components to match to the individual needs of each child based on developmental needs, specific AT tools, sources for each item, and examples of AT applications within daily routines. Following descriptive guidelines of the components of each of four AT toolkits, specific contents for each toolkit are identified. The chapter concludes with "maps" to implement AT in a format that links early childhood assessment tools to AT solutions to support each child's participation with family members and other children.

WHY ASSISTIVE TECHNOLOGY TOOLKITS?

The notion of toolkits is widely used in curricular methods for education and special education with particular focus areas including literacy development, behavioral strategies and supports, mathematics instruction, and science exploration. The origin of the toolkit approach is based in the concept of packaging solutions and guides to address specific needs for educational training and program development (Judge, 2006). Toolkits proliferate in many areas of health, human service, and education as a means to overcome barriers that are found in the workplace, school, and community.

In special education, toolkit approaches are available to address a spectrum of initiatives that target staff, program, and resource development in a number of topic areas. In the area of AT, toolkits in education most often address the needs of school-age children to gain access to literacy and learning using computer-based tools. One example of computer-based AT is IntelliTools Classroom Suite®, a curriculum-referenced software program that enables students with disabilities to participate in curriculum through digital media to adapt curriculum content across a range of topics and grade levels (IntelliTools, 2007). Developing toolkits focused on AT with young children with disabilities is based on the models demonstrated in elementary school applications. Judge (2006) reported that AT toolkits were used in academic contexts but were not available to address the learning, sensorimotor, and communication needs of young children. Initiatives to develop appropriate AT tools for use in early childhood settings developed from survey and interview research with early childhood practitioners (Judge, 2006; Stoner, Parette, Watts, Wojcik, & Fogal, 2008).

In response to reported gaps between research to support the effectiveness of AT applications with young children and actual practice in the field, Judge (2006) surveyed early childhood special education professionals and found that each had specific preferences for items with the highest utility value to use in classrooms with young children with disabilities. As a result, Judge developed a conceptual model for AT toolkits for young children that included the purpose, suggested item, and features of each item. Stoner et al. (2008) followed a similar process to identify the perceptions of early childhood teachers regarding implementing AT services and devices. Teachers surveyed by Stoner et al. reported that their perceptions of AT included devices or computers and that perceived challenges to implementing technology included the need for technical support, investment of time, and training. In an effort to address teachers' perceived barriers to implement AT with young children, Parette, Stoner, and Watts (2009) established user groups among teachers and equipped them with toolkits containing personal computer systems with software including IntelliTools®, Boardmaker with Speaking Dynamically Pro®, Writing with Symbols 2000®, and Clicker 5®. Following a series of training and user group meetings, Parette et al. reported the effectiveness of user groups to problem solve and expand their application of AT tools in early childhood classrooms.

Additional examples of toolkit approaches include inexpensive methods by Krupp and Villalobos (2007) to include children with severe disabilities in classroom activities to participate in news reports with News-2-U and an AT toolkit with sequenced communication VOCAs (Step-by-Step from AbleNet and Sequencer® from Adaptivation); two-choice VOCA (Rocking Plate Communicator® from Enabling Devices); single switches (Big Red Switch® and Jelly Beamer Wireless Switch® from AbleNet); and computer interface switches (PowerLink 3 Control Unit® and Switch Click® from AbleNet. Rush and Helling (2006) also described an AAC assessment toolkit that consisted of forms to identify necessary equipment prior to assessment and obtain it from equipment loan programs. The toolkit also included a number of AAC devices, such as a dry-erase board, photographs, symbols, a display board with Velcro-friendly fabric, multiple-message communication devices, and switch interface for computer and toy activation. The AAC TechConnect Toolkit is another example of an AAC toolkit that is commercially available and includes many of the previous items in addition to more extensive low- and high-tech evaluation tools for purchase (McBride & Bardach, 2009). Each of the examples demonstrate resources that aim to put AT and AAC tools in the hands of practitioner teams in order to improve the process of assessing and selecting the most appropriate technology systems for individuals with disabilities and their family members.

Judge (2006), Stoner et al. (2008), and Parette et al. (2009) developed the conceptual organization and contents of AT toolkits through seeking the perspectives of providers to identify essential AT tools and barriers to service delivery for all children who may benefit from AT solutions to participate in daily learning environments. These researchers also considered multiple levels of AT that include theoretical foundations regarding comprehensive aspects of developmental, learning, and participation goals for all children. Judge, in particular, proposed a model for designing AT toolkits that include a framework for addressing the learning, sensorimotor, and communication needs of young children. Judge suggested that tools for communication including the following: a visual schedule; calendar and list of activities; picture communication symbols and BoardMaker® software; communication boards with objects, pictures, and symbols; picture symbol display books/boards; and simple SGDs. AT tools for movement included a weighted vest; positioning devices (sitting, standing); switches; and adaptive seating equipment. Furthermore, items for learning included adaptive scissors, a touchscreen for computer use, pencil grips, electronic toys, switch-accessible toys/games, a slantboard/clipboard, talking books, and adaptive keyboards. The combination of low- and high-tech AT tools proposed by Judge provides a comprehensive approach to training and expanding AT services in early childhood programs.

Based on the model proposed by Judge (2006), Sadao et al. (2009) further developed an AT toolkit to support early childhood assessment and intervention and link to AT supports to meet individual goals to participate with peers in daily routines. As a special initiative of the Supporting Early Education Development Systems Project (SEEDS), a statewide technical assistance project for early childhood special education operated through the Sacramento County Office of Education in California, the SEEDS Workgroup on Early Education Technology (SWEET) formed to develop training and resources for providers and families in early childhood programs to increase awareness and use of AT for young children. The SWEET AT toolkit was developed to meet the needs for access to low-tech, inexpensive tools and adaptations designed to assist young children with disabilities to learn, communicate, play, grow, and participate with peers and family members. The SWEET AT toolkit is organized as a guide for developing and using AT in early intervention and early childhood settings. Research-based content was selected to provide recommended items and activities to promote development and learning in coordination with curriculum milestones identified in many available assessment measures widely used in early childhood programs. These well-established tools include the Assessment, Evaluation, and Programming System for Infants and Children (AEPS®; Bricker, 2002), and the Carolina Curriculum (Johnson-Martin, Attermeier & Hacker, 2004). Items are primarily available from online companies and discount retailers. Guidelines to assemble and use the SWEET AT toolkit are available on the SEEDS web site (http://www.scoe.net/seeds/ resources/at/atToolkit.html). Two containers are recommended to assemble a complete AT toolkit—one for AT tools that are purchased or created and one for additional supplies to create further AT adaptations.

In addition to guidelines for assembling an AT toolkit with low- and high-tech equipment and supplies, the SWEET AT toolkit includes handouts for each of the tools that are developed. The SWEET AT toolkit handouts provide examples for application, instructions for assembly, sources for equipment to purchase, supplies to make the items, and references that support the application of the selected tool. The handouts can be downloaded and may be used for both AT assessment and intervention.

Developing the SWEET AT toolkit provides a comprehensive model that enables programs serving young children with disabilities in their initiatives to build AT services. At whatever stage a program finds itself in the process of system development, the contents, supplies, and detailed application guides offer a comprehensive resource to improve AT service delivery. Additional adaptations of AT toolkits to focus on targeted areas of communication, play, literacy, and computer are discussed in the following sections.

ASSISTIVE TECHNOLOGY TOOLKIT FOCUS AREAS

Mistrett (2001, 2004) described the functional nature of AT to support early childhood development regarding movement, communication, and use of materials to take part in daily activities with family members and peers. Judge (2006) further categorized AT toolkits into areas to target the development of communication, movement, and learning for young children. Grant and Singer (2004) brought attention to the importance of computer use as a learning tool for children with disabilities to communicate, play, and learn. Drawing on both functional and development approaches to intervention with young children with disabilities, the authors of this book adapted the AT toolkit approach developed by Judge (2006) and Sadao et al. (2009). The authors of this book expanded AT toolkits in four categories: communication, play, literacy, and computer use, which also

Table 9.1. AT toolkit categories and tools for participation in daily activities

Communication	Play	Literacy	Computers
Communication photographs	Adapted toy	Page fluffers and turners	Mouse house
Communication book	Various switches	Baggie book (plastic-bag encased pages)	Switch interface
Eye-gaze communicator	Battery interrupter	Slantboard	Touch window/screen
Low-tech visual scene	Plug adapter	Head pointer on baseball cap/visor	Software
Single-message voice output communication aid	Battery-operated spinner		
Step-by-Step/Sequencer			

provide the format for this book and encompass developmental foundations and functional skills to enable children with disabilities to explore, learn, and participate in early learning environments. Table 9.1 shows each of the four categories with examples of AT tools. Although each of the AT tools potentially overlap in multiple categories, the primary target category for each tool is illustrated.

Assistive Technology Toolkit for Communication

A collection of tools to target communication development in young children with disabilities is designed to consider sequentially more complex skills and opportunities to participate in communicative interactions. Communication photographs are listed as a beginning communication tool in Table 9.2. A collection of photographs within the AT toolkit for communication can be generated from digital photographs of items contained within the toolkit, such as toys, adapted books, or other items in the environment. Using communication photographs can then be assessed with individual children to determine responsiveness to photographs or the need for more tangible communication tools, such as real objects. By using photographs, children can progress to a communication book, which can be made from a small photograph album. Photographs may be laminated and attached with Velcro to each page of the communication book rather than inserted into the page covering, thus allowing easy removal and storage in the book.

An eye-gaze communicator is another type of tool that evaluates access methods for children who have limited ability to reach, grasp, or point to pictures. Photographs or icons may be attached to the corners of a transparent plastic photograph frame to allow the communication partner to observe eye-gaze patterns to indicate possible choice and selection through direction of the child's eye gaze. From this basic level of choice making, a low-tech visual scene provides a next step in the sequence of communication development to provide a means for communicative interchanges and turn taking using photographs or icons in the context of a visual scene that depicts an environment familiar to the child, such as a playground, dress-up corner, or reading nook. The adult can determine the child's ability to respond to questions by using pictures to "express" answers and comments about the activity shown in the visual scene.

Vocal expression is represented as the next step in communication development and uses a single-message VOCA that can be purchased commercially or made from voice recorders found in talking greeting cards. A single, repeatable message is recorded and activated within the context of reading a book, playing a game, singing a song, or participating in a routine that the child enjoys. By observing the child's ability to activate the VOCA and degree of assistance needed, providers can determine the appropriateness of this type of tool to support communication. Next, a sequential-message VOCA, such as a Step-by-Step from AbleNet or Sequencer from Adaptivation, can be introduced within the context of a conversation, song, game, or story with multiple messages for the child

Table 9.2. AT toolkit for communication

Targeted developmental stage	Item definition and examples	Item sources	Item applications
Prelinguistic communication and preliteracy	*Communication book* Digital photographs of favorite toys, people, activities, and places organized in a photograph album	Discount stores Digital camera for photographs Lamination Velcro to attach photographs to pages of album	Categorize photographs with a picture of topics on the front page Prior to each activity (e.g., snack, art, music, outdoor play), guide child to select topic and choose items in which to play
Prelinguistic communication and preliteracy	*Communication photographs of kit items* Digital photographs of every item in the toolkit stored in a photograph album	Discount stores Digital camera for photographs Lamination Velcro to attach photographs to pages of album	Child will indicate choice of toy/game by choosing photograph out of two choices Ask child to pick the next toy/game he or she wants to play with; build choices as needed
Prelinguistic communication to make choices of activities; emerging language to indicate feelings and expanded vocabulary	*Eye-gaze board* Clear plastic photograph frame or clipboard Allows photographs, symbol cards, or small objects to be attached for hands-free viewing by child/user Orient vertically in between child and communication partner so joint referencing is clear	Clear plastic PVC pipe Wood Cardboard	Identify child's understanding of objects, pictures, symbols, gestures, and/or spoken words Improve expressive language skills Help establish choice-making skill Improve ability for joint attention during communication
Emerging language with expanding receptive vocabulary	*Low-tech visual scene* Photograph or graphic of a familiar environment with associated vocabulary props	File folders Page covers Contact paper BoardMaker PCS symbols (http://www.mayer-johnson.com) Photographs Sticky-back foam Velcro dots	Create a scene for every environment to use in communicating "What did we see?" Increase number of words expressed by locating familiar pictures and pairing them with the activity (slide/playground scene)
Prelinguistic and emerging communication/language	*Single-message VOCA* Purchase or make with voice recording module	Express One http://www.attainment.com Voice recording module http://www.augresources.com	Use single words and messages to request favorite activities Participate in storytelling by having repetitive lines of a story recorded and ready to be activated
Emerging communication and language; developing language	*Sequential-message VOCA* Step-by-Step Sequencer	Step-by-Step http://www.AbleNet.com Sequencer http://www.adaptivation.com	Record series of messages in conversation script Record lines of story and have child take turns "reading" pages with peers and teacher Record songs and "sing"

to "tell" and "respond" with others. Observing the child's adaptation and use of the sequential-message VOCA and other tools described provides a basis for team decisions regarding appropriate selections for AT to support communication development. The tools listed and described are not exhaustive; yet, they do represent increasing complexity in communication development. Based on prior assessment background and knowledge of an individual child's readiness, early childhood teams will decide on the level of complexity and select a corresponding AT tool to introduce to the child.

Assistive Technology Toolkit for Play

Adaptations for play include simple modifications from adapting colored markers with sponge rollers for improved grasp to buying electronic toys with a variety of switches (see Chapter 6). The toy items listed in the AT toolkit for play in Table 9.3 represent toys to support participation in play beginning with cause-and-effect experiences to interacting with peers. The adapted toy example can be a number of toys that are battery operated and can be purchased already switch ready or adapted after the fact. Adapted toys ready for switch use are commercially available from companies such as Enabling Devices and include animals that move, bubble blowers, and vehicles. Toy stores and electronic stores sell battery-operated toys that can be adapted with battery interrupters and plug adapters, which are inexpensive and can be ordered from online sources listed by AbleData (http://www.abledata.com), a comprehensive database to locate materials to adapt toys and electronic devices. Adapted toys require switch activation, and key items in the toolkit are various switches that include small and large pressure-activated switches, such as the Jelly Bean and Big Red Switches, and sip-and-puff switches, which are all available from AbleNet or Don Johnston.

Beyond cause-and-effect play that allows the child to activate toys through switch access, a battery-operated spinner is essential to include in the AT toolkit for play. Battery-operated spinners provide a means to choose toys and take turns in games. Ready-made spinners with overlays are available from AbleNet or can be made from children's pottery wheels, available in toy stores. The collection of items listed provide a means for early childhood team members to determine the physical, motivational, and play development stage of each child and to match appropriate play adaptations needed to engage in progressively advanced stages of play.

Assistive Technology Toolkit for Literacy

Exposure to books begins with physical access. The examples of tools listed in Table 9.4 offer a means for providers to allow each child to explore books at his or her own pace and access method. Page fluffers and turners are listed first as a method to adapt existing books, such as board books, with favorite early themes including animals, vehicles, toys, people, body parts, and clothing. Materials to create easier physical access to separating pages (fluffers) were reviewed extensively in Chapter 7 and include any durable material that can be attached between pages to create easier access to the book. Page turners are attached to page edges, providing material to grip and turn pages. By observing which materials work for each child, practitioners can determine the appropriate access methods for engaging each child with books.

Beyond physical access, creating an adapted book in the form of baggie books fills a number of purposes. Baggie books are attributed to King-DeBaun (2007b), who developed the instructions to create these from teacher-made books and zipper bags that are stapled together. Creating a baggie book provides a flexible tool as the pages can be designed to include any content that is relevant to the child, such as family photographs, a story

Table 9.3.   AT toolkit for play

Developmental stage	Item definition amd examples	Item sources	Item applications
Cause-and-effect play	*Adapted toy* Battery-operated toy with switch capacity	Frog with moving tongue and legs available from http://www.enablingdevices .com	Increase participation in circle time by activating toy when responding to story's repetitive line sequence
Cause-and-effect play Participatory play for older children	*Homemade switch* Allows easier physical access to switch adapted toys, computers, and environmental controls through the use of a single device/switch	Materials for homemade switch available from http://www.rjcooper.com	Connect homemade switch to adapted toy Take turns in activating with peer Develop thematic unit with battery-operated frog from Enabling Devices and *Jump Frog, Jump* book
Cause-and-effect play Participatory play for older children	*Battery interrupter* Adapter that allows switch activation of battery-operated toys Attach battery interrupter to battery casing between battery connection and toy Connect plug to switch or voice output communication aid	Materials for battery interrupter available from http://www.enablingdevices.com	Activate toy with repeated line
Cause-and-effect play Participatory play for older children	*Plug adapter* Adapter that allows various size switch plugs to fit and work with a variety of jack sizes	Electronic stores Internet	
Participatory and interactive play	*Battery-operated spinner* A device that rotates like a clock at variable intervals and can be adapted to be activated by a switch	Purchase All-Turn-It spinner from http://www.ablenet.com Create adapted child's pottery wheel from toy stores	Allow child to play a game with peers using a switch to "roll the dice" (increase peer-to-peer interactions) Use the spinner by hitting the switch to indicate random greetings

sequence of recent outings, or favorite books that can be protected in the plastic bags. In addition, props are made with matching items to attach to the pages of the book with Velcro, thus extending attention and engagement with the book content. Observation and interaction with the baggie book will add assessment information to plan appropriate book adaptations that are needed regarding physical, cognitive, linguistic, and sensory access discussed in Chapter 7.

Physical access to books can be further observed and supported using a slantboard, a tool that is easily made with a three-ring binder, approximately 3 inches in depth and

Table 9.4. AT toolkit for emergent literacy

Developmental stage	Item definition examples	Item sources	Item applications
Preliteracy: Book handling	*Page fluffers* Attached to book page to increase space between for turning	Sponges Furniture stoppers Clothes pins Paper clips	Increase access to books by allowing page turning with hand or wand
Emergent literacy: Picture and word awareness Rhyme awareness	*Baggie book* Baggies stapled together to form a binding with separate book pages for protection and easy access	Zipper bags Velcro dots http://www.feinersupply.com Sticky-back foam Instructions in SWEET AT toolkit http://www.scoe.net/seeds/res ources/at/atToolkit.html	Create story with photographs or Boardmaker PCS based on familiar theme, such as the zoo, with repetitive lines and props to match pictures Take turns with peer Provide opportunities for picture labeling using props attached to book pages with Velcro
Emergent literacy: Book handling Print awareness Receptive vocabulary Early literacy: Phonological awareness	*Slantboard* Slanted surface such as a three-ring binder covered with Velcro-friendly fabric on one side and shelf liner on other side Rough Velcro on back of books, base of voice output communication aid, or toy	Purchase from http://www.augresources.com Create with three-ring, 3-inch binder and microfiber fabric cover from office supply and craft stores	Group or individual book time Increase access to books to allow one-handed access. Places book in visual field. Provides support for wrist movement and position
Preliteracy: Book handling Emergent literacy: Identifying pictures, words, print	*Head pointer baseball cap/visor* Allows easier physical access to a child's environment if head control is a strength	Ball cap Visor Strapping material Pencil Shelf liner Electrical zip ties	Child can touch and manipulate objects Child can turn pages of a book Child can access touchscreen or computer keyboard for learning opportunities

covered with Velcro-friendly material. Rough Velcro is placed on the back of a book to attach to the slanted surface of the binder, thus stabilizing the book. In addition, a piece of nonslip shelf liner can be placed under the binder to prevent movement. Further access to books for children who require a head pointer to turn pages and to point to pictures can be made with a simple adaptation to a baseball cap or visor. Instructions to create the baseball cap/visor head pointer are available in the SWEET AT toolkit.

Assistive Technology Toolkit for Computers

Adapted computer use potentially offers children with disabilities the necessary tools to advance cognitive, language, literacy, and preacademic skills. The tools included for computer use are listed in Table 9.5 and are designed to provide improved physical access, maximum engagement, concept development, and structured learning.

Initially for access, the mouse house (Burkhart, n.d.) is included as a means to operate one-click programs that provide a cause-and-effect-operation. The mouse house is constructed with a small photograph album that is emptied to create a "house" for a computer mouse to be activated with a simple up-and-down movement on the top cover of the album. Instructions to build the mouse house are available from http://www.lburkhart.com/mhouse.htm.

Although the mouse house provides an initial starting point for physical access to computer use, alternate access methods may be needed, such as a Switch-Click®, USB computer switch, adapted mouse, joystick, head pointer, and eye tracker. Ready-made computer interfaces that are commercially available for children and include multiple means of access were reviewed in Chapter 8. A switch interface is also included in this toolkit in order to link existing switches that may be available to use with computers and those that are available commercially from companies such as Don Johnston. A touch

Table 9.5.   AT toolkit for computer use

Developmental stage	Item definition examples	Item sources	Item applications
Physical access for direct touch Cause and effect	*Touch window/screen* Touch windows or screens for computers allow items on the computer screen to be selected directly by touching the items with fingers or stylus	Touch windows/screens are available as add-on devices to existing computers Available from http://www.abilityhub.com/mouse/touchscreen.htm http://www.magictouch.com	Develop the concept of cause and effect Direct selection accuracy Recreation, games, and independent play Preacademic and academic programs
Cause and effect Single switch	*Mouse house* A homemade adaptation to a computer mouse that allows it to function like a single switch	This can be fabricated using a small photograph album, sponge or foam, Velcro, and simple tools Instructions at http://www.lburkhart.com/mhouse.htm	Attach USB plug to computer and position mouse house Take turns activating with single-switch game with peer
Physical access for switch use	*Switch interface* Adaptive device that is connected to a computer that allows a switch to control various mouse functions	Computer switch interfacing device can be purchased from http://www.donjohnston.com http://www.enablemart.com	Develop the concept of cause and effect Switch training for motor accuracy Recreation/game programs Preacademic and academic programs
Cause and Effect Concept development Vocabulary development Language development Preacademic skills	*Software* Adaptive software is useful to practice motor accuracy with switches, enhance play and social interactions, and reinforce learning in all areas of development	Cause and effect: Marble Soft-Simtech http://www.marblesoft.com Concept development: Soft Touch http://www.softtouch.com Language development: Laureate Learning http://www.laureatelearning.com	Provide cause and effect software program/game Switch training for motor accuracy Recreation/game programs Preacademic and academic programs

window/screen provides an alternate access method for children who are not responsive to switch activation. Often, young children respond to directly touching the computer screen rather than activating a switch, an act that is one level removed from immediate activity on the computer screen (Grant & Singer, 2004). Further assessment to determine the appropriate computer access method may also be conducted using guidelines for switch assessment by Justice (2006).

A collection of software or demonstration software that is available for trial use is also included in the AT toolkit for computers. Types of software were discussed in Chapter 8, and recommended programs for determining the child's interest and responsiveness included programs from Marblesoft, SoftTouch, and Laureate Learning. Including programs that provide cause-and-effect experiences, opportunities to observe switch use, responsiveness to various sizes and visual display representations, receptive understanding of vocabulary, and memory for sequences of pictures will help gather information regarding appropriate computer software to match the child's needs. The tools selected and highlighted thus far provide a starting point for team assessment and intervention planning in providing appropriate AT tools for computer use.

COMPONENTS OF ASSISTIVE TECHNOLOGY TOOLKITS FOR YOUNG CHILDREN

The AT toolkits for each of the four categories discussed previously are designed to augment early intervention and early childhood services for young children with disabilities and their family members. The tools highlighted in each category provide a starting point to design AT strategies that will overcome barriers to participation for each child. Each of four AT toolkits is further described in Tables 9.2–9.5. The following components are included in each toolkit as a guide for team members to select AT solutions in partnership with family members.

Developmental Sequence for Technology Applications

Each toolkit begins by considering the developmental stages of young children. Generally, low-tech AT tools are targeted for early developmental stages of communication, play, literacy, and computer use. For example, communication photographs and photograph books often provide a means for children in prelinguistic stages of communication development to link photographs with actual objects. Recognizing a photograph as a representation of favorite toys, activities, pets, places to go, feelings, games, and so forth provides a means to make choices and develop more abstract representation of the actual item or event. By attaching meaning to photographs, children can then progress to increasingly abstract symbols that have meaning, including hearing a spoken word, seeing a line drawing or icon, recognizing a sight word, and eventually attaching meaning to individual sounds and letter representations to gain literacy skills. Identifying developmental stages and skills that correspond to each item in the AT toolkits also provides practitioners another method to match appropriate tools to the needs of each individual child.

Item Definitions and Examples

AT toolkit items are defined with examples in Tables 9.6–9.9. Developing each of the AT toolkits is not limited to one specific item to target developmental stages or support functional skills for participation with others. Rather, the type of item has many variations and providers have many choices to complete each toolkit.

Item Source

Each of the items and variations within each AT tool can be obtained through several sources, including vendors with online purchasing or local stores. Where applicable, specific vendors and their web sites are identified for the sources for AT toolkit items in Table 9.5. General sources are also listed for those tools that are available in retail settings such as discount and hardware stores and other community outlets. There are two caveats in listing sources for the AT items: 1) being cautious because web sites often become outdated and obsolete and 2) listing of a particular vendor is not considered an endorsement by the authors but only the identification of reliable and established sources.

Item Applications

Examples in each AT toolkit include strategies to apply the AT tools within natural environments. Beyond describing tools, sources, and selections according to developmental levels, examples for application are meant to guide early childhood providers in developing and implementing IFSP/IEP goals. As identified by Stoner et al. (2008), early childhood teachers perceived that AT services required computer-based equipment, extensive time, and training. Application examples aim to address some of the perceived barriers to implementing AT to create scenarios in which daily routines become the context for AT services and equipment to be used.

Contents of Assistive Technology Toolkits for Young Children

AT toolkits require at least two containers—one for AT equipment that is purchased or made and another for supplies that can be used to create further AT adaptations as needed (Sadao et al., 2009). Collecting equipment that is targeted for specific skills and developmental stages is listed for each of the four toolkits. Tables 9.6–9.9 cover supplies for communication, play, literacy, and computers consecutively. The list is not exhaustive, but provides an assortment of ideas to consider for a set of supply kits.

Table 9.6.   AT toolkit for communication: suggested equipment and supply contents

AT communication equipment: container 1	AT communication supplies: container 2
Communication book with digital photographs of toolkit items (homemade)	Voice recording modules (http://www.augresources.com)
Eye-gaze board (homemade)	Page savers (nonglare)
Visual scene (homemade)	1 small photograph binder for mouse house 2 photograph albums for communication book and voice output communication aid (VOCA)
I Talk, Step-by-Step (Ablenet)	Microfiber mitt
Express One, talking photograph album, talking picture frame (Attainment)	Foam doorknob hanger
Photograph album VOCA (homemade)	Clear clipboard/plastic picture frame (8 × 10)
Boardmaker PCS (Mayer-Johnson)	Clear contact paper
	Hot glue gun
	Hot glue gun refills
	Glue sticks
	Velcro dots, hard and soft (one roll of each)
	Velcro strips, hard and soft (one roll of each)
	Stapler
	Scissors
	Magnetic paper
	Sticky-back foam
	Sticky tack
	Car sponge
	Sponge rollers for grasping markers
	Double-sided carpet tape

Table 9.7.   AT toolkit for play: suggested equipment and supply contents

AT play equipment: container 1	AT play supplies: container 2
Visual scene (homemade) I Talk, Step-by-Step (Ablenet) Express One, talking photograph album, talking picture frame (Attainment) Battery-operated toy R.J. Cooper Switches (Big Red, Jelly Bean, Soft Switch, Buddy Button)	Voice recording modules (http://www.augresources.com) Battery interrupter (Enabling Devices, Linda Burkhart) Switch interface (Don Johnston) Switch plug adapters (Linda Burkhart) Page savers (nonglare) Microfiber mitt Foam doorknob hanger Batteries Hot glue gun Hot glue gun refills Glue sticks Masking tape Duct tape Zipper bags Scissors Nonslip shelf liner Sticky tack Sponge rollers for grasping markers Styrofoam ball for grasping pencil Bicycle grips

Table 9.8.   AT toolkit for emergent literacy: suggested equipment and supply contents

AT literacy equipment: container 1	AT literacy supplies: container 2
Visual scene (homemade) Head pointer cap/visor (homemade) I Talk, Step-by-Step (Ablenet) Express One, talking photograph album, talking picture frame (Attainment) Adapted book Baggie book Battery-operated toy R.J. Cooper Switches (Big Red, Jelly Bean, Soft Switch, Buddy Button)	3-inch binders Page savers (nonglare) Tempo loop display fabric to cover binder Microfiber mitt Clear contact paper Hot glue gun Hot glue gun refills Glue sticks Masking tape Duct tape Zipper bags Velcro dots, hard and soft (one roll of each) Velcro strips, hard and soft (one roll of each) Stapler Scissors Foam, paper clips, hair ties for page fluffers Highlighter tape (http://onionmountaintech.com) Magnetic paper Nonslip shelf liner Zip ties Baseball cap with pencil Sticky-back foam

Table 9.9.   AT toolkit for computer use: suggested equipment and supply contents

AT computer equipment: container 1	AT computer supplies: container 2
Head pointer cap/visor (homemade) R.J. Cooper switches (Big Red, Jelly Bean, Soft Switch, Buddy Button) Magic touchscreen (KeyTec) USB computer switch click (TASH, Don Johnston) Mouse house (homemade, Linda Burkhart) Boardmaker PCS (Mayer-Johnson) Computer software (Marblesoft, Ablenet/Soft Touch) or freeware	Switch interface (Don Johnston) Zip ties Baseball cap with pencil

APPLICATIONS: TOOLKIT ASSESSMENT AND INTERVENTION PLANNING MAPS

Aligning outcomes across developmental milestones, assessment findings, functional skill target areas, and daily intervention contexts is a major initiative in early childhood programs serving young children with disabilities. Focusing on outcome measurement at the federal and state levels is a driving force in most early childhood programs, resulting in attention to measuring and defining outcomes as goals to assess both individual child progress and program effectiveness to serve young children with a range of developmental and educational needs. The development of crosswalks in early childhood programs provides a framework to align research-based developmental levels expected for typically developing children, curriculum goals in early childhood programs for children with disabilities, and actual outcomes as measured with periodic progress assessments. For example, the Early Childhood Outcomes (ECO) Center (2006) has developed numerous crosswalks to align commonly used developmental assessment tools with federal outcome measures for early childhood programs. The crosswalk model has also been adapted for use with the AT toolkits in assessment and intervention planning with young children. The crosswalk concept is shown in the form of maps to lead practitioners to use the AT toolkits, moving from assessment to intervention with AT in an activity-based format.

An AT toolkit map is shown for each of the AT Toolkits in Tables 9.10–9.13. By aligning OSEP outcomes and commonly used early childhood assessment/curriculum guides, practitioners will find that AT tools allow children to overcome barriers to be part of ongoing learning activities with peers. Furthermore, the AT toolkit maps serve to extend AT practices into typical early childhood settings.

SUMMARY

AT services support early intervention and early childhood programs to include all children in learning activities (Weikle & Hadadian, 2003). By developing and applying AT toolkits, practitioners can provide AT assessment and intervention with appropriate AT solutions for each child. This chapter reviewed the theoretical and research-based contributions from the field to contribute to developing AT toolkits. The practicality of AT toolkits gained support in research conducted with early childhood teachers who increased their use of AT through a community of users and availability of AT toolkits (Parette et al., 2009).

The availability of AT toolkits has the potential to coordinate with a universal design approach to early education by engineering classrooms and home environments with adaptations that work for all children. AT toolkits can assure that transdisciplinary team members consider AT for children with IFSPs/IEPs and use the kit to promote inclusion efforts in home, school, and community settings. Creating toolkits for every inclusion team increases the likelihood of successful inclusive opportunities for young children by providing basic, easy-to-use adaptations that may support a child's integration into learning environments not readily accessible without such accommodations. Having the tools readily available for professionals, early intervention and early childhood staff, special education providers, other educators, and therapists to demonstrate to parents and general education teachers promotes the ease of use and access. Judge et al. (2008) emphasized that an AT toolkit offers a solution to the challenge of limited access to AT equipment and related services by providing the tools in the classrooms where opportunities for participating in activities generally occur.

The four AT toolkits outlined and described in this chapter offer a means to programs serving young children with disabilities for bridging the gaps between theory, research, and practice. Perceptions of high-tech and high-cost AT services and barriers

Table 9.10. AT communication toolkit map: Linking assessment to participation in home, preschool, child care, and community

OSEP outcomes	AEPS® communication goals	Environments/ activities	Example: barriers to participation	Applying AT for communication
1: Positive social relationships	Participates in established social routines	PS and CC: Greeting COMM: Riding in car	Child is nonverbal No opportunity to greet others	Photograph album VOCA placed within reach of child that says GOOD MORNING, FRIENDS
1: Positive social relationships	Initiates and maintains interaction with adult	PS and CC: Free choice play time	Child is nonverbal Physical limitations to select	Eye-gaze board and communication photographs Hold up and note gaze/reach to choose toys
2: Knowledge and skills	Uses 50 words to express a variety of communicative functions (requesting, commenting, greeting, refusing)	H: Requesting food PS: Requesting art supplies CC: Requesting songs for music	Child is nonverbal and cannot physically select photographs Adults and peers tend to anticipate needs and wants	Communication book or communication can Determine number of choices to present Observe photograph selection method (eye gaze, point, lean, head turn)
2: Knowledge and skills	Uses two- to three-word combinations to express a variety of communicative functions	H: Family event photographs PS and CC: Prepare and review field trips	Child is passive participant Adult narrates events in photographs	Visual scene Assist child to express phrase using sentence strip on chart and complete sentence by placing Velcro photograph in slot
2: Knowledge and skills	Repeats familiar nursery rhyme	PS and CC: Music circle	Adult or peers provide verbal repetition of song/rhyme	Talking photograph frame with repeated line Step-by-Step to segment rhyme
2: Knowledge and skills	Recalls event in sequence	PS: Closing circle COMM: Riding bus H and CC: Greeting	Child is nonverbal Adult misses child cues, does not wait for response More verbal children respond	Step-by-Step to review events of the day at school, on bus, or at home while greeting each new communication partner

Key: H, home; PS, preschool; CC, child care; COMM, community; OSEP, Office of Special Education Programs; AEPS®, Assessment, Evaluation, and Programming System for Infants and Children; VOCA, voice output communication aid.

to service delivery can be balanced with a complete selection of low-tech and low-cost AT solutions. Small beginnings that show the success of AT tools with low-tech supports enable teams to document success and convince administrators and funding sources of the importance to reach all children and find AT solutions for continued learning and achievement. Access to high-tech solutions is essential for many children

Table 9.11.   AT play toolkit map: linking assessment to participation in home, preschool, child care, and community

OSEP outcomes	Play goals—HELP for preschoolers	Environments/ activities	Example: barriers to participation	Applying AT for play
1: Positive social relationships	5.4: Responsibilities /rules	PS: Circle time CC: Reading a story	Opportunity: nonverbal, cannot request playtime Access: physical limitations Attitude: peers request play activities for child	VOCA/SGD with repetitive line recorded and props for group participation in stories, songs, and group activities.
1: Positive social relationships	5.5: Social interactions and play	H: Family events PS: Greeting CC: Prepare for field trips COMM: Riding in car	Opportunity: nonverbal, cannot greet others Access: child is passive participant Attitude: adult narrates events in photographs	Talking photograph frame with family pictures and a recording of each person Photograph album VOCA placed within reach of child and it says GOOD MORNING, FRIENDS Visual scene Assist child to express phrase using sentence strip on chart and complete sentence by placing Velcro photo in slot
1: Positive social relationships	5.6: Social manners	PS: Board game CC: Board game	Opportunity: nonverbal, expresses emotions through screaming Access: fine motor limitations Attitude: adults play for child	Switch-adapted battery, battery-operated spinner Build up game pieces, enlarge game board, and provide simple messages for Boardmaker game icons Feeling symbols matched with single-message voiceovers placed in a clear, plastic carrying case for pictures/voice-overs to indicate feelings
1: Positive social relationships	5.7: Social language	H: Playtime PS: Computer time CC: Center time	Opportunity: limited access to play and computer stations Access: unable to communicate feelings Attitude: adults speak for child	Communication book, communication photograph album, and PCS symbols to identify and label feelings Using multiple-message VOCA/SGD (Go Talk, Cheap Talk, Activity Pad, Super Talker) programmed with words to identify feelings Auditory cues at transition time

Key: H, home; PS, preschool; CC, child care; COMM, community; OSEP, Office of Special Education Programs; VOCA, voice output communication aid; SGD, speech-generating device; PCS, Picture Communication Symbol.

Table 9.12. AT literacy toolkit map: linking assessment to participation in home, preschool, child care, and community

OSEP outcomes	Literacy goals—Brigance examples	Environments/ activities	Example: barriers to participation	Applying AT for literacy
1: Positive social relationships	Excitement and love of language and print materials F: General knowledge and comprehension F.1: Response to experience with books	H: Bedtime stories PS: Circle time CC: Literacy center COMM: Road signage	Opportunity: child is unable to handle books Access: limited speech inhibits indicating interests in books and signs Attitude: parents and peers speak for child during storytime	Use adapted books with page fluffers and page turners to increase physical access to books Use a Go Talk 4 by Attainment to label familiar signs in the environment, such as a stop sign; child hits picture of sign when seen in route to child care Provide a Step-by-Step or Sequencer to record repeated lines and story text for the child to press when the page is turned
2: Knowledge and skills	Comprehension and meaning from print materials F: General knowledge and comprehension F.6: Directional/ positional concepts	H: Computer station PS: Computer center CC: Computer laptop COMM: Library	Opportunity: child has limited opportunities to read books Access: limited speech inhibits verbal expression about what is happening in a story Attitude: parents and peers suggest what child is thinking and speak for him or her	Use My Own Bookshelf, a computer software program, to create stories about the child's daily routines that can be read onscreen using a single function switch click and include prepositional concepts
2: Knowledge and skills	Phonological awareness (ability to hear, identify, and manipulate the sound structure of oral language) I: Basic reading skills I.8: Matches initial consonants with pictures	H: Playtime PS: Game center CC: Free choice play COMM: Mommy and Me program	Opportunity: child watches other children during free play but does not participate Access: oral motor difficulties inhibit speech production Attitude: parents and peers tend to talk for the child	Adapted See 'n Say spinner; child presses switch to activate spinner and matches letter to its sound
2: Knowledge and skills	Alphabetic principle H: Readiness H.2: Recites alphabet	H: Storytime PS: Storytime CC: Storytime COMM: Grocery shopping	Opportunity: does not usually participate in circle time because of physical challenges Access: physical access to books is difficult Attitude: adults turn pages of book	Baggie book and page fluffers to turn pages of alphabet book (e.g., *Chicka Chicka Boom Boom*) with accompanying letter props and voice output for each letter on each page and alphabet software program for letter identification

Key: H, home; PS, preschool; CC, child care; COMM, community; OSEP, Office of Special Education Programs; Brigance, Brigance Inventory of Early Development II.

199

Table 9.13. AT computer toolkit map: linking assessment to participation in home, preschool, child care, and community

OSEP outcomes	Ounce Scale goals and examples	Environments/ activities	Example: barriers to participation	Applying AT for computer use
3: Action to meet needs	Gains control of head and body Physical development	PS and H: Computer time	Child has physical needs and cannot sit unattended in a chair	Provide cushions for support in chair at computer station
2: Knowledge and skills	Responds to sights and sounds Communication and language	PS and H: Computer time	Child is nonverbal Physical limitations to select	Gazes at computer screen as adult activates cause-and-effect software images
2: Knowledge and skills	Pays attention to what is happening in the environment Cognitive development	PS and H: Computer time	Child has visual impairments and physical needs Adults and peers tend to anticipate needs and wants	Observe method of attending to a computer screen with animated pictures from Wheels on the Bus software (eye gaze, point, lean, head turn, lean)
2: Knowledge and skills	Explores the environment; learns how things work Cognitive development	PS and H: Computer time	Child is passive participant Adult demonstrates computer cause-and-effect software by pressing touchscreen while child observes	Cause-and-effect software with touchscreen on computer Adult models touchscreen effects Next adult uses hand over hand to assist child to touch screen to activate software Child touches screen to activate a change in the screen effects
2: Knowledge and skills	Plays beside other children Social-emotional	PS and H: Computer time	Physical access Complex manipulations	Mouse house Activate cause-and-effect activities on computer Turn taking with another child with typically developing peer demonstrating mouse house
3: Action to meet needs	Reaches toward things	PS and H: Computer time	Child is unable to use hands for reaching Child can gaze toward preferred objects and has some head control	Use a baseball cap head pointer to touch screen on computer to activate cause-and-effect software
2: Knowledge and skills	Makes things happen Cognitive development	PS and H: Computer time	Adult or peers activate computer screen by hitting the keyboard for cause and effect	Child activates touchscreen using cause-and-effect software
2: Knowledge and skills	Follows simple directions and suggestions consistently Communication and language	PS and H: Computer time	Child is nonverbal Adult misses child cues, does not wait for response More verbal children respond	Dual switch for clicking and scanning options Child can follow a two-step direction on the computer screen
2: Knowledge and skills	Expects results when playing with toys and other objects	PS and H: Computer time	Physical access to books is limited	Hits switch to turn pages of Wheels on the Bus online book

Key: H, home; PS, preschool; CC, child care; COMM, community; OSEP, Office of Special Education Programs.

200

to become literate adults who can fully participate in the information age. The technology divide is disappearing, and AT toolkits offer a means to overcome barriers to become members of many communities, both on- and offline.

QUESTIONS

1. What kinds of tools are important to include in an AT toolkit for young children with disabilities?

2. Why include low-tech tools in a toolkit?

3. Name three toolkit items that are essential for increasing access to play environments. Describe how to use them in play situations.

4. How might you employ a toolkit in your work setting to increase the use of AT?

5. What other items would you suggest to include in a toolkit for supporting the use of computers in a preschool classroom not already included here?

TIPS

○ Follow the suggestions provided in this chapter for starting an AT toolkit.

○ Check on the availability of tools already purchased to start a toolkit.

○ Organize the toolkit into functional containers.

○ Include a separate supply container with batteries and other essential materials.

○ Compose a list of items included in your toolkit with a brief description of how to use each tool.

○ Peruse various AT vendor catalogs online to get ideas for new toolkit items.

○ Schedule monthly make-and-take sessions with other staff to create low-tech items to include in your toolkit.

Resources

CHAPTER 1

Let's Play Project

http://letsplay.buffalo.edu/

The Let's Play Project at the University of Buffalo has provided research and training information concerning AT and play since the mid-1990s. The web site provides downloadable handouts, handbooks, links, and PowerPoint presentations on all aspects of AT, play, and universal design. There is also an assessment for universal design for play.

National Early Childhood Technical Assistance Center (NECTAC)

http://www.nectac.org/topics/atech/atech.asp

NECTAC provides technical assistance to state-level representatives on all aspects of early childhood issues and includes a topical focus area on AT, including downloadable handouts and annotated links.

Supporting Early Education Delivery Systems (SEEDS) Project

http://www.scoe.net/seeds/resources/at/at.html

The SEEDS Project, a California technical assistance initiative, includes a section on AT on their web site. The materials include downloadable training modules; annotated links to AT for infants, toddlers, and preschoolers; and an AT toolkit with 19 activity-based examples.

Tots n Tech Research Institute

http://www.asu.edu/clas/tnt/

A technical assistance partnership between two universities, Thomas Jefferson and Arizona State, Tots n Tech Research Institute provides research and application on AT for infants and toddlers with disabilities and their families. In addition to technical and resource briefs, the web site includes a section filled with ideas for using AT with young children with disabilities.

Wisconsin Assistive Technology Initiative (WATI)

http://www.wati.org/

The WATI is a state-level technical assistance system that includes a web section on AT for K–12. The site includes a downloadable handbook covering all the essential information on AT use with children.

CHAPTER 2

Augmentative and Alternative
Communication Rehabilitation Engineering Research Center

http://www.aac-rerc.com

The AAC-Rehabilitation Engineering Research Center (AAC-RERC) is a grant-sponsored program through the National Institutes of Health on Disability and Rehabilitation Research (NIDDR). AAC-RERC conducts research and training and publishes information on AT for people using AAC. The web site offers information and resources concerning all aspects of AAC including funding sources such as Medicare and report writing for funding of AAC devices.

AbleData

http://www.abledata.com

Abledata is an NIDRR-sponsored grant that offers a web site providing information about state AT projects, AT companies, and other information on AT. Web browsers can download a guide to funding sources for AT.

AblePlay

http://www.ableplay.org

The web site provides information on rating toy products used to adapt play for children with disabilities. The site focuses on play equipment and materials.

Family Center on Technology and Disability Resources

http://www.fctd.org

The Family Center on Technology and Disability Resources is another grant funded by the Office of Special Education Programs (OSEP) that provides an extensive web site of information on funding services and AT devices. The project mails out CDs covering information on all aspects of AT. An AT fact sheet can be downloaded that reviews the basics in acquiring AT funding sources.

Lekotek

http://www.lekotek.org

Lekotek provides information on how to assess and rate toys and equipment.

National Assistive Technology Assistance Partnership (NATTAP)

http://www.resnaprojects.org/nattap/

The NATTAP is a project authorized under the ATA of 1998. In collaboration with the Rehabilitation Engineering and AT Society of North America (RESNA), NATTAP provides resources on the benefits of AT, state contacts for AT programs, and information about starting a lending library with sample policies and forms.

CHAPTER 3

Center for Applied Special Technology (CAST) Universal Design Book Builder

http://bookbuilder.cast.org/

This site is part of the NCAGC web site and provides free access to create, share, publish, and read digital books for diverse learners.

Universal Design for Learning

http://www.cast.org/index.html

This web site includes the National Center on Accessing General Curriculum (NCAC). Universal design for learning resources for young children are defined as a framework for designing curricula that enable all individuals to gain knowledge, skills, and enthusiasm for learning. Resources for planning and designing universal design for learning environments for all children are available on this site.

CHAPTER 4

Assistive Technology Training Online (Buffalo)

http://atto.buffalo.edu/registered/ATBasics.php

The AT Training Online provides basic information for providers and family members regarding AT for special populations. The focus of the materials is primarily on school-age students, with many applications for families of younger children.

Early Childhood Tech Integrated Instructional System, Western Illinois

http://www.wiu.edu/ectiis/

This web site is a free online training program for families and early childhood professionals.

Family-Centered Care Resources

http://www.medicalhomeinfo.org/health/family.html

Links to research-based resources and policy guides for developing family-centered approaches are available on this web site, which is sponsored by the American Academy of Pediatrics.

Texas Assistive Technology Network: Online Training Modules

http://www.texasat.net/default.aspx?name=trainmod.home

Training modules are provided for providers, families, and teams to develop AT services in school settings. Although materials are focused on school-age populations, the evaluation module provides guidelines in AT assessment that can be applied with young children.

CHAPTER 5

AACIntervention.com

http://aacintervention.com/resources.htm

Resources for early communication overlays and activity boards

Barkley Center

http://aac.unl.edu

Early vocabulary lists based on core vocabulary research

Enabling Devices

http://enablingdevices.com

Communicator feature comparison chart for low- and mid-tech devices

Georgia Project for Assistive Technology

http://www.gpat.org/

AT for AAC in preschool; professional presentation materials

JFK Assistive Technology Quick Guides

http://www.jfkpartners.org

Information for parents and providers in early childhood on range of AT topics

**National Center to Improve
Practice (NCIP) Project on Baby Power!**

http://www2.edc.org/ncip/library/ec/Power_7.htm

Applications of AT with young children, specifically in communication development

Picture Dictionary

http://www.pdictionary.com/

Source for online photographs and pictures for communication tools

Speaking of Speech

http://www.speakingofspeech.com/Preschool_Page.html
Ready made overlays for songs, games, and activities

Trainland Tripod

http://trainland.tripod.com/pecs.htm
Source for pictures made with Boardmaker

University of Buffalo Assistive Technology Basics

http://atto.buffalo.edu/registered/ATBasics/Populations/aac/index.php
Julie Maro and Lorie Tufte overview of AT and AAC

University of Washington Augcomm

http://depts.washington.edu/augcomm/03_cimodel/commind1_intro.htm
Continuum of Communication Independence Model and examples

CHAPTER 6

Fisher Price

http://www.fisher-price.com/US/special_needs

Fisher Price provides a special needs section on their web site dedicated to young children with disabilities through a partnership with the Let's Play! Project. The site explores play and toy tips to support development in various domains. The site includes an age-by-age guide for play activities and toy selection.

Toys"R"Us

http://www.toysrus.com

The Toys"R"Us web site offers a toy guide and toys for kids with disabilities.

CHAPTER 7

Augmentative and Alternative Communication Messaging and Vocabulary

http://aac.unl.edu/vocabulary.html

Research-based vocabulary lists are provided for all levels of communication and learning, from preschool to adult. Teachers will find this a valuable resource to develop core vocabulary activities and to pair print with pictures in emergent literacy activities.

Advisor

http://www.e-advisor.us/storyboxes/index.php?fontsize=normal&hicontrast

The resources found on this web site will assist families and early childhood professionals to develop literacy tools in the form of story boxes for young children with visual impairments.

Augmentative Communication Community Partnerships

http://www.accpc.ca/elp-ts-intduringstory.htm#ex1234

Early literacy downloads in Boardmaker and Classroom Suite formats are available at no cost.

Baltimore City Schools

http://www.bcps.k12.md.us/boardmaker/adapted_library.asp

Hundreds of downloadable book resources and topic boards in Boardmaker format are available at no cost.

Center on the Social and Emotional Foundations for Early Learning

http://www.vanderbilt.edu/csefel/resources/strategies.html

Scripted stories for young children to support social-emotional development, positive behavior, and relationships are provided at no cost for teachers. In addition, many teacher resources for positive social development are available.

Clifford's Interactive Storybooks

http://teacher.scholastic.com/clifford1/

Four interactive stories about Clifford the Big Red Dog in Flash format, presented by Scholastic.

Creative Communicating

http://www.creativecommunicating.com

Many tips are provided for adapting books and making literacy-rich environments for young children of all ages at no cost. Subscription resources are also available for cost that allow downloading of adapted books in multiple formats.

GenieBooks in PowerPoint

http://www.auburn.edu/%7Emurrag1/bookindex.html

Decodable books for beginning readers in HTML or PowerPoint, with books identified by phonics.

Inkless Tales

http://www.inklesstales.com/stories/

A variety of online early reader/emergent and Dolch stories are available at no cost from this web site.

Judith Kuster's Web Site

http://www.mnsu.edu/comdis/kuster2/sptherapy.html

Examples of materials that can be adapted for therapy are included in downloadable formats.

Kennedy Center's Storytime Online

http://www.kennedy-center.org/multimedia/storytimeonline/

This web site provides four video storybooks online at no cost. Real media player is required to open and navigate the stories.

Kids' Corner from Wired for Books

http://wiredforbooks.org/kids.htm

Online audio stories from various children's books are available at no cost. Real media player is required.

Language Is Key

http://www.walearning.com/

Training resources are available that focus on developing language through shared book-reading strategies in multiple languages. A DVD or VHS is available for purchase, and free parent handouts in seven languages are provided.

Literacy Instruction for Individuals with Autism, Cerebral Palsy, Down Syndrome, and Other Disabilities

http://aacliteracy.psu.edu/

Janice Light and David McNaughton developed this web site based on their research that provides guidelines for teaching literacy to children with special needs, particularly those with complex communication needs. Specific guidelines and strategies to teach emergent and early literacy skills and multiple examples are provided with video demonstrations.

Magic Keys

http://www.magickeys.com/books/

Children's books online with more than 30 illustrated children's stories in html format at no cost.

Miami-Dade County Public Schools

http://prekese.dadeschools.net/BMD/activityspecific.html

Boardmaker downloads for vocabulary development, literacy centers, shared reading, and phonological awareness are available at no cost.

New York City Public Schools

http://schools.nyc.gov/Offices/District75/Departments/Literacy/AdaptedBooks/default.htm

Downloadable adapted books in Boardmaker, PowerPoint, Writing with Symbols, and PDF formats are available at no cost.

**Perkins Scout: Emergent Literacy Resources
for Braille and Prebraille Skills**

http://www.perkins.org/resources/scout/literacy-and-braille/emergent-literacy.html

Resources for teachers to provide emergent literacy experiences for young children with visual impairments are found on this web site.

Preschool Rainbow

http://www.preschoolrainbow.org/book-themes.htm

The web site includes information about organizing and creating a thematic unit and includes preschool book themes available with activities.

Reading Is Fundamental (RIF) Reading Planet

http://www.rif.org/readingplanet/content/read_aloud_stories.mspx

Reading Planet offers a collection of read-aloud books that changes monthly.

Snee

http://www.snee.com/epubkidsbooks/

Snee provides 16 free e-publications of children's picture books.

Special Education Technology, British Columbia

http://www.setbc.org/pictureSET/SubCategory.aspx?id=18

Activities, games, and songs in downloadable Boardmaker format are available for young children and school-age students.

Starfall

http://www.starfall.com/

Starfall is designed for first-grade readers and has more than 75 reading/writing resources that are also useful for prekindergarten, kindergarten, and second grade.

Stories to Read Online

http://www.beenleigss.eq.edu.au/requested_sites/storiesontheweb/storiesontheweb.html

This web site provides links to about 100 stories for early childhood and elementary-age children.

Storyline Online

http://www.storylineonline.net/

Storyline Online provides 19 stories read by members of the screen actors' guild, including modern classics such as *Stellaluna* and the *Polar Express*. Stories are read and displayed through streaming video.

StoryPlace Preschool Library

http://www.storyplace.org/preschool/other.asp

The web site links the reader to 15 stories and associated books and activities for young children.

Thames Valley Public Schools Speech and Language Resources

https://apps.tvdsb.on.ca/employees/dptspeced/Speech%20and%20Language%20Resources.htm#Picture%20Books

Many Boardmaker® downloads for children's books are available at no cost.

CHAPTER 8

Animoto

http://www.animoto.com

The Animoto web site uses personal photographs to create 30-second video clips.

ConnSense

http://www.connsensebulletin.com/software.html

Connecticut Special Education Network for Software Evaluation provides monthly software reviews focused on children with special needs.

Early Connections: Technology in Early Childhood Education

http://www.netc.org/earlyconnections/preschool/software.html

Early Connections provides a brief overview of software considerations for young children.

SuperKids Software Review

http://www.superkids.com

SuperKids provides an online resource of reviews conducted on a variety of educational software programs.

Tar Heel Readers

http://www.tarheelreader.org

Tar Heel Readers, an online source based out of the University of North Carolina at Chapel Hill, includes a collection of free downloadable and readable books using PowerPoint or Flash Player. The books come in a variety of subject areas and provide an option to create your own. The books can be used with a touchscreen, switches, and IntelliKeys.

CHAPTER 9

Augmentative and Alternative Communication TechConnect

http://www.aactechconnect.com/

AAC TechConnect provides AAC evaluations, AAC toolkits, online resources, and workshops for purchase.

National Assistive Technology Technical Assistance Partnership (NATTAP)

http://www.resnaprojects.org/nattap/at/stateprograms.html

The NATTAP lists the 56 state and territory programs that are funded under the ATA of 1998. State ATA programs work to improve the provision of AT to individuals with disabilities of all ages through comprehensive statewide programs of technology-related assistance, such as device loan programs.

SWEET Assistive Technology Toolkit

http://www.scoe.net/seeds/resources/at/atToolkit.html

The SWEET AT toolkit was developed to meet the need for access to low-tech, inexpensive tools designed to assist young children with disabilities to learn, play, grow, and participate with peers and family members. The SWEET AT toolkit is online and includes guides for creating and implementing an AT toolkit in early childhood settings.

References

Acheson, M.J. (2006). The effect of natural aided language stimulation on requesting desired objects or actions in children with autism spectrum disorder. (Doctoral dissertation, University of Cincinnati, 2006). OhioLINK Electronic Theses and Dissertations Center. Retrieved July 29, 2009, from http://www.ohiolink.edu/etd/view.cgi?acc_num=ucin1147311601

American Academy of Pediatrics. (2003). Policy statement: Family-centered care and the pediatrician's role. *Pediatrics, 112* (3), 691–696. Retrieved May 24, 2010, from http://aappolicy.aappublications.org/cgi/content/full/pediatrics;112/3/691

American Academy of Pediatrics. (2008). *New and improved definition of family-centered care.* Retrieved June 27, 2009, from http://www.medicalhomeinfo.org/health/family.html

American Speech-Language-Hearing Association. (2002). *Augmentative and alternative communication: Knowledge and skills for service delivery.* Retrieved July 21, 2009, from http://www.asha.org/policy

American Speech-Language-Hearing Association. (2003). *Speech-language pathologists and early intervention: ASHA practice policies documents support role.* Rockville, MD: Author.

American Speech-Language-Hearing Association. (2005). *Evidence-based practice in communication disorders.* Retrieved July 22, 2009, from www.asha.org/policy

American Speech-Language-Hearing Association. (2006). *Fact sheet: Natural environments for infants and toddlers who are deaf or hard of hearing and their families.* Retrieved June 19, 2009, from http://www.asha.org/advocacy/federal/idea/nat-env-child-facts.htm

Americans with Disabilities Act (ADA) of 1990, PL 101-336, 42 U.S.C. §§ 12101 *et seq.*

Angelo, D.H. (2000). Impact of augmentative and alternative communication devices on families. *Augmentative and Alternative Communication, 16,* 37–47.

Assistive Technology Act (ATA) of 1998 PL 105-394, 29 U.S.C. §§ 3001 *et seq.*

Assistive Technology Act Amendments of 2004, PL 108-364, 29 U.S.C. §§ 3001 *et seq.*

Bailey, R.L., Parette, H.P., Stoner, J.B., Angell, M.E., & Carroll, K. (2006). Family members' perceptions of augmentative and alternative communication. *Speech, Language, and Hearing Services in the Schools, 37,* 50–60.

Bakkaloglu, H. (2008, May). The effectiveness of activity-based intervention program on the transition skills of children with developmental disabilities aged between 3 and 6 years. *Educational Sciences: Theory and Practice, 8,* 393–406.

Balajthy, E. (2005, January/February). Text-to-speech software for helping struggling readers. *Reading Online,* 8(4). Available at http://www.readingonline.org/articles/balajthy2

Banajee, M., Dicarlo, C., & Stricklin, S.B. (2003). Core vocabulary determination for toddlers. *Augmentative and Alternative Communication, 19,* 67–73.

Banerjee, R., & Horn, E.M. (2005). Use of sociodramatic play to develop literacy skills in early childhood settings. In E.M. Horn & H. Jones (Eds.), *Young exceptional children: Supporting early literacy in young children* (Monograph Series No. 7; pp. 101–112). Longmont, CO: Sopris West.

Barton, E.E., & Wolery, M. (2009). Teaching pretend play to children with disabilities: A review of the literature. *Topics in Early Childhood Special Education,* 28(2), 109–125.

Beck, J. (2002). Emergent literacy through assistive technology. *Teaching Exceptional Children,* 35, 44–48.

Berk, L E. & Winsler, A. (1995). *Scaffolding children's learning: Vygotsky and early childhood education.* Washington, DC: National Association for the Young Children.

Bernard-Opitz, V., Sriram, N., & Nakhoda-Sapuan, S. (2001). Enhancing social problem solving in children with autism and normal children through computer-assisted instruction. *Journal of Autism and Developmental Disorders,* 31(4), 377–384.

Beukelman, D.R., & Mirenda, P. (2005). *Augmentative and alternative communication: Supporting children and adults with complex communication needs* (3rd ed.). Baltimore: Paul H. Brookes Publishing Co.

Bevan-Brown, J. (2001). Evaluating special education services for learners from ethnically diverse groups: Getting it right. *Journal of the Association for Persons with Severe Handicaps*, 26, 138–147.

Binger, C., & Light, J. (2006). Demographics of preschoolers who require AAC. *Language, Speech, and Hearing Services in Schools*, 37, 200–208.

Binger, C., & Light, J. (2007). The effect of aided AAC modeling on the expression of multi-symbol messages by preschoolers who use AAC. *Alternative and Augmentative Communication*, 23, 30–43.

Bishop, K., Woll, J., & Arango, P. (n.d.). *Family-centered care projects 1 and 2 (2002–2004)*. Algodones, NM: Algodones Associates.

Bishop, K., Woll, J., & Arango, P. (1993). *Family/professional collaboration for children with special health care needs and their families*. Burlington: University of Vermont, Department of Social Work.

Bowser, G., & Reed, P.R. (1995). Education TECH points for assistive technology planning. *Journal of Special Education Technology*, 12(4), 325–338.

Bowser, G., & Reed, P. (2000). *Considering your child's need for Assistive Technology*. LD Online. Retrieved May 24, 2010, from http://www.ldonline.org/article/6246/

Bowser, G., & Reed, P.R. (2002). *Education TechPoints*. Retrieved May 24, 2010, from http://www.educationtechpoints.org/

Bowser, G., & Zabala, J. (2004). *SETT and re-SETT: Concepts for AT implementation*. Retrieved November 11, 2006, from http://www.unmedu/cdci/tripscy/localpdf/SETT_Implem_CTG.pdf

Brady, N.C. (2000). Improved comprehension of object names following voice output communication aid use: Two case studies. *Augmentative and Alternative Communication*, 16, 197–204.

Bredekamp, S., & Copple, C. (1997). *Developmentally appropriate practice in early childhood programs*. Washington, DC: National Association for the Education of Young Children.

Bricker, D. (2002). Assessment, Evaluation, and Programming System for Infants and Children (AEPS® 2nd ed.). Baltimore: Paul H. Brookes Publishing Co.

Bricker, D., Pretti-Frontczak, K., & McComas, N. (1998). *An activity-based approach to early intervention*. Baltimore: Paul H. Brookes Publishing Co.

Brigman, G., Lane, D., Switzer, D., Lane, D., & Lawrence, R. (1999). Teaching children school success skills. *Journal of Educational Research*, 92, 323–329.

Buckleitner, W. (1999). *The state of children's software evaluation: Yesterday, today and in the twenty-first century*. Retrieved December 28, 2009, from http://www.childrenssoftware.com

Burkhart, L.J. (n.d.). *Mouse house instructions*. Retrieved January 18, 2010, from http://www.lburkhart.com/mhouse.htm

Burkhart, L.J., & Musselwhite, C. (2000–2001). *Anatomy of a conversation: Social scripts*. Retrieved January 18, 2010, from http://www.lburkhart.com/chat_ideas.htm

Buysse, V., & Hollingsworth, H.L. (2009). Program quality and early childhood inclusion: Recommendations for professional development. *Topics in Early Childhood Special Education*, 29(2), 119–128.

Cafiero, J. (2001). The effect of an augmentative communication intervention on the communication, behavior, and academic program of an adolescent with autism. *Focus on Autism and Other Developmental Disabilities*, 16, 179–189.

California Department of Education. (2008). *The California preschool learning foundations* (Vol. 1). Sacramento: CDE Press.

California Department of Education. (2009). *The California infant/toddler learning and development foundations* (Vol. 1). Sacramento: CDE Press. Available at http://www.cde.ca.gov/sp/cd/re/itfoundations.asp

Calvert, S.L., Strong, B.L., & Gallagher, L. (2005). Control as an engagement feature for young children's attention to and learning of computer content. *American Behavioral Scientist*, 48(5), 578–589.

Campbell, P.H., Milbourne, S., Dugan, L.M., & Wilcox, M.J. (2006). A review of evidence on practices for teaching young children to use assistive technology devices. *Topics in Early Childhood Special Education*, 26(1), 3–13.

Chai, A.Y., Zhang, C., & Bisberg, M. (2006). Rethinking natural environment practice: Implications from examining various interpretations and approaches. *Early Childhood Education Journal*, 34, 203–208.

Chard, D.J., & Dickson, S.V. (1999). Phonological awareness: Instructional and assessment guidelines. *Intervention in School and Clinic*, 34, 261–271.

Chiara, L., Schuster, J.W., Bell, J.K., & Wolery, M. (1995). Small-group massed-trial and individually distributed-trial instruction with preschoolers. *Journal of Early Intervention*, 19, 203–217.

Children's Technology Review. (2009). *Active learning associates*. Retrieved December 28, 2009, from http://www.childrenssoftware.com

Clay, M.M. (1993). *An observation study of early literacy achievement*. Portsmouth, NH: Heinemann.

Clendon, S., Gillon, G., & Yoder, D. (2005). Initial insights into phoneme awareness intervention for children with complex communication needs. *International Journal of Disability, Development and Education, 52*, 7–31.

Cook, R.E., Klein, M.D., & Tessier, A. (2004). *Adapting early childhood curricula for children in inclusive settings.* Upper Saddle River, NJ: Pearson Merrill Prentice Hall.

Copley J. & Ziviani, J. (2007). Use of a team-based approach to assistive technology assessment and planning for children with multiple disabilities: A pilot study. *Assistive Technology, 19* (3), 109–125.

Cress, C.J. (1998). Communication milestones for young nonspeaking children: Assessment and intervention strategies. Presentation at the ISAAC Biennial Conference, Dublin, Ireland.

Cress, C.J. (2002). Expanding children's early augmented behaviors to support symbolic development. In J. Reichle, D.R. Beukelman, & J.C. Light (Eds.), *Exemplary practices for beginning communicators: Implications for AAC* (pp. 219–272). Baltimore: Paul H. Brookes Publishing Co.

Cress, C. (2006). *Early intervention in AAC: Spontaneous to symbolic.* Presentation at the California Speech & Hearing Association Conference, San Francisco.

Cress, C.J., & Marvin, C.A. (2003). Common questions about AAC services in early intervention. *Augmentative and Alternative Communication, 19*, 254–272.

Culatta, B., Aslett, R., Fife, M., & Setzer, L.A. (2004). Project SEEL: Part I. Systematic and engaging early literacy instruction. *Communication Disorders Quarterly, 25*, 127–144.

Cunningham, P.M., & Cunningham, J.W. (1992). Making words: Enhancing the invented spelling-decoding connection. *Reading Teacher, 46*, 106–115.

Dada, S., & Alant, E. (2009). The effect of aided language stimulation on vocabulary acquisition in children with little or no functional speech. *American Journal of Speech-Language Pathology, 18*, 50–64.

Dahlgren Sandberg, A., & Hjelmquist, E. (1996). Phonologic awareness and literacy abilities in nonspeaking preschool children with cerebral palsy. *Augmentative and Alternative Communication, 12*, 138–153.

Dahlgren Sandberg, A., & Hjelmquist, E. (1997). Language and literacy in nonvocal children with cerebral palsy. *Reading and Writing: An Interdisciplinary Journal, 9*, 107–133.

Daugherty, S., Grisham-Brown, J., & Hemmeter, M.L. (2001). The effects of embedded skill instruction on the acquisition of target and nontarget skills in preschoolers with developmental delays. *Topics in Early Childhood Special Education, 21*, 213–221.

DeBruin-Parecki, A. (2009). Establishing a family literacy program with a focus on interactive reading: The role of research and accountability. *Early Childhood Education Journal, 36*(5), 385–392.

Desired Results for Developmental Progress. (2008). *Guide to using the DRDP instruments for preschool special education.* Retrieved April 10, 2008, from http://www.draccess.org/assessors/GuideToUsingDRDP.html

DiCarlo, C., Banajee, M., & Buras-Stricklin, S. (2000). Embedding augmentative communication within early childhood classrooms. *Young Exceptional Children, 3*(3), 18–26.

Dolch, E.W. (1948). *Problems in reading.* Champain, IL: Garrard Press.

Dowden, P. (2002). *Likes and dislikes checklist.* Retrieved November 11, 2006, from http://depts.washington.edu/augcomm/original_modules/module_customizing/custom_vocab_likesanddislikes.htm

Dowden, P. (2004). *Continuum of Communication Independence.* Retrieved October 24, 2009 from http://depts.washington.edu/augcomm/03_cimodel/commind1_intro.htm

Dowden, P., & Mariner, N. (1995). *Observing communication in context.* Retrieved November 11, 2006, from http://depts.washington.edu/augcomm/01_vocab/forms_vocab/custom_vocab_observform.html

Drager, K., Light, J., Carlson, R., DiSilva, K., Larsson, B., Pitkin, L., & Stopper, G. (2004). Learning of dynamic display AAC technologies by typically developing 3-year-olds: Effect of different layouts and menu approaches. *Journal of Speech-Language Hearing Research, 47*, 1133–1148.

Drescher, P.L. (2009). *Access to computers for students with physical disabilities: Assessing students needs for assistive technology* (5th ed.). Wisconsin Assistive Technology Initiative (WATI), a state network sponsored by the Wisconsin Dept. of Public Instruction, Madison, WI.

Dugan, L., Milbourne, S., Campbell, P., & Wilcox, M. (2004). *Using assistive technology with infants and toddlers: Evidence-based practice.* Retrieved August 16, 2005, from http://tnt.asu.edu

Dunst, C.J. (2004). An integrated framework for practicing early childhood intervention and family support. *Perspectives in Education, 22*, 1–16.

Dunst, C.J., Boyd, K., & Trivette, C. M. (2002). Family-oriented program models and professional helpgiving practices. *Family Relations: Interdisciplinary Journal of Applied Family Studies, 51*(3), 221–229.

Dunst, C.J., Bruder, M.B., Trivette, C.M., Hamby, D., Raab, M., & McLean, M. (2001). Characteristics and consequences of everyday natural learning opportunities. *Topics in Early Childhood Special Education, 21,* 68–92.

Dunst. C.J., & Shue, P. (2005). Creating literacy-rich natural learning environments for infants, toddlers and preschoolers. In E.M. Horn & H. Jones (Eds.), *Young exceptional children: Supporting early literacy in young children* (Monograph Series No. 7; pp. 15–30). Longmont, CO: Sopris West.

Dunst, C.J., Trivette, C.M., & Hamby, D.W. (2007). Meta-analysis of family-centered help giving practices research. *Mental Retardation and Developmental Disabilities Research Reviews, 13,* 370–378.

DynaVox. (2009). *Implementation toolkit: AAC communication goal grid & introduction.* Retrieved on October 24 from: http://www.dynavoxtech.com/training/toolkit/paths.aspx?id=5

Early Childhood Outcomes Center. (2005). *Crosswalk between OSEP child outcomes and the ounce scale.* Retrieved December 10, 2009, from http://www.fpg.unc.edu/~eco/assets/pdfs/ounce_crosswalk.pdf

Early Childhood Outcomes Center. (2006). *Crosswalk between OSEP child outcomes and the Brigance Inventory of Early Development II.* Retrieved January 10, 2010 from http://www.fpg.unc.edu/~eco/assets/pdfs/BriganceIED-IIcrosswalk7-3-06.pdf

Early Childhood Outcomes Center. (2009). *Instrument crosswalks.* Retrieved December 12, 2009, from http://www.fpg.unc.edu/~eco/pages/crosswalks.cfm#Crosswalks

Early Childhood Technology Integrated Instructional System. (2004). *Center for best practices in early childhood at Western Illinois University.* Retrieved November 11, 2006, from http://www.wiu.edu/ectiis/

Education for All Handicapped Children Act of 1975, PL 94-142, 20 U.S.C. §§ 1400 *et seq.*

Education of the Handicapped Act Amendments of 1986, PL 99-457, 20 U.S.C. §§ 1400 *et seq.*

Edyburn, D. (2001). *Models, theories, and frameworks: Contributions to understanding special education technology.* Retrieved July 1, 2009, from http://cte.jhu.edu/accessibility/primer/resources/index.html

Edyburn, D.L. (2002). Born digital: Technology in the life of students starting kindergarten, high school, and college. *Special Education Technology Practice, 4*(4), 48.

Erickson, K.A., & Clendon, S.A. (2009). Addressing the literacy demands of the curriculum for beginning readers and writers. In G. Soto & C. Zangari (Eds.), *Practically speaking: Language, literacy, and academic development for students with AAC needs* (pp. 195–215). Baltimore: Paul H. Brookes Publishing Co.

Erickson, K.A., & Koppenhaver, D.A. (1995). Developing a literacy program for children with severe disabilities. *The Reading Teacher, 48,* 676–684.

Erickson, K.A., Koppenhaver, D.A., Yoder, D.E., & Nance, J. (1997). Integrated communication and literacy instruction for a child with multiple disabilities. *Focus on Autism and Other Developmental Disabilities, 12,* 142–150.

Escobar, R., Leslie, S., & Wright-Ott, C. (n.d.). *Self-initiated mobility is the way to go.* Retrieved January 30, 2010, from http://www.seatingandmobility.ca/ISS2002/ToSunnyHill2/iss2002html/031_SELFInitiatedMobility.htm

Falkman, K.W., Sandberg, A.D., & Hjelmquist, E. (2002). Preferred communication modes: Prelinguistic and linguistic communication in non-speaking preschool children with cerebral palsy. *International Journal of Language and Communication, 37,* 59–68.

Fey, M., Yoder, S.F., Brady, N., Finestack, L.H., Bredin-Oja, S.L., Fairchild, M., & Sokol, S. (2006). Early effects of responsivity education/prelinguistic milieu teaching for children with developmental delays and their parents. *Journal of Speech, Language, and Hearing Research, 29,* 526–547.

Foley, B.E. (1993). The development of literacy in individuals with severe congenital speech and motor impairments. *Topics in Language Disorders, 13*(2), 16–32.

Forgan, J.W., & Weber, R.K. (2001). *Linking software evaluation to the IEP: Part three.* Retrieved December 28, 2009, from http://findarticles.com/p/articles/mi_go2827/is_8_31/ai_n28891773/?tag=content;col1

Fox, L., & Hanline, M.F. (1993). A preliminary evaluation of learning within developmentally appropriate early childhood settings. *Topics in Early Childhood Special Education, 13,* 308–327.

Gallagher, P., & Lambert, R.G. (2006). Classroom quality, concentration of children with special needs, and child outcomes in Head Start. *Exceptional Children, 73,* 31–52.

Gately, S.E. (2004). Developing concept of word. *Teaching Exceptional Children, 36*(6), 16–22.

Gayle's Preschool Rainbow. (n.d.). Retrieved October 10, 2009, from http://www.preschoolrainbow.org/

Gebers, J.L. (2003). *Books are for talking, too!* (3rd ed.). Austin, TX: Pro-Ed.

Georgia Project for Assistive Technology. (2005). *AT Manual.* Retrieved May 28, 2010, from http://www.gpat.org/resources.aspx?Page

Req=GPATPol

Gillette, Y. (2005). *Communication Independence Model: For people with severe communication disabilities.* Retrieved October 27, 2009, from http://www.speechpathology.com/articles/article_detail.asp?article_id=215

Glennen, S.L., & Calculator, S.N. (1985). Training functional communication board use: A pragmatic approach. *Augmentative and Alternative Communication, 1,* 134–141.

Glennen, S.L., & DeCoste, D.C. (1997). Service delivery in AAC. In S.L. Glennen & D.C. DeCoste (Eds.), *The handbook of augmentative and alternative communication* (pp. 21–34). San Diego: Singular Publishing Group.

Goldman, A. (2009). Assistive technology for infants and toddlers with disabilities: Who will pay? *Perspectives on Augmentative and Alternative Communication, Division 12 Newsletter. American Speech-Language-Hearing Association,* 33–35.

Goosens', C. (1989). Aided communication intervention before assessment: A case study of a child with cerebral palsy. *Augmentative and Alternative Communication, 5,* 14–26.

Goosens', C., Crain, S., & Elder, P. (1992). *Engineering the preschool environment for interactive, symbolic communication.* Birmingham, AL: Southeast Augmentative Communication Conference.

Grabe, M., & Grabe, C. (2007). *Integrating technology for meaningful learning* (5th ed.). New York: Houghton Mifflin.

Grant, D., Justice, P., & Maltby, K. (2001). *Beyond the book: Infusing literacy and assistive technology into the classroom.* Presentation at the 2001 CSUN International Conference on Technology and Persons with Disabilities, Los Angeles.

Grant, D., & Singer, G. (2004). Computer assisted instruction for toddlers with disabilities. *Closing the Gap, 23,* 1–3.

Grisham-Brown, J., Hemmeter, M.L., & Pretti-Frontczak, K. (2005). *Blended practices for teaching young children in inclusive settings.* Baltimore: Paul H. Brookes Publishing Co.

Grisham-Brown, J., Pretti-Frontczak, K., Hawkins, S.R., & Winchell, B.N. (2009). Addressing early learning standards for all children within blended preschool classrooms. *Topics in Early Childhood Special Education, 29,* 131–142.

Grisham-Brown, J.L., Pretti-Frontczak, K.L., Hemmeter, M.L., & Ridgley, R. (2002). Teaching IEP goals and objectives in the context of classroom routines and activities. *Young Exceptional Children, 6*(1), 18–27.

Grisham-Brown, J.L., Schuster, J.W., Hemmeter, M.L., & Collins, B.C. (2000). Using embedded strategy to teach preschoolers with significant disabilities. *Journal of Behavior Education, 10,* 139–162.

Hanline, M.F., Nunes, D., & Worthy, M.B. (2007). *Augmentative and alternative communication in the early childhood years.* Washington, DC: National Association for the Education of Young Children.

Hart, B., & Risley, T. (1975). Promoting productive language through incidental teaching. *Education and Urban Society, 10,* 407–429.

Hart, B., & Rogers-Warren, A. (1978). A milieu approach to teaching language. In R.L. Schiefelbusch (Ed.), *Language intervention strategies* (pp. 193–235). Baltimore: University Park Press.

Haugen, K. (2001). *Evaluating software for young learners: Kids Can!* Retrieved December 28, 2009, from http://www.ataccess.org/resources/atk12/selectsofthecklist.pdf

Haugland, S.W. (2005). Selecting or upgrading software and websites in the classroom. *Early Childhood Education Journal, 32*(5), 329–340.

Head Start. (2000). *Head Start child outcomes framework.* Retrieved May 28, 2010, from http://www.hsnrc.org/CDI/pdfs/UGCOF.pdf

Head Start. (2003). *Head Start child outcomes: Setting the context for the National Reporting System.* (National Head Start Training and Technical Assistance Resource Center Publication No. 76.) Washington, DC: Head Start Bureau.

Heath, S.B. (1983). *Ways with words: Language, life, and work in communities and classrooms.* New York: Cambridge University Press.

Hemmeter, M.L. (2000). Classroom-based interventions: Evaluating the past and looking to the future. *Topics in Early Childhood Special Education, 20,* 56–61.

Hemmeter, M.L., & Grisham-Brown, J.L. (1997). Developing children's language skills in inclusive early childhood classrooms. *Dimensions of Early Childhood, 25,* 6–13.

Hemmeter, M.L., McCollum, J.A., & Hsieh, W. (2005). Practical strategies for supporting emergent literacy in the preschool classroom. In E.M. Horn & H. Jones (Eds.), *Young exceptional children: Supporting early literacy in young children* (Monograph Series No. 7; pp. 59–74). Longmont, CO: Sopris West.

Hemmeter, M.L., Smith, B.J., Sandall, S., & Askew, L. (Eds.). (2005). *DEC recommended practices workbook: Improving practices for young children with special needs and their families.* Missoula, MT: Division for Early Childhood.

Hitchcock, C., Meyer, A., Rose, D., & Jackson, R. (2002). *Technical brief: Access, participation, and progress in the general curriculum.* Retrieved June 19, 2009, from http://www.cast.org/publications/

ncac/ncac_techbrief.html--

Hitchcock, C.H., & Noonan, M.J. (2000). Computer-assisted instruction of early academic skills. *Topics in Early Childhood Special Education, 20*(3), 145–158.

Hofmann, R. (1985). Educational software: Evaluation? No! Utility? Yes! *Journal of Learning Disabilities, 18*(6), 358–360.

Horn, E., Lieber, J., Li, S.M., Sandall, S., & Schwartz, I. (2000). Supporting young children's IEP goals in inclusive settings through embedded learning opportunities. *Topics in Early Childhood Special Education, 20,* 208–223.

Hourcade, J.J., Parette, H.P., & Huer, M.B. (1997). Family and culture alert! Considerations in assistive technology assessment. *Teaching Exceptional Children, 30*(1), 40–44.

Huer, M.B., & Saenz, T.I. (2002). Thinking about conducting culturally sensitive research in *Augmentative and Alternative Communication. Augmentative and Alternative Communication, 18* (4), 267–273.

Hunt, P., Doering, K., Hirose-Hatae, A., Maier, J., & Goetz, L. (2001). Across-program collaboration to support students with and without disabilities in general education classrooms. *Journal of the Association for Persons with Severe Handicaps, 26,* 240–256.

Hunt, P., Soto, G., Maier, J., Liboiron, N., & Bae, S. (2004). Collaborative teaming to support preschoolers with severe disabilities who are placed in general education early childhood programs. *Topics in Early Childhood Special Education, 24*(3), 123–142.

Hunt, P., Soto, G., Maier, J., Müller, E., & Goetz, L. (2002). Collaborative teaming to support students with augmentative and alternative communication needs in general education classrooms. *AAC Augmentative and Alternative Communication, 18,* 20–35.

Hutinger, P.L. (1996). Computer applications in programs for young children with disabilities: Recurring themes. *Focus on Autism and Other Developmental Disabilities, 11,* 105–114.

Hutinger, P., Bell, C., Daytner, G., & Johanson, J. (2005). *Disseminating and replicating an effective emergent literacy technology curriculum: A final report.* Macomb, IL: Western Illinois University, Center for Best Practices in Early Childhood. Available at http://www.wiu.edu/thecenter/reports.php or as a PDF at http://www.wiu.edu/thecenter/finalreports/ELiTeCFinalRpt2.pdf

Hutinger, P.L., Bell, C., Daytner, G., & Johanson, J. (2006). Establishing and maintaining an early childhood emergent literacy curriculum. *Journal of Special Education Technology, 21*(4), 39–54.

Hyun, E. (1996). New directions in early childhood teacher preparation: Developmentally and culturally appropriate practice (DCAP). *Journal of Early Childhood Teacher Education, 17*(3), 3–19.

Hyun, E. (1998). *Making sense of developmentally and culturally appropriate practice (DCAP) in early childhood education.* New York: Peter Lang.

Hyun, E., & Marshall, J.D. (2003). Teachable-moment-oriented curriculum practice in early childhood education. *Journal of Curriculum Studies, 35,* 111–127.

Iacono, T.A. (1999). Language intervention in early childhood. *International Journal of Disability, Development and Education, 46,* 383–420.

Individuals with Disabilities Education Act Amendments (IDEA) of 1991, PL 102-119, 20 U.S.C. §§ 1400 *et seq.*

Individuals with Disabilities Education Act Amendments (IDEA) of 1997, PL 105-17, 20 U.S.C. §§ 1400 *et seq.*

Individuals with Disabilities Education Act (IDEA) of 1990, PL 101-476, 20 U.S.C. §§ 1400 *et seq.*

Individuals with Disabilities Education Improvement Act (IDEA) of 2004, PL 108-446, 20 U.S.C. 1400 *et seq.et seq.et seq.*

IntelliTools (2007). *The research basis for IntelliTools products.* Petaluma, CA: Cambium Learning Technologies. Retrieved on May 24, 2010, from http://www.intellitools.com/ about/research/index.aspx

Jewitt, C. (2006). *Technology, literacy and learning: A multimodal approach.* New York: Routledge.

Johnson, J.W., McDonnell, J., Holzwarth, V.N., & Hunter, K. (2004). The efficacy of embedded instruction for students with developmental disabilities enrolled in general education classes. *Journal of Positive Behavior Interventions, 6,* 214–227.

Johnson-Martin, N.M., Attermeier, S., & Hacker, B.J. (2004). *The Carolina curriulum.* Baltimore: Paul H. Brookes Publishing Co.

Johnston, L., Beard, L.A., & Carpenter, L.B. (2007). *Assistive technology access for all students.* Columbus, OH: Pearson.

Johnston, S.S., McDonnell, A.P., & Hawken, L.S. (2008). Enhancing outcomes in early literacy for young children with disabilities: Strategies for success. *Intervention in School and Clinic, 43,* 210–217.

Jonassen, D.H., & Howland, J. (2003). *Learning to solve problems with technology: A constructivist approach.* Upper Saddle River, NJ: Merrill Prentice Hall.

Judge, S.L. (1998). Computer applications in programs for young children with disabilities: Current status and future directions. *Journal of Special Education Technology, 16*(1), 1–12. Retrieved May 28, 2010, from http://truddentechnology.hcpss.wikispaces.n

et/file/view/Computer+Applicaitons+in+ Programs.pdf/34305775/Computer+Applicai tons+in+Programs.pdf

Judge, S.L. (2000). Assessing and funding assistive technology for young children with disabilities. *Early Childhood Education Journal, 28*(2), 125–131.

Judge, S.L. (2001). Computer applications in programs for young children with disabilities: Current status and future directions. *Journal of Special Education Technology, 16*(1), 29–40.

Judge, S. (2002). Family-centered assistive technology assessment and intervention practices for early intervention. *Infants and Young Children, 15*(1), 60–68.

Judge, S. (2006). Construction of an assistive technology toolkit: Views from the field. *Journal of Special Education Technology, 21*(4), 18–24.

Judge, S., Floyd, K., & Jeffs, T. (2008). Using an assistive technology toolkit to promote inclusion. *Early Childhood Education Journal, 36,* 121–126.

Judge, S.L. & Parette, H.P. (1998a). *Assistive technology for young children with disabilities: A guide to family-centered services.* Cambridge, MA: Brookline Books.

Judge S.L., & Parette, H.P. (1998b). Family-centered assistive technology decision-making. *Infant-Toddler Intervention, 8,* 175–184.

Justice, L., Kaderavek, J., Bowles, R., & Grimm, K. (2005). Language impairment, parent–child reading, and phonological awareness: A feasibility study. *Topics in Early Childhood Special Education, 25,* 143–156.

Justice, L.M., & Pullen, P.C. (2003). Promising interventions for promoting emergent literacy skills: Three evidence-based approaches. *Topics in Early Childhood Special Education, 23,* 99–113.

Justice, P. (2006). Feature Matching Checklist Adaptive Switch Assessment. Unpublished assessment.

Kaiser, A.P., Yoder, P.J., & Keetz, A. (1992). The efficacy of milieu teaching. In S.F. Warren & J. Reichle (Eds.), *Causes and effects in communication and language intervention* (pp. 63–84). Baltimore: Paul H. Brookes Publishing Co.

Kalan, R. (1991). *Jump, frog, jump!* New York: HarperCollins.

Kalyanpur, M., & Harry, B. (1999). *Culture in special education.* Baltimore: Paul H. Brookes Publishing Co.

Kemp, C.E., & Parette, H.P. (2000). Barriers to minority family involvement in assistive technology decision-making processes. *Education and Training in Mental Retardation and Developmental Disabilities, 35*(4), 384–392.

King-DeBaun, P. (2007a). *Making language and literacy visible.* Retrieved December 11, 2009, from http://www.creativecommunicating .com/tips-mllv.cfm

King-DeBaun, P. (2007b). *Supported readings.* Retrieved January 18, 2010, from http://www .creativecommunicating.com/tips-sr.cfm

Kinsley, T.C., & Langone, J. (1995). Applications of technology for infants, toddlers, and preschoolers with disabilities. *Journal of Special Education Technology, 12,* 312–324.

Knowledge Share. (2009). *SuperKids: Education for the future.* Retrieved December 29, 2009, from http://www.superkids.com

Kohler, F.W., Anthony, L.J., Steighner, S.A., & Hoyson, M. (1998). Teaching social interaction skills in the integrated preschool: An examination of naturalistic tactics. *Topics in Early Childhood Special Education, 21,* 93–103.

Koppenhaver, D.A. (1991). *A descriptive analysis of classroom literacy instruction provided to children with speech and physical impairments.* Unpublished doctoral dissertation, University of North Carolina at Chapel Hill.

Koppenhaver, D.A., & Yoder, D.E. (1993). Classroom literacy instruction for children with severe speech and physical impairments (SSPI): What is and what might be. *Topics in Language Disorders, 13*(2), 1–15.

Krupp, R., & Villalobos, C. (2007). Short on time and money? Make simple at work for all students with severe disabilities. *Closing the Gap, 26*(2), 1, 20–22.

Lane, S.J., & Mistrett, S. (2002). Let's play. *Young Exceptional Children, 5*(2), 19–27.

Langone, J., Malone, D.M., & Kinsley, T. (1999). Technology solutions for young children with developmental concerns. *Infants and Young Children, 16*(4), 272–283.

Lau, C., Higgins, K., Gelfer, J., Hong, E., & Miller, S. (2005). Effects of teacher facilitation on social interactions of young children during computer activities. *Topics in Early Childhood Special Education, 25*(4), 208–217.

Lesar, S. (1998). Use of assistive technology with young children with disabilities: Current status and training needs. *Journal of Early Intervention, 21*(2), 146–159.

Liboiron, N., & Soto, G. (2006). Shared storybook reading with a student who uses AAC: An intervention session. *Child Language Teaching and Therapy, 22,* 69–95.

Lieb, Rebecca. (2005). *Most Americans have PCs and web access.* Retrieved May 15, 2010, from http://www.clickz.com/3559991

Lieber, J., Horn, E., Palmer, S., & Fleming, K. (2008). Access to the general education curriculum for preschoolers with disabilities: Children's school success. *Exceptionality, 16,* 18–32.

Lifter, K., Ellis, J., Cannon, B., & Anderson, S.R. (2005). Developmental specificity in targeting and teaching play activities to children with pervasive developmental disorders. *Journal of Early Intervention, 27*(4), 247–367.

Lifter, K., Sulzer-Azaroff, B., Anderson, S.R., & Cowdery, G.E. (1993). Teaching play activities to preschool children with disabilities. *Journal of Early Intervention, 17* (2), 139–159.

Light, J. (2005) *AAC interventions to maximize language development for young children* [AAC-RERC web casts]. Retrieved November 11, 2006, from http://www.aac-rerc.com/pages/news/webcasts2005.htm

Light, J., & Drager, K.. (2007). AAC technologies for young children with complex communication needs: State of the science and future research directions. *Augmentative and Alternative Communication, 23*, 204–216.

Light, J., Drager, K., McCarthy, J., Mellott, S., Parrish, C., Parsons, A., Rhoads, S., Ward, M., & Welliver, M. (2004). Performance of typically developing four and five year old children with AAC systems using different language organization techniques. *Augmen-tative and Alternative Communication, 20*, 63–88.

Light, J., Drager, K., & Nemser, J. (2004). Enhancing the appeal of AAC technologies for young children: Lessons from the toy manufacturers. *Augmentative and Alternative Communication, 20*, 137–149.

Light, J., & Kelford Smith, A. (1993). The home literacy experiences of preschoolers who use AAC systems and of their nondisabled peers. *Augmentative and Alternative Communication, 9*, 10–25.

Lloyd, L.L., Fuller, D.R., & Arvidson, H.H. (1997). *Augmentative and alternative communication: A handbook of principles and practices*. Boston: Allyn & Bacon.

Long, T., Huang, L., Woodbridge, M., Woolverton, M., & Minkel, J. (2003). Integrating assistive technology into an outcome-driven model for service delivery. *Infants and Young Children, 16*(4), 272–283.

Lonigan, C.J., Anthony, J.L., Bloomfield, B.G., Dyer, S.M., & Samwel, C.S. (1999). Effects of two shared-reading interventions on emergent literacy skills of at-risk preschoolers. *Journal of Early Intervention, 22*(4), 306–322.

Lonigan, C.J., & Whitehurst, G.J. (1998). Relative efficacy of parent and teacher involvement in a shared-reading intervention for preschool children from low-income backgrounds. *Early Childhood Research Quarterly, 13*(2), 263–290.

Losardo, A., & Bricker, D.D. (1994). Activity-based intervention and direct instruction: A comparison study. *American Journal on Mental Retardation, 98*, 744–765.

Macy, M.G., & Bricker, D.D. (2007). Embedding individualized social goals into routine activities in inclusive early childhood classrooms. *Early Child Development and Care, 177*, 107–120.

Malmskog, S., & McDonnell, A.P. (1999). Teacher mediated facilitation of engagement by children with developmental delays in inclusive preschools. *Topics in Early Childhood Special Education, 19*, 203–216.

Malone, D.M., & Langone, J. (1999). Teaching object-related play skills to preschool children with developmental concerns. *International Journal of Disability, Development, and Education, 46*(3), 326–335.

Martin, B. (1983). *Brown bear, brown bear, what do you see?* New York: Henry Holt.

Marvin, C.A., Beukelman, D.R., & Bilyeu, D. (1994). Vocabulary-use patterns in preschool children: Effects of context and time sampling. *Augmentative and Alternative Communication, 10*(4), 224–236.

Mastrangelo, S. (2009). Harnessing the power of play: Opportunities for children with autism spectrum disorders. *Teaching Exceptional Children, 42*(1), 34–44.

Matas, J.A., Mathy-Laikko, P., Beukelman, D.R., & Legresley, K. (1985). Identifying the nonspeaking population: A demographic study. Augmentative and Alternative Communication, 1, 17–31.

McBride, D., & Bardach, L. (2009). Augmentative communication evaluations: A "toolkit" approach. Presentation at the Assistive Technology Industry Association Conference, Orlando, FL.

McCathren, R.B., & Howard-Allor, J. (2005). Using storybooks with preschool children: Enhancing language and emergent literacy. In E.M. Horn & H. Jones (Eds.), *Young exceptional children: Supporting early literacy in young children* (Monograph Series No. 7; pp. 75–86). Longmont, CO: Sopris West.

McCormick, L. (1987). Comparison of the effects of a microcomputer activity and toy play on social and communication behaviors of young children. *Journal of the division of Early Childhood, 11*, 195–205.

McCormick, L. (2003). Ecological assessment and planning. In L. McCormick, D. Frome Loeb, & R.L. Schiefelbusch (Eds.), *Supporting children with communication difficulties in inclusive settings: School-based language intervention* (pp. 235–258). Boston: Allyn & Bacon.

McCormick, L. (2006). Planning and evaluation/monitoring. In M.J. Noonan & L. McCormick (Eds.), *Young children with disabilities in natural environments: Methods and* procedures (pp. 99–118). Baltimore: Paul H. Brookes Publishing Co.

McGee, L.M., & Richgels, D.J. (2006). Can technology support emergent reading and writing? Directions for the future. In M.C. McKenna, L.D. Labbo, R.D. Kieffer, & D. Reinking (Eds.), International handbook of literacy and technology (Vol. 2, pp. 369–377). Mahwah, NJ: Lawrence Earlbaum Associates.

McGee, L.M., & Richgels, D.J. (2008). Literacy's beginnings: Supporting young readers and writers (5th ed.). Boston: Allyn & Bacon.

Meinbach, A.M., Fredericks, A., & Rothlein, L. (2000). The complete guide to thematic units: Creating the integrated curriculum (2nd ed.). Norwood, MA: Christopher-Gordon Publishers.

Milbourne, S.A., & Campbell, P.H. (2007). CARA's kit: Creating adaptations for routines and activities. Philadelphia: Child and Family Studies Research Programs, Thomas Jefferson University.

Milbourne, S., & Campbell, P. (2008). Report of assistive technology training for providers and families of children in early intervention. Retrieved August 15, 2009, from http://tnt .asu.edu

Mills, S.C., & Roblyer, M.D. (2006). Technology tools for teachers. A Microsoft Office tutorial (2nd ed.). Upper Saddle River, NJ: Pearson Merrill Prentice Hall.

Mioduser, D., Tur-Kaspa, H, & Leitner, I. (2000). The learning value of computer-based instruction of early reading skills. Journal of Computer Assisted Learning. 16, 54–63.

Mirenda, P., & Iacono, T. (Eds.). (2009). Autism spectrum disorders and AAC. Baltimore: Paul H. Brookes Publishing Co.

Mistrett, S. (2001). Synthesis on the use of assistive technology with infants and toddlers (birth to age two). Final report to the Office of Special Education and Rehabilitative Services (OSERS), Contract No. HS97017002.

Mistrett, S. (2004, October). Assistive technology helps young children with disabilities participate in daily activities. Technology in Action, 1(4), 1–8.

Mistrett, S. (2005). Universal design for play: a toy guide for all children. Retrieved May 28, 2010, from http://letsplay.buffalo.edu/toys/guide/index.htm.

Mistrett, S., & Goetz, A. (2000). Playing with switches. Retrieved October 2, 2009, from http://www.buffalo.edu/letsplay

Mistrett, S., & Goetz, A. (2009). Suggestions for computer play for young children: Birth to two. Retrieved December 1, 2009, from http:// www.letsplay.buffalo.edu

Mistrett, S., & Lane, S.J. (2002). Let's play:

Assistive technology interventions for play. Young Exceptional Children, 5(2), 19–27.

Mistrett, S.M., Lane, S.L., & Ruffino, A. (2004). Growing and learning through technology: Birth to five. In D. Edyburn, K. Higgins, & R. Boone (Eds.), The handbook of special education technology research and practice (pp. 273–307). Whitefish Bay, WI: Knowledge by Design.

Mistrett, S., Ruffino, A., Lane, S., Robinson, L., Reed, P., & Milbourne, S. (2004). Every kid can: Technology supports for young children. Retrieved June 25, 2009, from http://let splay.buffalo.edu/AT/EKC-wheel.pdf

Mistrett, S., Ruffino, A., Lane, S., Robinson, L., Reed, P., & Milbourne, S. (2006). Supports for young children: TAM technology. Buffalo, NY: University of Buffalo.

Moore, M., & Calvert, S. (2000). Vocabulary acquisition for children with autism: Teacher or computer instruction. Journal of Autism and Developmental Disorders, 30, 359–362.

Morrow, L.M. (2007). Developing literacy in preschool. New York: Guilford Press.

National Association for the Education of Young Children. (1996). Technology and young children: Ages 3 through 8. A position statement of the National Association for the Education of Young Children. Washington, DC: Author.

National Center for Family-Centered Care. (1989). Family-centered care for children with special health care needs. Bethesda, MD: Association for the Care of Children's Health.

National Early Childhood Technical Assistance Center (NECTAC). Assistive technology. Retrieved January 18, 2008, from http:// www.nectac.org

National Lekotek Center. (2008). Top ten tips for selecting toys for children with disabilities. Retrieved October 2, 2009, from http:// www.lekotek.org

National Reading Panel. (2000). Teaching children to read. An evidence-based assessment of the scientific literature. Retrieved February 26, 2008, from http://www.nichd.nih.gov/publi cations/nrp/smallbook.cfm

Nikolopoulou, K. (2007). Early childhood educational software: Specific features and issues of localization. Early Childhood Education Journal, 35(2), 173–179.

No Child Left Behind Act of 2001, PL 107-110, 115 Stat. 1425, 20 U.S.C. §§ 6301 et seq.

Noonan, M.J., & McCormick, L. (2006) Young Children with disabilities in natural environments: Methods and procedures. Baltimore: Paul H. Brookes Publishing Co.

Notari-Syverson, A., & Challoner, J. (2005). Supporting early literacy in natural environments for young children with disabilities. In E.M. Horn & H. Jones (Eds.), Young exceptional children: Supporting early literacy in *young children* (Monograph Series No. 7; pp. 1–14). Longmont, CO: Sopris West.

Novick, R. (1993). Activity-based intervention and developmentally appropriate practice: Points of convergence. *Topics in Early Childhood Special Education, 13,* 403–417.

Numeroff, L.J. (1995). *If you give a mouse a cookie.* New York: Harpercollins.

Odom, S.L. (2000). Preschool inclusion: What do we know and where do we go from here? *Topics in Early Childhood Special Education, 20,* 20–27.

Odom, S.L., Wolery, R.A., Lieber, J., & Horn, E. (2002). Social policy and preschool inclusion. In S.L. Odom (Ed.), *Widening the circle: Including children with disabilities in preschool programs* (pp. 120–136). New York: Teachers College Press.

Parette, H.P. (1998). Cultural issues and family-centered assistive technology decision-making. In Judge, S.L., and Parette, H.P. *Assistive technology for young children with disabilities: A guide to family-centered services.* Cambridge, MA: Brookline Books.

Parette, H.P., & Angelo, D.H. (1996). Augmentative and alternative communication impact on families: Trends and future directions. *Journal of Special Education, 30,* 77–98.

Parette, H.P., Boeckmann, N.M., & Hourcade, J.J. (2008). Use of writing with symbols: Software to support emergent literacy development. *Early Childhood Education Journal, 36,* 161–170.

Parette, H.P., & Brotherson, M.J. (1996). Family-centered assistive technology assessment. *Intervention in School and Clinic, 32*(2), 2–15.

Parette, H., & Brotherson, M.J. (2004). Family-centered and culturally responsive assistive technology decision making. *Infants and Young Children, 17,* 355–367.

Parette, H.P., Brotherson, M.J., & Huer, M.B. (2000). Giving families a voice in augmentative and alternative communication decision-making. *Education and Training in Mental Retardation and Developmental Disabilities, 35,* 177–190.

Parette, H.P., Hourcade, J.J., & Heiple, G. (2000). The importance of structured computer experiences for young children with and without disabilities. *Early Childhood Education Journal, 27*(4), 243–250.

Parette, H.P., & Judge, S.L. (1998a). Cultural issues and family-centered assistive technology decision-making. In S.L. Judge & H.P. Parette (Eds.), *Assistive technology for young children with disabilities: A guide to family-centered services* (pp. 188–210). Cambridge, MA: Brookline Books.

Parette, H.P., & Judge, S.L. (1998b). Expanding the vision of assistive technology with young children and families: Future directions and continuing challenges. In S.L. Judge & H.P. Parette (Eds.), *Assistive technology for young children with disabilities: A guide to family-centered services* (pp. 233–253). Cambridge, MA: Brookline Books.

Parette, H.P., & Stoner, J.B. (2008). Benefits of assistive technology user groups for early childhood education professionals. *Early Childhood Education Journal, 35,* 313–319.

Parette, H.P., Stoner, J.B., & Watts, E.H. (2009). Assistive technology user group perspectives of early childhood professionals. *Education and Training in Developmental Disabilities, 44*(2), 257–270.

Parette, H.P., & VanBiervliet, A. (2000). *Culture, families, and augmentative and alternative communication (AAC) impact: A multimedia instructional program for related services personnel and family members.* Washington, DC: U.S. Department of Education National Institute of Education.

Parette, H.P., VanBiervliet, A., & Hourcade, J.J. (2000). Family-centered decision making in Assistive Technology. *Journal of Special Education Technology, 15*(1), 45–55.

Parette, H.P., Wojcik, B.W., Stoner, J.B., & Watts, E.H. (2007, January). *Emergent writing literacy outcomes in preschool settings using AT toolkits.* Presentation at the Assistive Technology Industry Association (ATIA) Annual Meeting, Orlando, FL.

Paul, R. (2007). *Language disorders from infancy through adolescence: Assessment and intervention* (3rd ed.). St. Louis: Mosby-Year Book.

Pellegrini, A.D. (2001). Some theoretical and methodological considerations in studying literacy in social context. In S.B. Neuman & D.K. Dickinson (Eds.), *Handbook of early literacy research* (pp. 54–65). New York: Guilford Press.

Peterson-Karlan, G.R., & Parette, H.P. (2007). *Evidence-based practice and consideration of assistive technology effectiveness and outcomes.* Retrieved February 29, 2008, from http://www.atia.org/files/public/atobv4n1articleNINE.pdf

Piaget, J. (1962). *Play, dreams, and imitation in childhood.* New York: Norton.

Pierce, P.L., & McWilliam, P.J. (1993). Emerging literacy and children with severe speech and physical impairments (SSPI): Issues and possible intervention strategies. *Topics in Language Disorders, 13*(2), 47–57.

Preschool Rainbow, retrieved on October 20, 2009, from http://www.preschoolrainbow.org/book-themes.htm

Pretti-Frontczak, K. (2005). *Crosswalk between*

OSEP child outcomes and the AEPS. Retrieved March 10, 2010, from http://www.aepsinter active.com/downloads/AEPS_OSEPCrosswal k.pdf

Pretti-Frontczak, K.L., Barr, D.M., Macy, M., & Carter, A. (2003). Research and resources related to activity-based intervention, embedded learning opportunities, and routines-based instruction: An annotated bibliography. *Topics in Early Childhood Special Education, 23,* 29–39.

Pretti-Frontczak, K., & Bricker, D. (2001). Use of the embedding strategy during daily activities by early childhood education and early childhood special education teachers. *Infant-Toddler Intervention: The Transdisciplinary Journal, 11*(2), 111–128.

Pretti-Frontczak, K., & Bricker, D. (2004). *An Activity-Based Approach to Early Intervention* (3rd ed.). Baltimore: Paul H. Brookes Publishing Co.

QIAT Consortium. (2009). *Quality indicators for assistive technology services: Quality indicators.* Retrieved June 30, 2009, from http://natri.uky .edu/assoc_projects/qiat/qualityindicators. html

Quill, K. (1995). *Teaching children with autism: Strategies to enhance communication and socialization.* New York: Delmar Publishers.

Reed, P., & Bowser, G. (1998, November). *Education tech points: A framework for assistive technology planning and systems change in schools.* Paper presented at the CSUN Conference on Technology and Persons with Disabilities, Los Angeles.

Rehabilitation Act of 1973, PL 93-112, 29 U.S.C. §§ 701 *et seq.*

Reichle, J., Beukelman, D.R., & Light, J.C. (2002). *Exemplary practices for beginning communicators: Implications for AAC.* Baltimore: Paul H. Brookes Publishing Co.

Rittner, R.B. (2002). *Instructional software evaluation checklist.* Retrieved December 28, 2009, from http://urj.org//learning/teacheducate/ technology//?syspage=article&item_id=2365

Robinson, N., & Solomon-Rice, P. (2009). Supporting collaborative teams and families in AAC. In G. Soto & C. Zangari (Eds.), *Practically speaking: Language, literacy, and academic development for students with AAC needs.* Baltimore: Paul H. Brookes Publishing Co.

Romski, M.A., & Sevcik, R.A. (2005). Augmentative communication and early intervention: Myths and realities. *Infants and Young Children, 18,* 174–185.

Romski, M.A., Sevcik, R.A., & Forrest, S. (2001). Assistive technology and AAC in inclusive early childhood programs. In M.J. Guralnick (Ed.), *Early childhood inclusion: Focus on change* (pp. 465–480). Baltimore: Paul H. Brookes Publishing Co.

Rosenketter, S.E., & Knapp-Philo, J. (2006). *Learning to read the world: Language and literacy in the first three years.* Washington, DC: Zero-to-Three Press.

Roskos, K., & Christie, J. (2001). Examining the play-literacy interface: A critical review and future directions. *Journal of Early Childhood Literacy, 1,* 59–89.

Rouse, C., & Murphy, K. (1997). *Quick and easy: Ideas and materials to help the nonverbal child "talk" at home.* Solana Beach, CA: Mayer-Johnson.

Rowland, C., & Swiegert, P. (2000). *Communication matrix.* Retrieved November 11, 2006, from http://www.communicationmatrix.org

Ruffino, A.G., Mistrett, S.G., Tomita, M., & Hajare, P. (2006). The universal design for play tool: Establishing validity and reliability. *Journal of Special Education Technology, 21*(4), 25–37.

Rush, L., & Helling, C. (2006). Building and utilizing an AAC evaluation toolkit and process. *Closing the Gap, 25*(1), 11–12, 17.

Sadao, K.C. (2008, Summer). Assistive technology and early intervention: The SWEET training and technical assistance model. *Infant Development Association News, 36*(2), 1, 3, 6–7, 9, 12–13, 17.

Sadao, K., Brown, J., & Grant, D. (2009). Assistive technology toolkit to increase access to early learning environments for young children with disabilities. *American Speech-Language-Hearing Association, 18*(1), 11–20.

Sadao, K., & Robinson, N. (2007). *Handbook on developing and evaluating interagency collaboration in early childhood special education programs.* Retrieved January 30, 2010, from http://www.cde.ca.gov/sp/se/fp/documents/ eciacolbrtn.pdf

Sadao, K.C., Robinson, N.B., & Grant, D. (2007, Winter). It's all about access: Getting the word out about assistive technology in early intervention. *Closing the Gap Newsletter,* 1-4.

Sadao, K.C., Robinson, N.B., & Grant, D. (2008). *The SWEET assistive technology toolkit.* Available from http://www.scoe.net/seeds

Sandall, S., Hemmeter, M.L., Smith, B.J., & McLean, M. (2005). *DEC recommended practices: A comprehensive guide for practical application in early intervention/early childhood special education.* Longmont, CO: Sopris West.

Saracho, O.N., & Spodek, B. (2003). Recent trends and innovations in the early childhood education curriculum. *Early Child Development and Care, 173,* 175–183.

Sawyer, B., Milbourne, S., Dugan L., & Campbell, P. (2005). *Report of assistive technology training for providers and families of children in early intervention.* Retrieved August 16, 2005, from http://tnt.asu.edu

Scherer, M.J. (1995). A model of rehabilitation assessment. In L.C. Cushman & M.J. Scherer (Eds.), *Psychological assessment in medical rehabilitation* (pp. 3–23). Washington, DC: APA Books.

Scherer, M.J. (Ed.). (2002). *Assistive technology: Matching device and consumer for successful rehabilitation.* Washington, DC: APA Books.

Scherer, M.J. (2008, January). *Matching child and technology: Closer to a sure thing.* Retrieved July 1, 2009, from http://www.fctd.info/resources/newsletters/upload/FCTD_Jan08_Issue70w.pdf

Schrock, K. (2007). *Software evaulation form.* Retrieved January 10, 2010, from http://kathyschrock.net/1computer/page4.htm

Schwartz, I.S., Carta, J., & Grant, S. (1996). Examining the use of recommended language intervention practices in early childhood special education classrooms. *Topics in Early Childhood Special Education, 16,* 251–272.

Sevcik, R. (2006). Comprehension: An overlooked component in augmented language development. *Disability and Rehabilitation, 28,* 159–167.

Siegel, E.B., & Cress, C.J. (2002). Overview of the emergence of early AAC behaviors: Progression from communicative to symbolic skills. In J. Reichle, D.R. Beukelman, & J.C. Light (Eds.), *Exemplary practices for beginning communicators: Implications for AAC* (pp. 25–27). Baltimore: Paul H. Brookes Publishing Co.

Silver-Pacuilla, H., Reudel. K., & Mistrett, S. (2004). *A review of technology-based approaches for reading instruction: Tools for researchers and vendors.* Retrieved February 28, 2008, from http://www.nationaltechcenter.org/ matrix/default.asp

Singer, D., & Revenson, T. (1996). *A Piaget primer: How a child thinks* (rev. ed.). New York: Penguin.

Siraj-Blatchford, J., & Whitebread, D. (2003). *Supporting ICT in the early years.* Buckingham, England: Open University Press.

Skau, L., & Cascella, P. (2006). Using assistive technology to foster speech and language skills at home and in preschool. *Teaching Exceptional Children, 38,* 12–17.

Smilansky, S. (1968). *The effects of sociodramatic play on disadvantaged preschool children.* New York: Wiley.

Snow, C., Burns, S., & Griffin, P. (1998). *Preventing reading difficulties in young children.* Washington, DC: National Academies Press.

Soto, G. (2006). Supporting storybook reading participation for children who use augmentative and alternative communication. In L. Justice (Ed.), *Clinical approaches to literacy intervention* (pp. 295–327). San Diego: Plural Publishing.

Soto, G., Dukohvny, E., & Vestly, T. (2006). Increasing storybook reading for children who use AAC. In L. Justice (Ed.), *Clinical approaches to emergent literacy intervention* (pp. 289–320). San Diego: Plural Publishing.

Soto, G., & Hartmann, E. (2006). Analysis of narratives produced by four children who use augmentative and alternative communication. *Journal of Communication Disorders, 39,* 456–480.

Soto, G., Hartmann, E., & Wilkins, D.P. (2006). Exploring the elements of narrative that emerge in the interactions between an 8-year-old child who uses an AAC device and her teacher. *Augmentative and Alternative Communication, 22,* 231–241.

Soto, G., Müller, E., Hunt, P., & Goetz, L. (2001a). Critical issues in the inclusion of students who use augmentative and alternative communication: An educational team perspective. *Augmentative and Alternative Communication, 17*(2), 62–72.

Soto, G., Müller, E., Hunt, P., & Goetz, L. (2001b). Professional skills for serving students who use AAC in general education classrooms: A team perspective. *Language, Speech, and Hearing Services in Schools, 32*(1), 51–56.

Soto, G., Robinson, N., & Hanson, M. (2004). *Collaborative AAC services in inclusive early intervention settings.* California: San Francisco State University, Department of Special Education.

Soto, G., Yu, B., & Henneberry, S. (2007). Supporting the development of narrative skills of an 8-year-old child who uses an augmentative and alternative communication device: Case study. *Child Language Teaching and Therapy, 23,* 27–45.

Stahl, S.A., & Yaden, D.B., Jr. (2004). The development of literacy in preschool and primary grades: Work by the Center for the Improvement of Early Reading Achievement. *Elementary School Journal, 105,* 141–165.

Stephenson, J. (2009). *Book reading as an intervention context for children beginning to use graphic symbols for communication.* Retrieved December 9, 2009, from http://0-www.springerlink. com.opac.sfsu.edu/content/d418535001162812/?p=a83b4824041e4075bbd7387408a2d9d9&pi=1

Stoner, J.B., Parette, H.P., Watts, E.H., Wojcik, B.W., & Fogal, T. (2008). Preschool teacher perceptions of assistive technology and professional development responses. *Education and Training in Developmental Disabilities, 43*(1), 77–91.

Stowitschek, J.J., & Guest, M.A. (2006). Islands with bridges: Using the web to enhance ongoing problem-solving among educators of young children with special needs. *Infants and Young Children, 19*(1), 72–82.

Stremel, K. (2005). DEC recommended practices: Technology application. In S. Sandall, M.L. Hemmeter, B.J. Smith, & M. McLean (Eds.), *DEC recommended practices: A comprehensive guide for practical application in early intervention/early childhood special education* (pp. 147–162). Longmont, CO: Sopris West.

Strucker, J., Snow, C., & Pan, B.A. (2004). Family literacy for ESOL families: Challenges and design principles. In B.H. Wasik (Ed.), *Handbook on family literacy* (pp. 467–481). Mahwah, NJ: Lawrence Erlbaum Associates.

Sullivan, M.W., & Lewis, M. (1995). Contingency, means-end skills and the use of technology in infant intervention. *Infants and Young Children, 5*(4), 58–77.

Sweig Wilson, M., Fox, B.J., Pascoe, J.P. (2008). *Laureate's language development programs.* Winooski, VT: Laureate Learning Systems.

Tabors, P.O., & Snow, C.E. (2001). Young bilingual children and early literacy development. In S.G. Neuman & D.K. Dickinson (Eds.), *Handbook of early literacy research* (pp. 159–178). New York: Guilford Press.

Teale, W.H., & Martinez, M.G. (1988). Getting on the right road to reading: Bringing books and young children together in the classroom. *Young Children, 44*(1), 10–15.

Technology-Related Assistance for Individuals with Disabilities Act of 1988, PL 100-407, 29 U.S.C. §§ 2201 et seq.

Texas Assistive Technology Network. (2004). *Assistive technology evaluations: A team perspective.* Retrieved June 30, 2009, from http://www.texasat.net/default.aspx?name=trainmod.evaluation

Thousand, J., & Villa, R. (1992). Collaborative teams: A powerful tool in school restructuring. In R. Villa, J. Thousand, W. Stainback, & S. Stainback (Eds.), *Restructuring for caring and effective education: An administrative guide to creating heterogeneous schools* (pp. 73–108). Baltimore: Paul H. Brookes Publishing Co.

Turbill, J., & Murray, J. (2006). Early literacy and new technologies in Australian schools: Policy, research, and practice. In M.C. McKenna, L.D. Labbo, R.D. Kieffer, & D. Reinking (Eds.), *International handbook of literacy and technology* (Vol. 2, pp. 93–108). Mahwah, NJ: Lawrence Erlbaum Associates.

U.S. Department of Education. (1998). *To assure a free, appropriate education for all children with disabilities: Twentieth annual report to Congress on the implementation of the Individuals with Disabilities Act.* Washington, DC: Author.

U.S. Department of Health and Human Services, Health Resources and Services Administration, Maternal and Child Health Bureau. (2008). *The National Survey of Children with Special Health Care Needs Chartbook 2005–2006.* Rockville, Maryland: U.S. Department of Health and Human Services.

van Kleeck, A. (2004). Fostering preliteracy development via storybook-sharing interactions: The cultural context of mainstream family practices. In C.A. Stone, E.R. Silliman, B.J. Ehren, & K. Apel (Eds.), *Handbook of language and literacy: Development and disorders* (pp. 175–208). New York: Guilford Press.

Vandervelden, M., & Siegel, L. (1999). Phonological processing and literacy in AAC users and students with motor speech impairments. *Augmentative and Alternative Communication, 15*, 191–209.

Vandervelden, M.C., & Siegel, L.S. (2001). Phonological processing in written word learning: Assessment for children who use augmentative and alternative communication. *Augmentative and Alternative Communication, 17*, 37–51.

Venn, M.L., Wolery, M., Werts, M.G., Morris, A., DeCesare, L.D., & Cuffs, M.S. (1993). Embedding instruction into art activities to teach preschoolers with disabilities to imitate their peers. *Early Childhood Research Quarterly, 8*, 277–294.

Vernadakis, N., Avgerinos, A., Tsitskari, E., & Zachopoulou, E. (2005). The use of computer assisted instruction in preschool education: Making teaching meaningful. *Early Childhood Education Journal, 33*(2), 99–104.

Vohs, J. (1993, Fall/Winter). Natural environments for infants and toddlers: An inquiry into the origin and meaning of the term. *Early Childhood Bulletin,* 1–3. Retrieved June 19, 2009, from http://www.eric.ed.gov/ERICWebPortal/custom/portlets/recordDetails/detailmini.jsp?_nfpb=true&_&ERICExtSearch_SearchValue_0=ED452659&ERICExtSearch_SearchType_0=no&accno=ED452659

Wasik, B.A., & Bond, M.A. (2001). Beyond the pages of a book: Interactive book reading and language development in preschool classrooms. *Journal of Educational Psychology, 93*(2), 243–250.

Wasik, B.H., & Hendrickson, J.S. (2004). Family literacy practices. In C.A. Stone, E.R.

Silliman, B.J. Ehren, & K. Apel (Eds.), *Handbook of language and literacy: Development and disorders* (pp. 154–174). New York: Guilford Press.

Watson, J.A., Nida, R.E., & Shade, D.D. (1986). Educational issues concerning young children and microcomputers: Lego with logo? *Early Child Development and Care, 23,* 299–316

Weikle, B., & Hadadian, A. (2003). Can assistive technology help us to not leave any child behind? *Preventing School Failure, 47*(4), 181–186.

Weintraub, H., Bacon, C., & Wilcox, M. (2004). *AT and young children: Confidence, experience and education of early intervention providers.* Retrieved August 30, 2005, from http://tnt.asu.edu

Westby, C. (1985). Learning to talk, talking to learn: Oral-literate language differences. In C.S. Simon (Ed.), *Communication skills and classroom success: Therapy methodologies for language-learning disabled students* (pp. 181–213). San Diego: College-Hill Press.

Westerlund, C. (2000). Speech disorder. In M. Williams & C. Krezman (Eds.), *Beneath the surface: Creative expressions of augmented communicators* (p. 55). Toronto: ISAAC Press.

Whitehurst, G.J., Epstein, J.N., Angell, A.L., Payne, A.C., Crone, D.A., & Fischel, J.E. (1994). Outcomes of an emergent literacy intervention in Head Start. *Journal of Educational Psychology, 86*(4), 542–555.

Whitehurst, G.J., & Lonigan, C.J. (1998). Child development and emerging literacy. *Child Development, 69,* 848–872.

Wilcox, M.J., Guimond, A., Campbell, P.H., & Moore, H.W. (2006). Provider perspectives on the use of assistive technology for infants and toddlers with disabilities. *Topics in Early Childhood Special Education, 26*(1), 33–49.

Wilcox, M. J., Weintraub, H.L., & Aier, D. (2003, October). *Confidence in use of assistive technology by early interventionists.* Paper presented to the annual meeting of CEC, Division for Early Childhood, Washington, DC.

Wilkinson, K., & Albert, A. (2001) Adaptations of fast mapping for vocabulary intervention with augmented language users. *Augmentative and Alternative Communication, 17,* 120–132.

Williams, W.B., Stemach, G., Wolfe, S., & Stanger, C. (1995). *Lifespace access profile: Assistive technology assessment and planning for individuals with severe or multiple disabilities* (rev. ed.). Irvine, CA: Lifespace Access Assistive Technology Systems.

Wilson, L.L., Mott, D.M., & Batman, D. (2004). The asset-based context matrix: A tool for assessing children's learning opportunities and participation in natural environments. *Topics in Early Childhood Special Education, 24,* 110–120.

Wisconsin Assistive Technology Initiative. (2010). *Free materials.* Retrieved May 28, 2010, from http://www.wati.org/?pageLoad= content/supports/free/index.php

Wissick, C.A. (2006). Assistive technology centers: Getting technology into the hands of users. *Journal of Special Education Technology, 21*(4), 55–57.

Wolery, M. (2000). Recommended practices in child-focused interventions. In S. Sandall, M. McLean, & B. Smith (Eds.), *DEC recommended practices in early intervention/early childhood special education* (pp. 29–37). Longmont, CO: Sopris West.

Wolery, M., Anthony, L., Caldwell, N.K., Snyder, E.D., & Morgante, J.D. (2002). Embedding and distributing constant time delay in circle time and transitions. *Topics in Early Childhood Special Education, 22,* 14–25.

Wood, A. (1994). *Silly Sally.* New York: Scholastic.

Woods, J., & Goldstein, H. (2006). When the toddler takes over: Changing challenging routines into conduits for communication. *Focus on Autism and Other Developmental Disabilities, 18,* 176–181.

Yaroz, D.J., & Barrett, W.S. (2001). Who reads to young children? Identifying predictors of family reading activities. *Reading Psychology, 22,* 67–81.

Yoder, P.J., & Warren, S.F. (2001). Relative treatment effects of two prelinguistic communication interventions on language development in toddlers with developmental delays vary by maternal characteristics. *Journal of Speech, Language, and Hearing Research, 44,* 224–237.

Yoder, P.J., & Warren, S.F. (2002). Effects of prelinguistic milieu teaching and parent responsivity education on dyads involving children with intellectual disabilities. *Journal of Speech, Language, and Hearing Research, 45,* 1297–1310.

Zabala, J.S. (1995). *The SETT framework: Critical areas to consider when making informed assistive technology decisions.* Houston, TX: Region IV Education Service Center. (ERIC Document Reproduction Service No. ED381962)

Zabala, J. S. (2002). *A brief introduction to the SETT framework.* Retrieved July 1, 2009, from http://www .sbac.edu/~ese/AT/referral process/SETTUPDATE.pdf

Zabala, J. (2005). *Setting the stage for success: Building success through effective selection and use of assistive technology systems.* Retrieved

July 1, 2009, from http://www.ldonline.org/ld_indepth/technology/zabalaSETT2.html

Zabala, J., Bowser, G., Blunt, M., Hartsell, K., Carl, D., Korsten, J., Davis, S., Marfilius, S., Deterding, C., McCloskey-Dale, S., Foss, T., Nettleton, S., Hamman, T., & Reed, P. (2000). Quality indicators for assistive technology services in school settings. *Journal of Special Education Technology, 15*(4), 25–36.

Zabala, J.S., & Carl, D.F. (2005). Quality indicators for assistive technology services in schools. In D.L. Edyburn, K. Higgins, & R. Boone (Eds.), *The handbook of special education technology research and practice* (pp. 179–207). Whitefish Bay, WI: Knowledge by Design.

Zevenbergen, A.A., Whitehurst, G.J., & Zevenbergen, J.A. (2003). Effects of a shared-reading intervention on the inclusion of evaluative devices in narratives of children from low-income families. *Journal of Applied Developmental Psychology, 24*, 1–15.

Index

Page numbers followed by *f* indicate figures; those followed by *t* ndicate tables.